# GOD
# ON
# MUTE

Pete Greig

Engaging the Silence
of Unanswered Prayer

**Regal**

**From Gospel Light**
**Ventura, California, U.S.A.**

Published by Regal Books
From Gospel Light
Ventura, California, U.S.A.
Printed in the U.S.A.

Library of Congress Cataloging-in-Publication Data
Greig, Pete.
  God on mute / Pete Greig.
    p. cm.
  ISBN 0-8307-4324-3 (hard cover) — ISBN 0-8307-4390-1 (international trade paper)
  1. Prayer—Christianity. I. Title.
  BV210.3.G733 2006
  248.3'2—dc22                                                           2006033139

1   2   3   4   5   6   7   8   9   10   /   10   09   08   07

# ANI MA'AMIN

אני מאמין בשמש גם אם אינה זורחת
אני מאמין באהבה גם אם אינני חש בה
אני מאמין באלוהים גם אם הוא שותק

*I believe in the sun even when it isn't shining.*
*I believe in love even when I am alone.*
*I believe in God even when He is silent.*

*(Graffiti found in 1945 on the wall of a basement*
*in Köln, Germany, where a Jewish believer is thought*
*to have been hiding from the Gestapo.)*

*If you are hurting and secretly wondering*
*"Where is God?" and "Why has this happened to me?"*
*and "How come my prayers aren't working?"*
*then I dedicate this book to you . . .*

*. . . and to Samie.*

## AUTHOR'S NOTE ABOUT TERMINOLOGY

Many of the names of people mentioned in this book have been changed to protect their privacy. I have also endeavored to use language that is broadly inclusive. For instance, I prefer to refer to the pre-Christian books of the Bible as the *Hebrew Testament* out of respect for our Jewish forebears to whom they were originally given. However, I have submitted entirely to the traditional usage of the masculine pronoun for God, although I do this recognizing that men and women together reflect the character of their Creator and that we do so in equal measure (see Gen. 1:27).

# CONTENTS

**MAUNDY THURSDAY:**

# HOW

**AM I GOING TO GET THROUGH THIS?**

**GOOD FRIDAY:**

# WHY

**AREN'T MY PRAYERS
BEING ANSWERED?**

**HOLY SATURDAY:**

# WHERE

**IS GOD WHEN HEAVEN IS SILENT?**

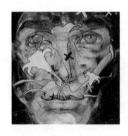

**EASTER SUNDAY:**

# WHEN

**EVERY PRAYER IS ANSWERED**

# FOREWORD

Pete Greig has written an extraordinarily honest book, so I need to begin this foreword honestly, with a confession: I love the subject of prayer (because I love to pray) and I have read a lot of books on the subject, but I haven't liked quite a few of them. Some have struck me as formulaic and full of easy answers, which is a euphemism for dishonest answers. They made unrealistic promises and were full of some of the unhelpful misguidance that Pete's book effectively, but gently, seeks to correct.

Several of these books were guilt-inducing, preoccupied with quantifying how much prayer is necessary for a *truly committed* Christian and shaming people for not praying enough, or the prescribed way, or whatever. This approach always hurts my prayer life, because after reading them, as soon as I say, "Dear God" or "Our Father," my next thought is, *I'm sure You're already disappointed in me because I haven't prayed enough this week. Oops, I probably didn't start this prayer right. Okay, let me start again . . . er . . .*

A few of these books, though, have been so important in my life that they made getting through all the others worthwhile—just to find these gems. I think, for example, of Richard Foster's *Prayer*, or C. S. Lewis's *Letters to Malcolm, Chiefly on Prayer* or Anthony Bloom's *Beginning to Pray*. The book you are now holding is the most recent member of this B-list. (There is no A-list. *B* in this case means *best, beautiful* and *be sure to recommend it to others*.) In fact, I just gave this manuscript to one of my sons and made him promise to pass it on to my other son when he finished.

I said this is an honest book, but it's not just politely honest; it goes a lot farther than that. I'm tempted to say "brutally honest," but there's nothing brutal about this book. It would be better to say "tenderly honest" or, even better, "compassionately honest," because compassion makes a veteran in prayer tell even painful or embarrassing or troubling truths so that beginners (and other veterans) will know they are not alone in their confusion, discouragement, doubt, anger and disillusionment with prayer. I think you'll find yourself saying, *Oh, thank God, I'm not the only one, after all, who has ever felt that way! I'm not the only person who has thought or asked that.*

Along with honesty, this is a book of theological depth. Pete draws from the Bible—not in a superficial proof-texty way, but reaching deeply and broadly into the biblical texts, with a mature sensitivity to context. Not only that, but he draws deeply from his own circle of friends and, of course, he draws deeply from his own experience. One senses that, for all his honest confessions of doubts and confusion, this is a man who talks and listens to God, not just a man who speaks and writes books on how others should do so.

Honest and deep. These qualities would be wonderful enough, but this book is also skillfully written. Pete's style reminds me of some of our best contemporary writers, like Don Miller and Annie Lamott. To have important things told with spark and flash, with a laugh and a tear and a wink, with irony and understatement and also great, naked, simple, open-eyed sincerity . . . reading doesn't get much better than that.

My conviction is that simply praying is one of the most important things we do, however inept or bumbling or insane we feel when we do it. One of my wisest friends, systematic theologian John Franke, has told me many things that have deeply helped me. Among them, he distinguishes between first- and second-order disciplines. Praying, giving to the poor and reconciling with an offended sister or brother in the church are first-order disciplines. Having a theology of prayer, or a theology of economics and development, or a theology about reconciliation are second-order disciplines. John taught me how important it is to stick with the first-order disciplines even when our second-order disciplines are shaky or even crumbling.

Praying is a first-order discipline. Just doing it is what matters most. But all of us know that if our second-order theology of prayer is in disarray—if it is wobbly or limping or even crippled by some recent tough experiences—we will find it hard to do the first-order discipline.

Nobody can do the first-order discipline for us. That's up to us. But what Pete does in these pages is so important: He helps us sort through our second-order theology of prayer, our thinking about prayer, our understanding of how it works and doesn't work and why. I think that will make it easier for us to actually do the thing that matters: stay in touch with God.

Having said all this, it only seems right to conclude this foreword with a prayer to take us forward:

*Gracious God, You are so wonderful, so powerful, so mysterious, so good that when we say a name for You—God, Father, Lord, Creator, Almighty, Holy One—we hardly know what we mean. Our best thoughts of You are like a baby crying, "Mama! Papa!" She knows so little about her parents. She has no idea of the depths of their minds or the range of their knowledge and experience. She knows nothing of their sorrows and very little of the depth of their love for her. But simply in calling out to them, with her limited understanding, she establishes the bond through which, over the years, she will come to know them more and more.*

*So I pray, Source of all our comfort and wisdom and strength, that You will meet each reader of this book as they read, reflect, digest and discuss the insights here . . . insights You have graciously given to Pete through his trials and struggles, his doubts and joys, his triumphs and setbacks in his walk with You.*

*You sent Your Holy Son, empowered by Your Holy Spirit, to liberate captives and free the oppressed. Many readers are captives to bad ideas and oppressed by misconceptions and false assumptions. Let these pages be liberating, freeing and life-giving. Help beginners to learn how to pray for the first time. Help the disillusioned to unlearn bad patterns and relearn better ones. And help the experienced to find reminders and refreshment and reassurance.*

*What a gift You have given us, almighty and ever-living God: the gift of Your attention, the gift of Your interest in what we have to say. Thank You. Thank You. Thank You. In the name of Jesus and in the power of the Holy Spirit. Amen.*

Brian McLaren
Laurel, MD, USA
www.brianmclaren.net

# HOW I DEVELOPED A POWERFUL MINISTRY TO BASKETBALL PLAYERS, THANKS TO MY INTERGALACTICALLY STUPID FRIEND

If your deepest, most desperate prayers aren't being answered, if life sometimes hurts so much that you secretly wonder whether God exists, and if He does whether He cares, and if He cares why on earth He doesn't just *do* something to help, then you're not alone. Surprisingly, the Bible reveals that Jesus—even Jesus—suffered the silence of unanswered prayer. The One who turned water to wine, healed the sick and even raised the dead, was also denied and apparently abandoned by the Father. What's more, as far as we can tell from the Gospel accounts, Christ's unanswered prayers seem to have been concentrated on His time of greatest need: the four days of His Passion.

On *Maundy Thursday,* Jesus asked the Father to spare Him from suffering, but every crucifix testifies to the agony of that unanswered prayer. Earlier that day, Jesus had prayed repeatedly for Christian unity. But look around you! Tragically (and for whatever reason), that crucial request also remains unanswered.

On *Good Friday*, we witness a third unanswered prayer. Nailed to a cross and slowly suffocating, the Son cried out to the Father with a chilling question: "My God," He gasped, "My

God, why have You forsaken Me?" And there was no response to the "why." No dove descending. No booming voice. No answer to prove the question wrong.

On *Holy Saturday,* the hopes and prayers of every disciple lay dashed and broken in the grave. But God did nothing. Said nothing. No sound but the buzzing of flies around the corpse of the Son.

And then, on *Easter Sunday,* God broke the silence. He awoke. He spoke. And for those of us who walk (however reluctantly) in Jesus' footsteps from Gethsemane and Golgotha to the Garden tomb, Easter Sunday offers irrepressible hope. That one ultimate miracle—the resurrection of the Son of God from the dead—assures us that every buried dream and dashed hope will ultimately be absorbed and resurrected into a reality far greater than anything we can currently imagine.

## More Prayer than Sex

When I asked my friend Mike if I could share his experiences of unanswered prayer in this book, he laughed laconically and said he'd prefer to be featured in the *Forbes* rich list. "Being held up as an example of unanswered prayer is not exactly what I dreamed about as a kid," he joked. I know how he feels. But however zealously we may pray for health, wealth and a happy home, sooner or later life goes wrong.

We all get hijacked eventually. One moment you're cruising from *A* to *B* at 30,000 feet, fiddling with the earphones and feasting on life's pretzels. The next, you're more scared than you've ever been before, caught in a situation you prayed you'd never be in, and heading somewhere that you never asked to go. The terror comes in many guises: a sudden trauma, a long-term illness, the loss of someone you love, the death of a dream.

Michael Stipe is right. Everybody hurts sometimes.

And when we hurt, most of us turn to prayer. Way more than you might think. Way more than we go to church, at any rate. The girl at the checkout hoping she's not pregnant, the businessman staring at his sales figures, the teenager laying flowers by the roadside. The Queen of England does it, football fans do it, priests and professors do it, surgeons do it, and so do terrorists. Even atheists backslide from time to time. More Americans say they pray every week than work, exercise or have sex. I read somewhere (but I find it hard to believe) that a whopping 20 percent of agnostics and atheists sheepishly admit to praying *daily*! So there's a lot of praying that goes on out there. "It is not possible for us to say, I will pray, or I will not pray, as if it were a question of pleasing ourselves," observed the great theologian Karl Barth. Prayer, he noted, is "a necessity, as breathing is necessary to life."[1]

But the brutal fact of the matter is that while most of us pray, prayer does not always seem to work, and it's not easy to be honest about this.

At university, I knew a guy called Captain Scarlet (nicknamed after the lead puppet in the cult TV series called *Captain Scarlet and the Mysterons*). Everyone liked Captain Scarlet because he was pretty much nuts and very, very enthusiastic about things no one else wanted to think about. He was a Christian, and he combined this with being about as positive about positive thinking as it is possible to be. For a while, Captain Scarlet believed that God wanted everybody on Earth, especially students and Africans, to be spectacularly wealthy, eternally healthy and as addicted to Kenneth Copeland teaching cassettes as he was. Which is, let's face it, a whole lot better than being penniless, depressed and into Marilyn Manson.

The Captain was the only 19-year-old I've ever known who viewed televangelists as aspirational role models. For the Captain, Jesus Christ was the King of ker-ching. Anyway, one time he told me that he had been healed of a serious back complaint that had been causing him a lot of pain, adding with complete seriousness, "It's just the symptoms I can't seem to get rid of." That's honestly what dear-old Captain Scarlet said, and I was so bewildered that I just said, "Wow!" and tried to give him a hug, which, because of his symptoms, turned out to be a bad idea.

I still don't agree with Captain Scarlet's view of faith. In fact, I think it's potentially dangerous to put so much faith in faith that we ignore the facts and kiss our brains goodbye. However, I'm not a cynic. I believe in the goodness and greatness of God, and I've spent most of my adult life trying to help others believe too. Maybe that's why, like Captain Scarlet, I sometimes find it so much harder to admit my disappointments and frustrations in prayer than I do to broadcast glad tidings of great joy to all mankind.

I'm convinced that miracles great and small do happen more often than people realize and that when one comes to us we should shout it from the rooftops! But let's be honest, too, about the reality of unanswered prayer so that we can think intelligently and relate sensitively around the deep questions of our lives.

## Glory Stories

A few years ago, one of my friends (whose sense of humor is, admittedly, warped) took it upon himself to send a spoof letter to a well-known Christian leader informing him that I had recently persuaded an entire basketball team to convert to Christianity. With a final flourish of creativity, my friend added that the team now had the catchy little phrase "Jumpin' for Jesus" embroidered on their shorts. Embarrassed, I phoned the leader to explain that the whole thing was a hoax and to apologize for the intergalactic stupidity of my friend. I explained that there was no basketball team. There had been no conversions. There would never be any shorts embroidered with the phrase "Jumpin' for Jesus."

The pastor just couldn't understand what I was saying. "Why," he wanted to know, "would someone fabricate a story like that? What's funny about it, anyway?" It's pointless explaining a joke to someone who didn't understand it the first time. Trust me. I've had a lot of experience, and I know. So I apologized to the perplexed leader and hung up the phone. A few weeks later, I was scanning the pages of a national magazine when an article caught my eye. It was reporting a revival among basketball players. I froze. The article was about me.

Christians are quick to spread glory stories, but disappointments tend to be brushed under the carpet because we don't want to discourage anyone at church or be a bad commercial at work. But God isn't like us. He doesn't get insecure about His performance, and He never asks us to cover up for Him.

When our prayers aren't answered and heaven is silent, there may be good reason to doubt God's existence. I know plenty of people who've gone that route. But there is also good reason to believe. I'm told that the chances of life beginning by cosmic fluke are something in the region of 1 in $1\mathrm{x}10^{40,000}$. That's a lot of zeros. Not impossible, of course, but cutting the Creator out of the equation takes an awful lot of faith. And if there is a God, there's pretty good reason to believe in the power of prayer too. "Ask and you will receive," Jesus promises, "and your joy will be complete" (John 16:24). But it is this very conviction—the belief that prayer works—that causes perplexity and pain when it doesn't. Unanswered prayer is only a problem for those of us who truly believe. For cynics, it is simply a reassurance that they were right all along.

## The Cheshire Cat's Grin

In my book *Red Moon Rising*, I described a time on the Mediterranean island of Ibiza when the Anglican priest asked a bunch of young missionaries sent out by our organization to pray for rain because the locals were suffering from serious drought. No one could possibly have been more surprised than we were when, minutes after we prayed, the heavens opened and unseasonal storms began lashing the island. When we learned that it hadn't rained so heavily on Ibiza in July since 1976, the timing of our prayer meeting seemed even more remarkable.

Somehow, a British journalist caught wind of the story and phoned me for an interview. As we talked, I could hear the cynicism in his thick London accent. "So you're the bloke," he smirked. "You're the bloke who's claimin' you made it rain in Ibiza!"

"No," I replied cautiously. "It would be ridiculous to think that we could make it rain. Wouldn't it?"

"Well, yeah," he had to concur.

"Look, we're just saying that we prayed for it to rain, and then it did. It's you that made the connection."

"I did?"

"Yes, and I can tell you're pretty dubious about the whole idea. I mean, we'd have to be a bunch of nutters to think that our prayers could control the weather, wouldn't we?"

"Erm, well, it's not exactly normal to . . ."

"Look, maybe you're right," I said. "If you want to believe that there's absolutely no connection between the fact that we prayed and then it rained, well, I can totally understand that. If you reckon there's no power in prayer and human beings are merely a bunch of highly evolved animals trapped in a meaningless universe without recourse to any higher power, I respect your opinion and . . ."

"Nah, don't get me wrong, mate." The voice on the line sounded flustered. "I mean, there's gotta be more to life. My mum's a Catholic." He paused as if this last statement explained everything, which in a way—if you've ever known an East End Catholic family—it did. "Yeah, fair play. You're probably right. There is somethin' to this whole prayer thing. To be absolutely honest with you, I do it myself, mate."

A number of people commented that the subsequent press coverage entitled "God Squad Claims First Miracle on Ibiza" was unusually favorable.

These days, it's pretty tricky to find a full-on, card-carrying materialist—someone brave enough to deny unequivocally the existence of a spiritual realm and the possibility of an occasional miracle. These people are still out there, don't get me wrong, but in an age of quantum physics and postmodern imagination, they are starting to look like an endangered species (which is ironic really, as they tend to be the ones advocating evolutionary progress).

More than 30 years ago, the prize-winning writer Annie Dillard noted, "Some physicists now are a bunch of wild-eyed, raving mystics. For they have perfected their instruments and methods just enough to whisk away the crucial veil, and what stands revealed is the Cheshire cat's grin!"[2] Years of cautious calculation, on the very cusp of new technology, have left many of our brightest physicists thinking more like theologians or philosophers than the wary rationalists they once were. Like the journalist who admitted to conversing with God, they too are increasingly open to spirituality and the extraordinary possibilities of prayer.

## Cry Baby

I heard recently about a couple, Jim and Molly, whose first child screamed and cried night after night until they thought they would go crazy. The couple prayed desperately that their daughter would stop crying just long enough to let them get some sleep—long enough to let them feel that they weren't the worst parents in the world. But their prayers made no notable difference. If anything, praying seemed to make her crying worse.

Eventually, Jim and Molly made a decision to stop asking God for help altogether. I guess if you ask God to make a baby stop crying once and it keeps on bawling, you hardly blink. Twice, three times, even for a whole week, you would just figure that God had more important things to do than act like some kind of cosmic pacifier. But when that crying drives your prayers to a place of desperation night after night and yet God remains silent, I guess your faith in prayer (or your faith in yourself) could just fade like a childhood photograph.

Jim and Molly's crying baby is now a happy, well-adjusted young adult, and her parents are dedicated members of their local church. Jim's the sort of guy who helps out with everything from evangelism programs to building projects. He leads a house group with Molly, and they rarely miss a Sunday. You get the picture: These are seriously dedicated Christians. Yet in an honest discussion one evening, Jim opened up about the damage that season of unanswered prayer had done to his relationship with God. He admitted that he no longer prays for any of his or Molly's personal needs and that he hasn't done so for 20 years. It's just too painful.

Paradoxically, Jim and Molly still pray for other people and for other situations, just not for themselves. Praying for the peace of a nation seems easier than praying for a peaceful night's sleep. They still expect the Father to do miracles for other people, just not for them.

Whatever the reason, I've written this book for people like Jim and Molly who have been disappointed by unanswered prayer, and for people like Captain Scarlet too. It seems to me that those of us who spend our time encouraging people to pray and share the amazing stories of answered prayer also have a sworn duty to care for those whose prayers appear not to be working.

## The Manifold Problems of Prayer

When people heard that I was writing a book on the subject of unanswered prayer, I got some extreme reactions. Just last week one woman, the wife of a vicar, said "Oh!" with evident disappointment before enquiring, "Will you be following it up with a book about the *answered* variety?" I tried to explain that *God on Mute* is really about a deeper kind of faith and that I'd already written a book about miracles, but I couldn't get through to her. The day before this exchange, another woman, the wife of a successful businessman, said a very different kind of "Oh!" In fact, it was more of an "Oooh!" before adding, "I'll buy an armful of those. We know so many people who need a book like that!"

As I write, a vivacious 23-year-old in our church is facing the possibility of a terminal diagnosis. Understandably, each day she swings between faith and grave fear. We're praying like crazy, but what will happen if our prayers don't work? When one of my relatives heard about this book, she broke down in tears. Her struggle is with chronic fatigue syndrome, a condition that has sapped her energy since leaving university 25 years ago. She is sometimes unable to lift even a small bag of potatoes, gets exhausted after any serious conversation, and has never been able to work. I'm also recalling the face of a man who received a clear word from God to abandon his safe career and launch out in business. It was a risk, but he felt sure that the Lord had spoken to him. Three years later, he was bankrupt and without a house. But by far, his greatest loss was the ability he once had to trust God simply.

Maybe your problems are less obviously painful than these scenarios. You're probably reading this because, like me and Captain Scarlet, some of your prayers simply aren't working and you want to know why. Maybe God seems a million miles away. Maybe you took a risk, stepped out of the boat, and sank. Maybe you're sick and tired of praying for healing or breakthrough. Maybe miracles happen to everyone else, but never to you. Maybe someone you love is rejecting God, no matter how hard you pray. Maybe you need a word from heaven, but God is on mute and the remote is lost down the back of some cosmic sofa.

Thousands of us carry around the pain of unanswered prayer in our hearts. Occasionally, we wonder why God does not respond to our requests, but generally we just get on with life and try to trust in Him. But it truly doesn't have to be like this.

There's a bit of a myth out there that when it comes to unanswered prayer, there are no answers and we just have to walk blindly through the veils of mystery and hope we don't trip up. Of course, it's true that there can be no explanation to the ultimate problems of suffering, but to the vast majority of questions there are, in fact, answers—good ones—that have helped millions of people for thousands of years to navigate disappointment without losing their way.

## The New Rock and Roll!

It's vital that we think about these issues, because people all over the world are getting very excited indeed right now about prayer. For instance, on Pentecost Sunday in 2005, more than 200 million Christians in at least 176 nations joined hands around the world for the first-ever global day of prayer. I'm part of a movement that started with a single prayer room in 1999 and somehow spread to 63 nations within its first 5 years. This was not by design. I'm as surprised as anyone else. Even Pepsi didn't spread that quickly!

Because of this explosion of intercession, I don't really do a job anymore. Getting hijacked by a prayer movement (of all things) isn't exactly a conventional career move, but one of the many upsides is the constant stream of encouraging e-mails recounting amazing answers to prayer.

I used to particularly appreciate receiving these stories during the long hours I spent sitting next to my wife's hospital bed. It was—and still is—thrilling to hear the accounts of people stepping into 24-7 prayer rooms and experiencing the presence of God. Equally miraculous are the stories about addictions being broken and lives being put back together by God. When I read stuff like this, I want to call my friends and say, "You'll never guess what's happened. This is *insane!*"

It occurs to me that a book about *unanswered* prayer needs plenty of these stories about the answered variety too. I mean, if (for example) you're sitting in hospital right now trying to make sense of your situation, the last thing you want is people trying to be "sensitive" by censoring all the good stuff out of their conversation. Even when your own prayers aren't being answered the way you want them to be, you can still be happy for others, and their encouragement can give you hope for your situation. I've had to live with this paradox for a few years now and I'm grateful that there's been so much good news alongside the depressing stuff. Maybe it's the paradox that keeps me sane!

It's precisely because we believe so passionately in the power of prayer that we must also make sense of unanswered prayer. And when we do begin to wrestle openly with this issue, it can never be a neat, academic exercise for polite theological discourse because the question of unanswered prayer touches the deepest, most painful experiences of our lives. We all have friends who have lost their faith because it seemed that God was not there when they needed Him most. Others, like Captain Scarlet and Jim and Molly, continue to believe but live with secret disappointments that drain the joy from their relationship with God.

### *Reader's Digest*, Cappuccino and the Cosmic Problem of Suffering

When my wife was first rushed to hospital, we looked in vain for a book that could help make a little sense of the chaos that we were going through. Samie (pronounced Sammy) didn't need a great, scowling theological tome on the problem of suffering. She didn't need the kind of paperback that uses pithy quotes and punchy allegories to prove that one's problems are not really problems. What she needed was an honest, practical book that had done the hard work for her and would fit on her bedside table between her *Reader's Digest* and a cappuccino.

I have waited five years, wanting to try to write the book that we were looking for. I know the need for it, yet I have been intimidated by the prospect of exposing my most intimate pain and private doubt to public scrutiny. I admit that I've also been daunted intellectually. Right now, my desk is piled so high with every imaginable book about suffering and prayer—by some of the cleverest people who've ever lived—that it's starting to look like the Manhattan skyline. One more purchase and I'll be getting fan mail from Amazon.com.

If there's one thing that all these books about suffering have made me realize, however, it's that I have neither the brains nor the years to add anything worthwhile to the pile. If you want to grapple with the issue of suffering, then I'd encourage you to go straight to the great teachers: St. John of the Cross, Elie Wiesel, Jürgen Moltmann, C. S. Lewis and, more recently, people like Henri Nouwen, Dorothee Sölle and Philip Yancey. This book inevitably draws from their insights, but mainly it's an altogether simpler book about the practicalities of prayer: how it works, why it doesn't always work, how to get better at it, how to navigate the disappointments without losing your faith.

And so here it is: an honest book about unanswered prayer that will fit between *Reader's Digest* and a cappuccino, written to help a few people who are hurting too. It's not going to answer all your questions, but I think it will help answer *some* of them. It takes the form of a journey through the four days of Christ's betrayal, death, burial and resurrection.

The journey begins on Maundy Thursday in the Garden of Gethsemane where Christ's "soul is overwhelmed with sorrow," and His prayers for deliverance go unanswered. It continues through Good Friday where Christ considers Himself forsaken by the Father in His hour of deepest need. Next we traverse the gloom and confusion of Holy Saturday, asking, "Where is God?" when Jesus Himself lies dead and buried. Finally—inevitably— Gethsemane, Golgotha and the burial Garden are engulfed by the good news of Easter Sunday.

The things that Samie and I have so far suffered along the way don't merit special telling. Plenty of people fight similar battles, or much worse. But the incomparable story of Christ's agony, abandonment and eventual resurrection—that story remains the hope for a hijacked world.

> *When you find yourselves flagging in your faith, go*
> *over that story again, item by item, that long litany*
> *of hostility he plowed through. That will shoot adren-*
> *aline into your souls!*
> HEBREWS 12:3, *THE MESSAGE*

## ENGAGING THE SILENCE

first
there is
   *prayer*
and where there is prayer
there may be
   *miracles*
but where miracles may not be
there are
   *questions*
and where there are questions
there may be
   *silence*
but silence may be
more than
   *absence*
silence
may be presence
   *muted*
silence
may not be nothing but
   *something*
to explore
defy accuse
   *engage*
and
this is
   *prayer*
and where there is prayer
there may yet be
   *miracles* . . .

# HOW

## AM I GOING TO GET THROUGH THIS?

*Abba, Father,*
*everything is possible for you.*
*Take this cup from me.*
MARK 14:36

In the Garden of Gethsemane, Jesus is wrestling for His life, in prayer. The location is significant: "Gethsemane" literally means "the Oil Press," and for Jesus it has become a place of intense pressure—spiritually, emotionally and physically. When life threatens to crush us, we too may wrestle in prayer. If God is our loving Abba, Father, for whom everything is possible, why—we may wonder—does He not just remove the cup of our suffering? Does He really care? Is He really there? I don't know the shape of your unanswered prayers—we each arrive in Gethsemane by different paths—but here's how it happened to me . . .

# Chapter One

# CONFETTI

*My soul is overwhelmed . . .*
JESUS, MARK 14:34

*What is most personal is most universal.*
HENRI NOUWEN, *THE WOUNDED HEALER*

*"Wake up!"* she gasped. "Something's wrong." Samie's whispers buffeted me out of a deep sleep, and I began mumbling and fumbling like a drunk, flailing frantically for the bedside lamp. Squinting in its light, I stared instinctively toward the old Moses basket beside the bed, but seven-week-old Daniel was soundly asleep, his lips pouting softly for his mother's milk.

"It's my leg." Samie's voice bristled with fear. "I can't feel it. It won't move . . ." Samie, pale as the moon, was sitting upright in bed, clutching her thigh. Then, suddenly, before I could laugh and tell her that she'd probably just been sleeping funny and that she should go back to sleep before she woke the baby, the fingers of her right hand began to curl into an old lady's fist. Her wrist twisted to a 90-degree angle. She let out a gasp—a yelp—of pain as shuddering spasms began to tremble up her arm.

Samie watched the convulsions in horror, as if some alien power had seized her hand and was now advancing malevolently along her arm toward her head. "What's happening to me?" she gasped, but I didn't know. Her elbow jabbed sideways and her hand became a cobra ready to strike. These strange contortions reached the curve of her neck and then, with a dreadful inevitability, an invisible violence took hold of Samie's head, thrusting her chin down toward her shoulder as if she was playing the fiddle. As if she was holding the phone to chat casually—hands-free—by shrugging that same shoulder toward her ear. I'd never before witnessed a seizure. I felt calm, yet breathless. My head was logical and my lungs were full of helium. Concentrating, I dialed the ambulance, carefully placing my finger on each pad.

It is a terror to wake in the night to see the face you love more than any other leering demonically. The image stains your memory like the Shroud of Turin, and it doesn't fade. By now, Samie's eyes—those beautiful, summer-blue eyes—had turned to moons of white and her whole body seemed to be shaking. I hoped she was unconscious, but then, with superhuman effort she forced out a single, desperate word: "P-p-p-pray."

And so I did. I prayed like I'd never prayed before, helplessly convinced that I was watching my wife die. I begged God to make the convulsions stop so that she could at least draw breath. I prayed in the name of Jesus. I tried to have faith. I invoked the power of His blood. I rebuked and renounced everything I could think of rebuking and renouncing. This was not prayer for a parking space or a sunny day. This seemed to me to be a matter of life and death. Samie was turning blue, and bloodied spittle was blotting the pillow. The ambulance was taking forever. My prayers weren't working.

In fact, it was probably only a matter of minutes before the paramedics strode into the house, their boots clomping loudly on the exposed wooden floorboards of our bedroom. They assessed the situation and carried Samie noisily down to the ambulance parked in the road outside, lights flashing like a cheap disco. Somehow, Danny slept peacefully through the whole ordeal, still blowing those tiny kisses of comfort, still dreaming no doubt about the milky warmth of his last feed. Would it, I wondered, be exactly that—his last feed?

· · · ·

The lights of the hospital were reassuringly bright, and the seizure soon exhausted itself. Samie slumped to sleep like a puppet whose strings had been cut. Concussed, I just stood there gazing at my wife, watching her breathing. Breathing slowly. Breathing softly. Her face was white, bleached like a flash photograph, and her blond hair was brown against the brightness of the pillow. I blinked. Everything seemed without shadows, overexposed.

My mind swirled back to the previous evening. Climbing into bed, I had prayed as usual for Hudson, asleep in the room next door, for our tiny new baby beside the bed and, yes, I had prayed for Samie too. "Watch over us, Lord," I'd whispered as I always did. We turned out the light that night, trusting God's protection implicitly. How, I now wondered, could we ever turn it back on?

But such doubts seemed dangerous in these hostile wards. Somewhere, they were doing tests. The chrome instruments, the beeping monitors and the smell of ether made prayer seem naïve, so I grabbed my phone and shuffled outside.

Cigarette butts lay strewn around the entrance to the hospital like soggy confetti at the door of a church. It was a miserable dawn at the dog-end of winter, but out here, standing in the smokers' ash under a gray sky, I felt closer to God and talked to Him as best I could. I told Him I trusted Him, repeating the same childish little phrases over and over again like a monk muttering the rosary: "Please make her better . . . heal her, Lord . . . don't let there be a problem . . ."

I went back inside, and a nurse assured me kindly that "Everyone's allowed one seizure in his or her lifetime." She was right. Loads of people go through stuff like that—and worse, by far. Anyway, if, for some strange reason, Samie had developed epilepsy, we would cope. People do. But what about our two children asleep at home with a babysitter? Why, I wondered darkly, hadn't my prayers made any notable difference when Samie and I needed God's help more than ever before?

Here I am, one of the leaders within a prayer movement that (according to one overexcited commentator) is "taking the world by storm," and (dare I admit it?) my deepest prayers are impotent. It's scarcely comforting that the disciples had the same problem when they prayed for a boy with epilepsy and that Jesus put it down to their lack of faith. No wonder the boy's father wept when he said, "I do believe; help me overcome my unbelief!" (Mark 9:24). It's a line I have tried myself (sometimes with the tears) many times since that night. But as subsequent seizures continued to assault Samie's body, I confess that it eventually became easier not to pray at all than to endure a minor crisis of faith after each episode.

## Bad News

Eventually, a doctor invited me to sit with him on a row of gray plastic seats attached to the wall in a corridor right next to an automatic door. "Bad news," he intoned. I chose to leave a seat between us, and so we sat there side by side, a little apart, as he began to say the words: "The CAT scan shows a growth in your wife's brain."

An ambulance man came through the automatic doors. It was a cold day in March and an icy breeze followed him in. "It's very large, I'm afraid . . . the size of an orange . . . it might have been growing very slowly over a protracted period, or it might be fast-growing and aggressive." I remember thinking that a row of plastic chairs in a corridor was the wrong place to be telling me this. And why an orange? The doctor said something about sending the scans electronically to a consultant at another hospital for analysis. He didn't know if it would be operable. He stood in his white coat, and I in my jeans. "Shall we go tell Samantha?"

I persuaded the doctor to delay breaking the news until Samie awoke. Her parents and sister had arrived at her bedside, but for more than an hour, as she continued to sleep peacefully, I didn't tell them the diagnosis because—for some old-fashioned reason—I thought Samie should be the first to know. Waiting with this terrible secret ticking in my mind like a time bomb, I willed my wife not to wake. I watched her. I watched the clock. I watched her family, who were talking low and reading celebrity magazines. I was lonelier than I had ever been before; yet strangely, I was also becoming aware of a kind of inner warmth. It was the comfort of huddling into a thick coat with deep pockets on a bitterly cold night. Doctors would probably call it shock, but to me it felt a lot like the presence of God.

I have talked to others about their experiences of trauma, and it is remarkable how often the crisis throws us upon God—whether or not we had faith in Him before. Suddenly, we are jolted into a state of intense vulnerability and instinctively reach for the Father's hand. Trauma itself rarely creates a crisis of faith. I guess hospital lights are just too bright to house the dark night of the soul. During the initial trauma of a car crash or a betrayal or a diagnosis like ours, we are simply too shocked and too scared to ask grave theological questions about unanswered prayer. For me, at least, those questions would come in the weeks, months and years of weary believing that lay ahead.

When Samie awoke, she immediately realized that something else was wrong. I took her hand, drew a deep breath and paused. I have no idea what words I used to tell my 29-year-old wife that she had a tumor the size of an orange growing within the confines of her skull, but I do remember her response vividly. For a moment she just stared at me in blank denial, her eyes pleading for a punch line, searching my face for a glimpse of absolution. Then a moaning sound began in her belly and she cried "*NO!*" so loud and so long that the entire ward heard her grief. It was the saddest, angriest sound I have ever heard, like the groan of a wounded animal. The doctor was shaking when he left the room.

· · · ·

After several hours, the news came back that the tumor was operable. We gasped with relief and began to prepare Samie for the ordeal that lay ahead. Kind relations cared for Hudson and Daniel, and each night I would leave the hospital to bathe them both and read Hudson his bedtime story. Would the words and pictures some day describe a mother he couldn't recall? Night after night I banished such thoughts and cuddled the kids a little too tightly. For me, putting Hudson and Danny to bed was the hardest thing of all during those days awaiting the operation. I would often tiptoe out of their bedrooms choking back the tears.

Samie didn't want to be left alone for more than a few minutes. Something was growing in her head. Seizures could assault her body at any moment. Her children had been taken from her. And soon a man would saw away a section of her skull and cut something from her brain. For a long time, she was too scared to sleep without sedatives. Then, one evening, a group of strangers drove two hours from Reading, near London, to pray all night in the hospital chapel just for Samie. That was the first night she slept peacefully without pills. The following morning when we found out about this covert prayer vigil, we recognized the evidence of God's love embedded in their extraordinary kindness.

As the day of the surgery approached, we also found great comfort in the promises of the Bible. I'm not just saying this because it's what Christians are supposed to say in situations like this. The Bible addressed our fears in a way no person could and gave words to things we were struggling to express. Almost every night we went to sleep clutching a verse for dear life. One of our favorites came from the fourth chapter of Paul's letter to the Philippians:

> Do not be anxious about anything, but in everything, by prayer and petition, with thanksgiving, present your requests to God. And the peace of God, which transcends all understanding, will guard your hearts and your minds in Christ Jesus (vv. 6-7).

We also gleaned hope from some less predictable sources. When we learned that actor and former pop star Martin Kemp (he was in the '80s rock band *Spandau Ballet*) had survived a brain tumor, we cut out a picture of him frolicking on a beach in Barbados from *Hello!* magazine and stuck it to the mirror above Samie's basin. The blessed icon of Saint Martin of the Most Sexy Six-Pack smiled benevolently down on us from above the sink, promising the possibility—however distant it seemed—of life after brain surgery.

## Praying Like a Man Falling Down Stairs

Outwardly, I tried to give an impression of stoic endurance, and there were times when I did feel very calm. But I was also scared that Samie might die if I didn't pray enough, or if I didn't have enough faith, or if I didn't fast enough, or if I didn't bind some disembodied principality, or if I didn't repent of some root sin, or if I didn't strap her body on a stretcher bound for Lourdes, or if I didn't agree with Benny Hinn. *Surely*, I thought, *God would not disqualify her on a technicality?*

I'm ashamed to admit that this was how my prayer life looked when it really counted. Samie's faith frequently amazed me, but I prayed at best like a child and at worst like a charlatan looking for snake oil. There were times (should I admit this to you?) when Samie's diagnosis merely stirred up the murkiest shallows of my soul, bringing to the surface my inner cravings for sin, sympathy and back-to-back Big Macs. What a contrast to the One who endured grief infinitely worse than ours yet somehow gouged the words from His heart on which human history would turn: "Not my will, but yours be done" (Luke 22:42).

When our souls, like Christ's, are overwhelmed with sorrow to the point of death, we do not necessarily pray like Jesus. In fact, we may barely pray at all. I've noticed that one of the common defense mechanisms against suffering is to glorify it by beatifying any person who manages to endure pain with some modicum of dignity. We are quick to describe such people as heroic. We consider them deep. We frequently declare them saints simply for having suffered. Our subconscious motive in doing this is, perhaps, to distance ourselves from the dreadful possibility that it really could be us in that wheelchair, or caught by that tsunami, or in danger of losing that baby. Of course, many saints do suffer, but in my experience there is nothing glorious—and far less that is glamorous—in the soul's response to profound trauma. Lying half naked and vomiting with fear in an MRI scanner does not automatically grant you a hotline to heaven.

The psychological trauma experienced by Jesus in the Garden of Gethsemane was extreme. Symptomatically, according to

Doctor Luke, "his sweat was like drops of blood falling to the ground" (Luke 22:44). Jesus, we now know, was probably suffering a rare physiological condition called haematidrosis in which, under extreme anguish, capillaries may rupture in the subcutaneous layer of skin near the sweat glands so that the sufferer emits sweat tinged with blood. Here is a man caught in the extremes of mental and spiritual torment. "My soul," He tells His disciples without exaggeration, "is overwhelmed with sorrow to the point of death" (Mark 14:34).

One of the most touching aspects of Christ's prayers at this agonizing time is how very simple and honest they are: "Abba, Father . . . everything is possible for you. Take this cup from me" (v. 36). The great theologian Karl Barth said that true prayer is primarily simple. "In the first instance, it is an asking," he said.[1] This is reassuring for those of us who struggle to issue anything more than six-year-old "Dear God" type requests when we are under intense pressure.

Sometimes we wonder why these prayers are not being answered, and well-meaning people tell us deep things about prayer not being a slot machine, or about the transforming inner power of contemplative prayer, or about fasting, spiritual warfare and the importance of gratitude. We nod and say, "Aha, that's really helpful," but our prayer lives continue to be a staccato succession of yells and groans like a man falling down stairs. And as we gurgle and bounce down the steps of life, these people seem to glide serenely past us on the escalator bound for heaven. Secretly, we may sometimes suspect that we're not really praying at all. So these words from Barth are reassuring:

> It is the fact that [a man] comes before God with his petition which makes him a praying man. Other theories of prayer may be richly and profoundly thought out and may sound very well, but they all suffer from a

certain artificiality because they miss this simple and concrete fact, losing themselves in heights and depths where there is no place for the man who really prays, who is simply making a request.[2]

In that hospital ward, awaiting Samie's surgery, I couldn't manage long, impressive prayers and complicated spiritual techniques. In fact, after many months, I ran out of words altogether. My prayers—if that's what they were—merely amounted to thinking about Samie, the kids or our bank account with a heavy sigh and groaning two words that might have been mistaken for blasphemy: "Oh, God." I didn't know if this even counted as prayer, but at that time it was about all I could manage. I have since come to find enormous riches in other forms of prayer —some of which we will touch on later in this book. But Karl Barth kindly reminds us that it's okay to pray like a six-year-old or a man falling downstairs. In fact, it's more than okay; it's possibly the most important kind of prayer there can be.

### Nostalgia for Normal

The day before the operation, Hudson and baby Daniel were brought in to see their mother, and photographs were taken for reasons we dared not voice. That night, as I slept on a mattress beside her bed—beneath the blessed icon of Saint Martin—Samie secretly wrote her goodbyes. She wrote a letter to me and a letter each for the boys to have and to read when they were older, telling them that their mummy had loved them utterly, that she had never wanted to leave them, and that Jesus loves them still.

Danny's letter was the hardest of all to write, because Samie realized that she didn't yet know anything about him. Who would this little bundle grow up to be? Mourning for memories that might never happen—family photographs in which she might not appear—the letters became shorter with every rewriting, until eventually she knew that she was done. She sealed the three simple messages neatly in three envelopes and hid them where she knew I would find them. There was peace in the completion of this task, and soon Samie too was able to sleep beneath Saint Martin's gaze.

The following day when they eventually called Samie to the operating room, we killed time by playing the quiz game "Who Wants to Be a Millionaire?" The truthful answer to the rhetorical question was "not us!" We wanted more than mere millions. What greater prize could there possibly be than to be ordinary again? What riches to live in a house, go to the supermarket on Thursdays, and simply to tuck the kids in their beds one more time, pink from the bath and smelling of soap.

Somewhere in the hospital, the surgeon was preparing for his third operation of the day. The orderlies came to take Samie down. Would she ever return? And if she did, would she still have her movement, her speech and the ability to understand? Silencing such thoughts, Samie held out her wrist—the one that had first convulsed—and allowed a man to put a needle in it. Her eyes closed and, in less than a minute, she was gone.

Chapter Two

# SEEKING MAGIC FRUIT AND FINDING TEARS

*Abba, Father, everything is possible for you. Take this*
*cup from me. Yet not what I will, but what you will.*
JESUS, MARK 14:36

*Father in heaven,*
*when the thought of you wakes in our hearts,*
*let it not wake like a frightened bird that flies about in dismay,*
*but like a child waking from its sleep with a heavenly smile.*
SØREN KIERKEGAARD

Samie and I had been married just a few months when we went on holiday to the Mediterranean island of Cyprus. After a week lounging on the beach, I was bored, so we packed our bags and hitched a ride on a cruise ship bound for the Israeli port of Haifa. Disembarking, I bought a loaf of freshly baked sesame bread and a super-sized orange from a street trader and settled down to watch a group of kids playing on swings and slides.

Suddenly, a moment of drama occurred: A little boy—about five years old—with a skull cap pinned to his dark curly hair was knocked to the ground by the force of the swing. For a split second he just sat there, dazed, the way kids do when they're trying to figure out if they're hurt or not. Then he just threw back his head and began bawling, "Abba! Abba!" Immediately, his father appeared from the crowd, scooped the boy up in his arms and carried him away from the arc of the returning swing.

## Abba, Father

As Jesus prays in Gethsemane, we are granted one of the most moving insights into the intimacy of His relationship with the one who sent Him. All three synoptic Gospels record that in His darkest hour, Jesus addressed His prayers to the "Father."

However, Mark's Gospel reveals, more particularly, that Jesus used the same word to address His Father as the child crying in the playground that day in Haifa: the intimate Aramaic word "Abba." Here, we see one of the rare occasions in which Mark, almost certainly writing his Gospel in Greek, chooses to use a word in the original language spoken by Jesus in order to drive home a point. He wants us to catch a glimpse of the extraordinary intimacy and humanity of Christ's interaction with the Almighty. This is the only time in the whole Bible in which Jesus addresses Yahweh as "Abba," and He is doing it at the time of His gravest vulnerability. It might well have been the very first word His lips had ever formed as a baby—the first word spoken by the Word incarnate—and now it would also be one of His last: "Abba."

Andrew Murray, a nineteenth-century South African writer, once said, "The power of prayer depends almost entirely upon our apprehension of who it is with whom we speak."[1] When life hurts, it becomes more important than ever to cry out to God like that child on the swing, remembering that He is first and foremost Abba, Father.

We don't know exactly what emotional resonances there were for Jesus in calling his heavenly Father "Abba." Was He taking the word that He had associated since childhood with Joseph, his stepfather, and attaching it to God? Or is it possible that Jesus had never called Joseph "Abba"—that Mary had shared with Him the circumstances of His conception and that the intimacy of this term was therefore reserved in Christ's heart for Yahweh alone? You decide! If the word "father" is full of positive human associations in your life, then by all means bundle them together, double their meaning, and apply them to the Creator God. But if, on the other hand, you had no dad, or he was absent, abusive or cold, then you, perhaps like Jesus who had no biological human father, can reserve for God alone the wonderful name "Abba," Father.

We tend to assume that there is a necessary depth of spirituality to which we must aspire, a technique we are somehow lacking, or a key of mystical revelation that will unlock the miracles we require. But Jesus consistently taught His followers that the key to powerful praying was to simply understand that the one to whom they were praying was their Father in heaven. He taught the disciples to begin their prayers, "Our Father." He told the crowds that God loves to give good gifts to them because they are His children (see Matt. 7:9-11). Jesus taught that the aim of prayer is the Father's glory (see John 14:13) and that the power of prayer is rooted in the Father's love. Ultimately, He addressed the most desperate prayers of His life to the One He knew as Abba.

God's voice can so easily be muted by our hurt, our self-hatred or our crazy preconceptions about who He really is, how He speaks and what we think He will say. But when we come to God repeatedly with some deep need—perhaps for healing, or to find a partner, or for a friend who's turned his back on Jesus—His eyes are not angry, bored or cold and passionless, assessing the merits of our request and the technique of our prayer. Whenever we come to God with an open wound of longing, we come to Abba, Father, who loves us deeply. "Cast all your anxiety on him," says the apostle Peter, "because he cares for you" (1 Pet. 5:7).

## Seeking Magic Fruit

In the first of his Narnia Chronicles, *The Magician's Nephew*, which is the prequel to *The Lion The Witch and The Wardrobe*, C. S. Lewis tells the story of a boy named Digory whose mother is dying. When Digory first encounters the great lion Aslan, he gathers his courage and asks, "May I—please, will you give me some magic fruit of this country to make Mother well?" It's a heart-rending request—a prayer of desperation—and yet, at the time, Aslan appears to ignore it completely:

> He had been desperately hoping that the Lion would say "Yes"; he had been horribly afraid it might say "No." But he was taken aback when it did neither.[2]

When God is silent in response to our deepest and most desperate prayers—saying neither yes with a miracle nor no with a clear sign that would at least let us know He had heard us—it is natural to conclude that God doesn't care. But a little while later, Digory dares to ask Aslan for help again:

> He thought of his Mother, and he thought of the great hopes he had, and how they were all dying away, and a lump came in his throat and tears in his eyes, and he blurted out:
> "But please, please won't you—can't you give me something that will cure Mother?" Up till then he had been looking at the Lion's great feet and the huge claws on them; now, in despair, he looked up at its face. What he saw surprised him as much as anything in his whole life.

For the tawny face was bent down near his own and (wonder of wonders) great shining tears stood in the Lion's eyes. They were such big, bright tears compared with Digory's own that for a moment he felt as if the Lion must really be sorrier about his Mother than he was himself.[3]

Digory's prayer remained unanswered, but everything had changed. Now, he knew that the great Lion—in whom all his hopes were resting—truly cared. Whenever we carry a burden to God in prayer, begging, "please, please, won't you, can't you" and yet God remains silent, we may assume that He is unmoved as long as our eyes remain downcast reverently at His feet. But when, in our pain and shame, we dare to lift our gaze to study His countenance, we find His face bent down near our own and, "(wonder of wonders) great shining tears" are in His eyes. What an incredible revelation! Our Jewish forefathers considered God's name so holy that it was never to be pronounced nor transcribed. And yet this same God invites us to speak to Him and to call Him "Abba."

## The "Cosmic Sadist"

If you're going through a particularly painful time and your prayers don't seem to be making any noticeable difference, pictures of lions and tears may sound a bit trite. We can't build our lives on stories in children's books. What's more, *The Magician's Nephew* was written by a man who apparently lived a thoroughly cosseted existence, sipping tea with Tolkien and discussing classics beneath the dreaming spires of Oxford.

However, Lewis was no stranger to pain, and this particular story in the Narnia Chronicles is actually his most autobiographical. Like Digory, C. S. Lewis at the age of 10 watched his mother suffer with cancer. At one point she recovered (as if by magic) in answer to his childish prayers only to die two months later. Suddenly orphaned, C. S. Lewis was dispatched to boarding school, where the headmaster was so sadistic that he would eventually, two years after Lewis's arrival, be declared insane.

Ironically, this poignant, semi-autobiographical story of Digory's quest for a magic fruit to cure his mother's illness finally found its way onto paper during one of the happiest periods of Lewis's later life. However, just months after the book's publication, the story would rise to haunt him when his wife-to-be, Joy Gresham, was diagnosed with the disease that had killed his mother. Suddenly, all Lewis's childhood terrors were revived and, once again, he prayed childish prayers and dared to hope for miraculous fruit.

During a remission, Lewis married Joy—such a poignant name—only for her to die 5 years later at the age of 45. Still fresh with grief, C. S. Lewis wrote a book so shocking that it was originally necessary to publish it under a pseudonym. In *A Grief Observed,* the man who charms our hearts with comforting images of a weeping lion reflects on the agony of his wife's protracted dying and dares to wonder whether God is, in fact, just a cosmic sadist or a spiteful imbecile who enjoys inflicting pain on people:

> What chokes every prayer and every hope is the memory of all the prayers [Joy] and I offered and all the false hopes we had. Not hopes raised merely by our own wishful thinking, hopes encouraged, even forced upon us, by false diagnoses, by X-ray photographs, by strange remissions, by one temporary recovery that might have ranked as a miracle. Step by step we were "led up the garden path." Time after time, when He seemed most gracious He was really preparing the next torture.[4]

After a good night's sleep, the sophic Oxford don reread these words and acknowledged that they had been more of a yell of pain than a thought. But, crucially, he leaves them in the book. C. S. Lewis did not, as the movie *Shadowlands* implies, lose his faith, but he certainly struggled in his own Gethsemane with this idea of God as a deeply compassionate father.

When the pain of life strips us bare of sentiment, children's stories will no longer do as a basis for theology and prayer. At such times, we must return from Narnia to the grim historical actualities of Jesus in the Garden of Gethsemane, overwhelmed as He was with sorrow to the point of death, sweating blood and pleading with God for His own deliverance. This is no bedtime story. In Gethsemane we find no cheap emotion, no space for religious sloganeering. Instead, we solemnly watch a man like us wrestling with His own soul, "overwhelmed with sorrow to the point of death" (Mark 14:34). This, then, is the context for Christ's sparse, 21-word prayer that teaches us to begin by bringing our pain to "Abba, Father."

## When God Is All You've Got

When my deep prayers don't work, I easily default to despair, anger or doubt. Although I believe that God can handle my hang-ups, the truth is that there is only temporary comfort in anger and no hope whatsoever in doubt.

One morning, I asked Samie if she ever doubted God's existence or His power to intervene. She was back in the hospital after a particularly vicious epileptic attack. It was really more of a confession on my part than a question for her. But without hesitation, Samie replied, "No! I never doubt God these days, Pete." Pausing, she examined my face with a mixture of affection and reproach. "How can I doubt God?" she continued more softly. "God is all I've got!"

It's amazing to me that the shock of Samie's diagnosis never caused her to struggle with the fundamentals of her faith.

As she prepared for surgery, enduring such inner turmoil, Samie's belief in God's existence, love and power proved resolute. In fact, her belief grew stronger in spite of such profound disappointment and unanswered prayer. Of course, such convictions are well founded. Our hope in the face of suffering is not to reject God but rather to rely on Him even more, choosing to call Him "Father" with a mixture of desperation and hope, militantly believing that although our prayers remain unanswered, it is not because God is callous or uncaring, for He is love.

At one moment in his autobiography, the atheistic philosopher Bertrand Russell speaks with bleak honesty on behalf of those who have no such faith in God:

> We stand on the shore of an ocean, crying to the night and to emptiness; sometimes a voice answers out of the darkness. But it is a voice of one drowning; and in a moment the silence returns. The world seems to me quite dreadful; the unhappiness of most people is very great.[5]

We all stand on the shore of that ocean—atheists, agnostics, God-lovers and God-haters alike—and we all eventually experience seasons of great unhappiness. But how tragic it is to be the one "crying to the night and to emptiness" without this profound comfort of knowing the love of God the Father.

The revelation of God's love—the tears in His eyes—may not solve any of our intellectual questions about why He leaves a particular prayer unanswered. (In many ways, the sight of those tears makes His unresponsiveness even harder to comprehend.) But it does touch an emotional need within us that is perhaps even deeper than the intellectual one: the need to know that what we are going through and the way that we are feeling *matters;* the need to know that our requests have been *heard;* the need to know that God—in whom we have placed all our hope—is near and He truly *cares.*

· · · ·

Soon after Samie's tumor was diagnosed, our baby Daniel contracted chicken pox. I remember all too well his perfect little baby body covered in prickly, red spots. They were even in his mouth and on his eyelids. His temperature soared, his skin itched, he sniveled, and when he sneezed his nose produced number-11 formations of snot that ran in two streaks down his face.

Watching our baby in such distress was painful. I yearned to tell him why he felt so terrible and that he wasn't going to feel like this for the rest of his life. But, of course, a five-month-old baby can't understand words, let alone the concepts of recovery and immunity. I gave him tepid baths and smeared him in Calamine lotion, but the relief was short-lived. All I could really do to soothe his distress was to hold him and wait out the days.

Pacing the landing and cuddling Danny one night, it occurred to me that perhaps my heavenly Father wanted to do the same thing for me. Eventually, Danny's crying subsided and he sank into a fitful sleep. At last, I found myself with the luxury of time to reflect on the events since his birth. What had happened to those normal, excited parents who were expecting the imminent arrival of their second child? Life no longer felt safe. In fact, it felt dangerous. How do you relax once you discover that the human body is a time bomb waiting to explode? Slowly, it was dawning on me that, in my early thirties, I would never again feel immune or immortal or invincible—which is to say that I would never again feel young.

There had been little time for processing such thoughts since the diagnosis. If life were a movie, Samie and I would, by now, have gazed into each other's eyes, found just the right words to express what we were going through, and cried a lot. But life doesn't come with a scriptwriter and a string quartet, and no such moment in our lives had arisen. Instead, here I was pacing the landing, up and down, plodding on from day to day trying to cope. In addition to dealing with my wife's critical condition, I also had two small and bewildered children to nurture, I had friends to visit whom I'd hardly seen in months, and, to cap it all off, I was worried about letting down an international movement to which I was supposed to be contributing leadership.

Around this time, one of our friends, an Earth-Mother type, told me that it was actually "a good thing" that Danny had contracted chicken pox because it is apparently so much worse to get it later in life. When I thanked her for this piece of information, she asked if it would be okay to throw a "pox party" to expose her unblemished children to Danny's highly desirable virus. I've been to some pretty lousy parties in my time, but it seemed to me that a pox party would be the worst of the lot. So I said no. You have to be firm with these people.

Twenty years from now, Danny will no doubt understand all about chicken pox, and he will probably look back and be glad that he's had it. When life hurts and we find ourselves struggling to make sense of unanswered prayer, we often wonder why God doesn't just click His fingers and make everything better. At such times of unknowing when there's nothing good in the pain and we're helpless and hopeless as a baby with chicken pox, there is comfort in trusting God to carry us through the turmoil in His arms. We may not be able to understand why He is allowing the situation to continue when He has the power to stop it, but, like Danny crying without comprehension in my arms, we can still trust Abba, Father.

## A Doxology in the Darkness

In 1900, Hudson Taylor, the great pioneer missionary to China, suffered a nervous breakdown. He was speaking in Boston at the time when he began to repeat the same two phrases over and over again: "You may trust the Lord too little but you can never trust him too much" and "If we believe not, yet he abideth faithful: he cannot deny himself" (2 Tim. 2:13, *KJV*).

Hudson Taylor repeated these two extraordinary sentences over and over before finally being escorted from the stage. He returned to London and then, on doctor's orders, moved to Switzerland in a state of complete mental and physical exhaustion. That was where the terrible news reached him that 58 of his fellow missionaries and 21 children had been massacred in the Boxer Revolution. The news was almost more than his aging heart and exhausted mind could endure. "I cannot read; I cannot think; I cannot even pray," he admitted to his wife, "but I can trust."[6]

With hindsight, we can see that Hudson Taylor's trust was well-founded: The blood of such martyrs was to become the seed of the Chinese Church, which has since grown into one of the most vibrant and sacrificial expressions of Christian faith in the contemporary world. But at the time, devastated by the pain of so many lives cut short, children killed and the gospel seemingly silenced, Hudson Taylor could find no such hope in the tragedy. Countless prayers for protection had come to nothing. Years of intercession and endeavor for the evangelization of inland China had seemingly been thwarted. Hudson Taylor could do nothing but trust, resting helplessly in the arms of the one who "abideth faithful," even when he was in doubt.

When we are hurting and the pain seems senseless, we may find it hard to think clearly or to pray diligently. But we can still trust, resting quietly in the Father's love for us (see Isa. 30:15). What does this mean in practice? In part it means meditating on the wonderful promises of Scripture with a hopeful heart for the future. It also means remembering the goodness of God poured out to us in the past, perhaps through things and places that remind us of happier times. And in the present, it means receiving the kindness of people as gifts from God. Whenever we choose to recognize and receive such blessings (especially the small ones) with a grateful heart, we open ourselves to the love of the Father. As Brennan Manning puts it:

> To be grateful for an unanswered prayer, to give thanks in a state of interior desolation, to trust in the love of God in the face of the marvels, cruel circumstances, obscenities, and commonplaces of life is to whisper a doxology in the darkness.[7]

In a letter written from prison, Anatoly Emmanuilovich Letivin, an old Russian Orthodox believer who had been persecuted all his life by the secret police, described this incomparable power of prayer to bring peace and to enlighten even the darkest moments of our lives:

> The greatest miracle of all is prayer. I have only to turn my thoughts to God and I suddenly feel a strength which bursts into my soul, into my entire being. What is it? Psychotherapy? No, it is not psychotherapy, for where would I, an insignificant, tired old man, get this strength which renews me and saves me, lifting me above the earth? It comes from without and there is no force on earth that can even understand it.[8]

The lives of people such as Letivin inspire us to accept the reality of the Father's love, even when times are hard. I don't know why your prayers haven't been answered. But I do know that the very best thing about our lives—the most incredible thing we've got going for us—is that the Creator of a million stars is entirely and eternally good, that He is utterly caught up in the details of our situation, and that He cares for us more than we care for ourselves.

God loves you, and not just out of a divine duty to love people whether He likes them or not. He loves you passionately with relentless fascination because it is the great delight of His being to do so. The God of the cosmos thinks you are amazing. You! Not just some heavenly, idealized version of the person you might one day become. You—the person who does such stupid things. You—the one with a peculiar sense of humor. You—the one with bad hair, bad breath and bad desires.

The Bible consistently exposes the depth of God's love for us. "Whoever touches you," says the prophet Zechariah to the people of God, "touches the apple of his eye" (Zech. 8:2). The royal poet Zephaniah says that God "will quiet you with his love" and "rejoice over you with singing" (Zeph. 3:17). Isaiah memorably portrays God as one who tattoos the name of His people on the palms of His hands (see Isa. 49:16). The Song of Songs is an entire hymn to the divine romance of God's passionate desire for, and pursuit of, His bride. The psalmist says, with a mixture of wonder and fear, "You hem me in—behind and before . . . Where can I flee from your presence?" (Ps. 139:5,7).

The apostle Paul kneels before the Father and prays that the believers in Ephesus would somehow comprehend the extravagance of God's love. Elsewhere, he suggests to the Christians in Rome that "our present sufferings are not worth comparing with the glory that will be revealed in us" (Rom. 8:18). In *us*! Not just in *Jesus* and not just *to* us or *for* us. The glory of God will be revealed *in* ordinary people like us who are currently having such difficulties.

Paul follows this verse with one of the most remarkable assurances in the entire canon of Holy Scripture: "In *all* things" he says, "God works for the good of those who love him, who have been called according to his purpose" (v. 28, emphasis added). Perhaps we are still reeling from that last promise and wondering whether Paul can really, honestly mean what he has just said when he concludes with another incredible assertion: "I am convinced, that neither death nor life . . . nor anything else in all creation, will be able to separate us from the love of God" (v. 38).

Not angels and not demons. Not cancer wards and not concentration camps. Not loneliness and not fear. Not bankruptcy, not bereavement, not barrenness. Nothing we endure has the innate power to tear us away from the ultimate reality of the fact that we are loved eternally by *Abba, Father*.

### Prayer

*Abba, Father, I know all this stuff about Your love in my head, but my heart gets hard to it and I'm tired. Please do whatever You've got to do (and I mean whatever) to unclench my fists. Pry open my eyes so that I can see Your tears and soften my heart so that it moves me deeply. I don't understand why You don't just answer my prayers, but I do choose to trust that You have heard me, that You actually do care and that You're somewhere out there on my case. Abba, Father, thank You for all the ways You have blessed me. I honestly don't know what I'd do, where I'd be or even who I'd have become without You. Abba, Father, I am going to try to trust You today. Amen.*

Chapter Three

# INTO THE MYSTERY

*Everything is possible for you . . .*
JESUS, MARK 14:36

In the Garden of Gethsemane, Jesus, having addressed Himself intimately to "Abba, Father," then proceeds to reverently acknowledge God's power: "Everything is possible for you" (Mark 14:36). In grasping the wonder of God's fatherly love, we must also recognize the awesome possibilities of His sovereignty.

C. S. Lewis cautions us to remember that for all his tears, Aslan is not a tame lion. An old Hebrew saying makes a similar point: "God is not a kindly old uncle; He is an earthquake."[1] This is the best news possible when we are struggling with unanswered prayer, for while there is comfort for the present in receiving God's fatherly love, there is also an irresistible hope for the future that is implicit in His omnipotence. An earthquake can shift things that a kindly old uncle can only smile at. Sometimes, the lion must roar.

The questions provoked by our experiences of unanswered prayer tend to call into question either God's love ("Don't You care?") or His power ("Can't You help?"). Having explored the Father's love in the previous chapter, we will now examine the implications of His power for those of us living with disappointments in prayer.

· · · ·

Samie and I spent the first week of our honeymoon in a remote cottage tucked away in the beautiful English Lake District. The closest town, Ambleside, boasted a tiny, one-screen cinema, so one night we decided, like the reckless young things we were, to take a risk and go see whatever happened to be showing.

I can't say that I recommend watching *Schindler's List* on your honeymoon. It's a powerful film and I've since purchased my own copy, but, as you may recall, the scenes of profound human suffering in Auschwitz are deeply disturbing, as are the questions raised by Oskar Schindler's reluctant heroism. By the end of the movie, Samie and I were shell-shocked. No one in the cinema moved until the final credits had rolled from the screen. Samie and I came out of the building in silence, climbed into our old Volvo 340 and began driving the winding country lanes back to our cottage.

We were miles from civilization when I noticed that the car was about to run out of gas. Instinctively I muttered a prayer: "Get us home safely, Lord. I really don't want to break down out here!" From there we willed the car, gasping and spluttering, all the way back to our cottage. Turning off the engine at last, I breathed a sigh of relief and walked into the house thanking God. And then, suddenly, it hit me.

"How on earth can I believe that God did that?" I said.

"Did what?" replied Samie.

"Got us home safely without running out of gas, just to save me the inconvenience of walking a few miles with a gas can?"

"Erm, because He loves us?" Samie ventured warily, bringing me back to the simple stuff.

"Yeah, I know," I continued, "but didn't He care just as much about all His people in that concentration camp crying out for help? Do we seriously believe that God heard my prayer for gasoline in Ambleside yet ignored their prayers for help in Auschwitz?"

"Darling, it's our honeymoon," Samie reminded me. "This really isn't a great time for a crisis of faith." A mischievous grin flashed across her face. "Pass me the car keys."

"What for?"

"If it helps you cheer up, let's keep driving until the car breaks down. You'll lose your dignity but keep your faith!"

As I said, *Schindler's List* isn't a great movie to watch on your honeymoon.

. . . .

Theologians refer to any systematic Christian response to the problem of suffering as "theodicy" (literally *théos diké*, the justice of God).[2] The problem to which theodicy seeks to respond is expressed succinctly in the first seven words of Christ's prayer in Gethsemane: "Abba, Father, everything is possible for you." In this juxtaposition of God's love and power, we have the very heart of the problem of suffering encapsulated in a single sentence: His love means that He must surely *want* to end most (but not necessarily all) suffering, and His power means that He must surely be *able* to end it. So why doesn't He? It's a profoundly important question, not least because so many people have lost their faith in the face of suffering.

Just before Christmas 2005, lightning struck a Presbyterian church in Malawi, killing 11 worshipers and injuring many others. Theodicy seeks to explain why God in His love and power allowed that tragedy to happen to a bunch of His people gathered in His name to worship. Have you ever wondered why God doesn't just speak in an audible voice or in a dramatic dream or send an angel to visit a cynical friend for whom you've been praying for years? Doesn't God care about him or her?

Yes! Isn't He able to reveal Himself to her? Of course! Theodicy
tries to make sense of such important questions.

Part of the problem we face is that Jesus promised, in the
most categorical terms, to respond to our requests. "I tell you
the truth," He said, "My Father will give you whatever you ask
in my name . . . Ask and you will receive" (John 16:23-24).
What, then, are we to make of our unanswered prayers? Did He
get it wrong? Was Jesus just exaggerating when He said that
everything is possible for God? Of course, the big get-out clause
is that little phrase "in my name," and admittedly there are
many prayers that go unanswered because they are blatantly
incompatible with God's character and purposes. But why do
so many prayers that appear to fit perfectly with God's revealed
will in Scripture remain unanswered? Can we really just say to
the mother in mourning, "It wasn't God's will to save your
baby?" Are we supposed to believe that the rape victim who
screams for help is praying out of line with the Father's purposes? These are extreme examples, admittedly, but they are not
uncommon.

And what about my *Schindler's List* question: How are we to
make sense of the idea that God provides for the details of our
lives—food on the plate and gas in the tank—when so many
people cry out to Him from the farthest clutches of despair, yet
suffer and die?

## Downsizing God

A few days after blowing out the candles on his third birthday
cake, Aaron Kushner was diagnosed with the premature aging
disease called *progeria*. His parents were told that he would
never grow to be more than three feet tall, would never have
hair on his head, would look like a wizened, old man and—
worst of all—that he would never reach adulthood. Devastated,

they tried to make the most of Aaron's short life, wanting his life to matter and for him to be remembered. All the while, they wrestled with their own profound questions about God's purposes and the evident limitations of prayer.

Aaron died at the age of 14. Years later his father, a rabbi, looked back on his son's short life and wrote these moving words:

> I am a more sensitive person, a more effective pastor, a more sympathetic counselor because of Aaron's life and death than I would ever have been without it. And I would give up all of those gains in a second if I could have my son back. If I could choose, I would forego all the spiritual growth and depth which has come my way because of our experiences, and be what I was fifteen years ago, an average rabbi, an indifferent counselor, helping some people and unable to help others, and the father of a bright, happy boy. But I cannot choose.[3]

It's true that our unanswered prayers can teach us great truths and make us more sensitive to others. We can be refined by suffering, which is comforting when we experience relatively minor trials. But when our loss is profound, it is understandable if we would rather trade every good thing wrought in our lives by affliction just to have that person or that wholeness or that hope back again. But, like the rabbi, we cannot choose.

Rabbi Harold Kushner wrote a book about the profound questions his son's life and premature death raised, which went on to become a surprise bestseller. *When Bad Things Happen to Good People* proposes that the only way to make sense of unmerited suffering without losing one's faith in God is to reduce our expectations of what God is able to do. Faced with the tension between God's love and God's omnipotence, Kushner argues that we should accept God's love but downgrade our expectations of His power. In particular, he says that we should stop expecting miracles—not because God won't do them, but because in many situations He simply can't do them: "God would like people to get what they deserve in life but He cannot always arrange it."[4]

In some respects, this is an attractive proposition. Nuns at a convent in Massachusetts wrote to Kushner to say that, although they disagreed with his theology, they were giving out five copies of his book a week because they found it to be such a comforting message. The nuns added that they figured they could correct peoples' theology later!

## Arbitrary Miracles

The American who sat opposite me in the quiet English pub wore a scruffy denim jacket, his ear pierced and his expression thoughtful as he simultaneously pulled and pummeled at my conscience.

Rob Morris is from Connecticut, and he spends a lot of his life trying to rescue children who are victims of sex trafficking. There was no mistaking the fire in his eyes as he described the little girls he had seen living in slavery in the brothels of Southeast Asia. Rob described one brothel where the girls are made to wear uniform red dresses with large number badges so that they can be easily chosen. The children choose to watch cartoons while predatory men drink beer and watch them through a glass screen in order to take their pick. Rob told me that on one occasion when investigators raided a brothel to rescue some children, they discovered that one of the girls had written a prayer for help all over the wall of her room. Had they been sent in answer to that little girl's heart cry to God? Had He seen her graffiti, heard her plea and intervened to save her life?

Such a hopeful possibility inspires Rob in his work, and yet he admitted that it also disturbs him deeply. It troubles him because there are hundreds of thousands of children like that girl, all crying out to God for help, and yet no one will ever rescue them. "Miracles seem so *random,*" he said. "One person gets rescued or healed or whatever, but a thousand others don't."

The abolitionist paused, searching my face for permission to say what he was really feeling. "Sometimes I think I'd actually find it easier if God didn't do miracles," he said. He looked around at the faces in the pub, but I could tell that his mind was lost in the streets of Southeast Asia, watching men watching girls watching cartoons. "I mean, if God never did miracles, we could just get on with using prayer like a meditation technique and trust Him for all the non-physical stuff. I could accept that. What confuses me is the fact that God does sometimes seem to intervene dramatically and supernaturally in answer to prayer. He does it *sometimes,* so why doesn't He do it all the time? Miracles just seem so *arbitrary.*" Rob paused, staring into his drink as if looking for answers. "Is it just some kind of lottery who gets a miracle and who doesn't?"

Rob looked up from his drink. It was my turn to stare into mine.

When wrestling with the questions of unanswered prayer—whether you're a rabbi with a dying child, a man on a mission in a Bangkok brothel, or somebody who's prayed a thousand times for healing—it's natural to question the apparent limitations of God's power with regard to miraculous intervention. *Is everything* really *possible for the Father?* you sometimes wonder darkly. Maybe He's limited in how many miracles or in what kind of miracles He can do.

Few people state this doubt as brazenly as Kushner. More often, they say things that sound very spiritual and faith-filled, such as, "Prayer isn't about changing reality. It's about changing the way we *look* at reality." They elevate the contemplative and internal dimensions of prayer at the expense of the primary type of prayer that is petitionary: the act of asking God to do or to change some actual thing.

## Psychoanalyzing God

However, Jesus did not tell His disciples that if they had faith as small as a mustard seed they would be able to shift their *attitude* toward the mountain. He said that the mountain itself would move. Reality would shift in obedience to their faith, and, Jesus added, "Nothing will be impossible for you" (Matt. 17:20-21). It is clear from Christ's subsequent ministry and that of His disciples—not to mention the testimony of the Church down two millennia—that God can and does do miracles. The omnipotence of God is a consistent theme of the entire Bible—even when it creates great problems of faith for the writers.

If we go right back to the earliest book of the Bible, we find that at the conclusion to Job's litany of agonizing experiences, God finally appeared and revealed His power. When (to coin Kushner's title) bad things happen to this good person called Job, God does not say, "I feel your pain, son, and I'd like to help, but I can't." Quite the reverse! God rolls back the clouds to unveil an awesome vision that, far from diminishing Job's expectations of His power, renders him speechless. "Where were you," God rumbles, "when I laid the earth's foundation? Tell me, if you understand. Who marked off its dimensions? Surely you know . . . who laid its cornerstone—while the morning stars sang together and all the angels shouted for joy?" (Job 38:4-7).

God's answer to Job's archetypal cry of "why?" is simply, "look at Me" (see Job 38–41). "My ears had heard of you but now my eyes have seen you," cries Job in awe, as if his sufferings have simply evaporated (42:5). The book of Job is therefore both the most frustrating and enlightening treatment of unanswered prayer in the Bible, because God's solution to so much misery is merely and ultimately to reveal His greatness.

The great psychoanalyst Carl Jung found the story so disturbing that he wrote a book called *An Answer to Job,* setting himself face to face with what he considered to be "the unvarnished spectacle of divine savagery and ruthlessness."[5] So troubled was Jung by Job's predicament that he attempted to psychoanalyze God, concluding with a suggestion so bizarre that it would be hard to take seriously if it had not come from one of the most respected thinkers of the nineteenth century. Jung proposed that God was in fact so ashamed of His behavior toward Job that He sent Jesus to die in penance for His own injustice. Jesus, said Jung, was given to the world as a guilt response because God felt bad and needed to grow in His own moral consciousness![6]

Jung had every right to rage against the apparent injustices of a God who permits suffering. He was, remember, writing just seven years after the holocaust in a continent devastated by war. But he missed the fundamental point of the book of Job. No matter how much we might wish such a graphic depiction of tragedy to explain the reasons for suffering—to answer the great "why" of life—this ancient text concludes with an epiphany of God's power that extinguishes Job's need for such an explanation. The book, we discover, is not so much about why bad things happen to good people as it is about who God is and how—when faced with the gross unfairness of life—we are to respond. It is a message that defies the cheap comfort of easy explanations but leaves us in no doubt about God's power.

With its awesome conclusion, the message of the book of Job ultimately contradicts Kushner's theodicy of divine weakness. And what of the Garden of Gethsemane? Do we have the text wrong? Did Jesus in fact pray, "Abba, Father, a few things are possible for You. I wish You were able to take this cup from me, but I know You can't"? No! Christ's prayer in Gethsemane unequivocally asserted the Father's absolute power over *every-thing*. Through Good Friday and Easter Saturday, Rabbi Kushner and all those who doubt God's miracle-working power today might seem thoroughly vindicated. But with Easter Sunday comes the ultimate revelation for all time that our God *can* work miracles in the physical realm. He is Abba, Father. Yet He is also the sovereign Lord.

It saddens me to see how many people today—particularly many of my friends in the emerging church scene—are quietly downgrading their belief in miraculous healing in response to their own disappointments in prayer. Admittedly, miraculous healings are rarer than we would like them to be and much rarer than many preachers would lead us to believe (we will explore this in more detail in chapter 7). Undeniably, there have been many terrible abuses of people's gullibility and des-peration (Jesus predicted that this would happen). Without doubt, there are also many painful questions that have been provoked by a belief in miracles (not least, as my friend Rob points out, their apparently arbitrary nature). But belief in God's power to perform miracles has never been an optional extra to the Christian faith. Every clause of the Apostles' Creed hinges upon a miracle: the creation of the world, the virgin conception of Jesus, the resurrection of Jesus from the dead, the ascension of Jesus into heaven, the bodily resurrection of the saints and the life everlasting. It's quite a list!

We shall see later that there may be some limited truth in Kushner's argument in so far as there are areas in which God, in His sovereignty, may choose to restrict His own power. However, while Kushner's view of God as *intrinsically* limited may seem comforting at a superficial level, it simply does not hold up to scrutiny. Biblically, it is not consistent with the revelation of God in the Hebrew and New Testaments. Historically, Kushner's downsizing is not consistent with extensive human experience of

God's miraculous intervention in every age. Philosophically, it is not consistent with any monotheistic definition of divinity. Even personally, it is, ultimately, not comforting to abandon all hope of miracles by shrinking our view of God's power to the size of our own pain. As Samie said to me from her place of despair, "God is all I've got."

## Ceasing to Plead

We've seen that some theists, like Kushner, seek to reconcile their belief in God's love with their experience of suffering by limiting their expectations of His power. "God loves us," they insist, "but He simply can't do everything we need Him to. That's why our prayers are unanswered."

Other people insist that God, by definition, must be omnipotent. So, instead of questioning His power like Kushner, they doubt His goodness. This is what Jung did when he concluded his analysis of Job by questioning the sincerity of God's love. "God is guilty," these people say in response to suffering. "The reason He doesn't answer our prayers is that He is not good."

However, there is a third position, as espoused by the holocaust survivor Elie Wiesel and many like him. These people resign themselves to the idea that the suffering of this world is ultimately a mystery and beyond human comprehension. To them, Kushner's pragmatism seems ridiculous and inadequate. But so too does Jung's hubris in attempting to psychoanalyze God. "We can ask God the questions," they say, "But we will never be able to understand why such terrible things happen."[7]

In his remarkable memoir simply titled *Night*, Wiesel describes a previously pious teenager angrily losing his faith in God's love during—of all things—a prayer meeting. A crowd of 10,000 men had gathered in Auschwitz to mark Rosh Hashanah, the end of the Jewish New Year, but for that teenage boy, it was to become his initiation into unbelief. Wiesel writes:

> I heard the voice of the officiant rising up, powerful yet at the same time broken, amid the tears, the sobs, the sighs of the whole congregation, *"All the earth and the Universe are God's!"* He kept stopping every moment, as though he did not have the strength to find the meaning beneath the words. The melody choked in his throat.
>
> And I, mystic that I had been, I thought: "Yes . . . But these men here, whom You have betrayed, whom You have allowed to be tortured, butchered, gassed, burned, what do they do? They pray before You! They praise Your Name!"
>
> *"All creation bears witness to the greatness of God!"*
>
> Once, New Year's Day had dominated my life. I knew that my sins grieved the Eternal; I implored His forgiveness. Once, I had believed profoundly that upon one solitary deed of mine, one solitary prayer, depended the salvation of the world.
>
> This day, I had ceased to plead. I was no longer capable of lamentation. On the contrary, I felt very strong. I was the accuser, God the accused. My eyes were open and I was alone—terribly alone in a world without God and without man. Without love or mercy. I had ceased to be anything but ashes, yet I felt myself to be stronger than the Almighty, to whom my life had been tied for so long. I stood amidst that praying congregation, observing it like a stranger.[8]

In the face of great suffering, many thousands of people have come to the same tragic conclusion as Elie Wiesel. Angry at God, they have "ceased to plead." Some may not abandon the community of faith altogether, but they remain "amidst that praying congregation, observing it like a stranger." They may still believe in God, but they doubt His intentions.

## Finding God in Hell

Unsurprisingly, Hitler's holocaust—during which at least five million people were herded together and systematically slaughtered—is cited more than any other global atrocity as evidence in the case against God. Here, we are told, is the ultimate example not just of man's brutality to man but of God's disregard for people—His *own* people.

For this reason, an American rabbi, Dr. Reeve Robert Brenner, surveyed hundreds of holocaust survivors to find out how their experiences had affected their beliefs about God.[9] Dr. Brenner's conclusions were extraordinary. First, he discovered that the horrors of the Holocaust had no impact at all on the religious convictions of a remarkably high percentage (almost half) of the survivors. Somehow these people had endured hell on Earth without losing their faith in Yahweh. "It never occurred to me to question God's doings while I was an inmate of Auschwitz, although of course I understand that others did," wrote one survivor. "If someone believes God is responsible for the death of six million because he didn't somehow do something to save them, he's got his thinking reversed. We owe God our lives for the few or many years we live, and we have the duty to worship him."[10]

According to Dr. Brenner's research, about 11 percent of Holocaust survivors did lose their faith in God (although he observes that their professions of atheism seemed more like an emotional shift than a theological one because so many of them continued to believe in God enough to be angry with Him). However, the really extraordinary discovery made by Dr. Brenner was that 5 percent of the Holocaust survivors in his survey had actually abandoned atheism and begun to believe in God as a direct result of their experiences in the Nazi laboratories of death.

If we project that extraordinary statistic onto the total number of European and Russian Jews that survived the Holocaust (around three-and-a-half million people), it is equivalent to 177,000 survivors coming to faith through the concentration camps. To put it another way, it would be like 5 percent of the total population of Los Angeles turning to Yahweh in just five years. In Christian terms, this might be described as one of the most fruitful "revival" movements in any one people-group during the last 70 years. However, it becomes astounding when considered against the backdrop of the concentration camps, so often held up as primary evidence against the benevolence of God.

When we look at situations of unanswered prayer and conclude that there is no God or that if there is a God, He is either a powerful sadist or an impotent but kindly old uncle, His removal from the equation of our suffering solves nothing. However problematic His existence may seem, without God—this bankruptcy, this broken marriage, this four-year-old with leukemia, this congregation killed by lightening, this mother mowed down by a drunk driver—the tragedies of life are reduced to meaningless losses in the great evolutionary casino. Without God, we are hopelessly alone in a twisted reality, contorting without spiritual comfort and without the hope, however distant, of supernatural intervention. As the poet W. H. Auden puts it, "Nothing can save us that is possible, we who must die demand a miracle.[11]

## Possibilities

A story is told of the Nobel Prize-winning Russian novelist Alexander Solzhenitsyn when he was imprisoned by Stalin in a Siberian gulag. One day, slaving away in sub-zero temperatures, he finally reached the end of his endurance. Discarding his shovel, he slumped onto a bench and waited for a guard to beat him to death. He'd seen it happen to others and was waiting for the first blow to fall.

Before this could happen, an emaciated fellow prisoner approached Solzhenitsyn silently. Without a word of explanation, the prisoner scratched the sign of the cross in the mud and scurried away. As Solzhenitsyn stared at those two lines scratched in the dirt, the message of the cross began to converse with his sense of despair. "In that moment, he knew that there was something greater than the Soviet Union. He knew that the hope of all mankind was represented in that simple cross. And through the power of the cross, anything was possible."[12] Picking up his shovel, Alexander Solzhenitsyn slowly went back to work.

Nothing but the message of God's suffering could have inspired Solzhenitsyn to return to work that day. Only the presence of God at Golgotha could imbue the gulag with fresh possibilities. More than just the comforting knowledge of divine empathy (great as that is), the cross rekindled in Solzhenitsyn the actual hope that everything was possible for God—even in a Siberian concentration camp, where all the evidence suggested otherwise. In fact, especially in such a place.

The Christian gospel is the story of a God who breaks the rules of plausibility—often when we least expect it and in ways we could never have predicted. Living with unanswered prayer, I need a big God; an awesome, unspeakably amazing God; a death-defying, eternal God; a God who dies in Siberian concentration camps and senseless car crashes in order to destroy death and release an indestructible life. I need a God whose promises are certain; a God who's been there before and can walk with me and counsel me and pray for me and prepare a place for me and who can even make all things work together for good. This, then, is the confession we cannot afford to compromise, even when it propels us into the realms of mystery and confusion: Our God is our Father, loves us completely, is all-powerful and will ultimately make all things new.

> *"He will wipe every tear from their eyes. There will be*
> *no more death or mourning or crying or pain, for the*
> *old order of things has passed away." He who was seat-*
> *ed on the throne said, "I am making everything new!"*
>
> REVELATION 21:4-6

. . . .

## Prayer for Trust in Jesus

*O Christ Jesus,*
*when all is darkness*
*and we feel our weakness and helplessness,*
*give us the sense of Your presence,*
*Your love, and Your strength.*
*Help us to have perfect trust*
*in Your protecting love*
*and strengthening power,*
*so that nothing may frighten or worry us,*
*for, living close to You,*
*we shall see Your hand,*
*Your purpose, Your will through all things.*

ST. IGNATIUS OF LOYOLA

Chapter Four

# NAKED PRAYER

*Take this cup from me . . .*
JESUS, MARK 14:36

*If people cannot speak about their affliction they will be
destroyed by it, or swallowed up by apathy . . . without the
capacity to communicate with others there can be no
change. To become speechless, to be totally without
any relationship, that is death.*
DOROTHEE SÖLLE, *SUFFERING*[1]

A nightmare came true for the brother of a close friend when he
was confirmed HIV positive. Research suggests that those who
manage to maintain an optimistic attitude toward the disease
tend to survive for a longer time without it developing into full-
blown AIDS. So, of course, this terrified young man now hardly dares to be anything other than "fine" and "feeling great" all
the time. He's scared of being scared.

In the Garden of Gethsemane, Jesus was utterly honest
about His fear. He knew that His mission was to "suffer many
things" (Luke 9:22), but He still asked God to take the cup of
suffering away from Him. This is not the kind of thing that
messiahs are supposed to pray. In fact, it's a prayer that runs
counter to God's revealed purposes! But in this heart-rending
request, we are assured that it's okay to grieve and cry, to plead

with God and to wonder why. In fact, it's more than okay—it's affirmed as something that expresses His heart. God accepts our honesty. But as we've seen, when life gets tough it's easy to forget who God is. It's even easier to pretend to be something or someone we're not.

· · · ·

My prayer life really took off the day I became an atheist. It was just before my eighteenth birthday. Admittedly, I was never very good at being an atheist, but I really did give it my best shot. Some days I relapsed into a rather pathetic state of beige agnosticism, and I confess that, once or twice, I gave up altogether and backslid for a few glorious hours of shameless faith in Jesus Christ as my personal Lord and Savior. Embarrassingly, my attempts at apostasy also triggered a minor revolution in my prayer life, through which I learned a lot about being utterly honest with God in prayer. Here's how it happened.

In a matter of months so many things had gone wrong in my 17-year-old world that I gradually became depressed and eventually began to question my faith. It began when I left school with worse grades than anyone expected. I was scheduled to take my driving test the day after receiving these disappointing results, and the test went fine until I somehow managed to get stuck behind a yellow steamroller on its way to work. Nothing in months of rehearsing three-point turns and emergency stops had prepared me for the possibility of getting caught behind a vehicle the size of a large shed rumbling at the speed of a small snail along a very busy road. Kids on bikes and old people on electric carts were passing us on the pavement. Because it was my driving test, I was way too nervous to attempt passing the truck. So instead, I cruised along at a little over five miles an hour for the majority of the examination. I did this faultlessly.

Personally, I think the cautious approach was commend-able. Even now, I insist that the testing official should have considered what an exceptionally safe driver I was going to be as soon as he let me loose on Britain's roads. Instead, I think he imagined me becoming one of those "careful" drivers who pull travel trailers so slowly along congested motorways on public holidays that they create back-ups longer than the Great Wall of China. Whatever the reason, the testing official failed me. With the benefit of hindsight, my advice to people who get stuck behind steamrollers these days is to seriously consider passing them.

A few weeks after getting my bad grades and failing my driv-ing test, my first girlfriend chucked me, and, of course, I was heartbroken. It's easy to be flippant about it now, but at the time it honestly felt as if my whole world had shattered.

That was not the only broken dream. My friend Steve and I had been planning to embark on a two-man mission from God. We wanted to go into local schools to conduct assemblies, put on concerts and tell people about Jesus. Surprisingly, we were already beginning to receive invitations from educational establishments when this whole dream fell apart in the most tragic way. A friend of Steve's committed suicide and, under-standably, he was devastated. Steve moved away to live with some people who could help him get his head back together. Without him, I could see that the school project wasn't going to work. Steve was black, effortlessly cool, could play the guitar, and sang like Luther Vandross. Without Steve, I was nothing. Without Steve, hundreds of kids were going to be left gaping at an uncoordinated white guy, who didn't even have a girlfriend and couldn't drive a car, attempting to persuade them about the wonders of the Christian religion.

Steve's problems made mine seem pretty insignificant, but when our plans fell apart so suddenly, I couldn't help feeling let down. Not by Steve, but by God. In fine Sunday School tradition, I had offered Him my five loaves and two fishes, but instead of saying thanks and multiplying my packed lunch for the benefit of the adoring crowds, it felt to me as though He'd just thrown it all back in my face.

Around this time, most of my friends went away to university and, without anything to do, I was left licking my wounds, kicking my heels and looking for work. Eventually, I landed myself a job as a toilet cleaner in the New East Surrey Hospital. As a former professional, I can promise you that hospital toilets are the very worst kind to clean—not so much the pinnacle of a career in sanitary services!

Gradually, the world was turning gray. I was withdrawing from others and becoming utterly unmotivated to do anything other than sleep. I would cycle home from the hospital every day after work and crawl into bed long before it got dark. I felt stupid and unwanted, and God didn't seem particularly bothered about it. Self-pity became despondency. It was a short passageway from despondency to doubt.

It happened during a service at the ancient old church that I had attended all my life. We stood to sing a hymn when suddenly, as I looked around at the congregation doing the same stuff we did every Sunday evening, I just knew that the whole thing was a meaningless circus. Life was hurting like hell, and God didn't seem to care. I stepped out of the pew and strode purposefully down the aisle and out into the cold night air. "I don't believe You exist," I yelled angrily, and tears began burning down my cheeks.

All the next day, I continued to tell God that He didn't exist. I felt abandoned, and I told Him that too. And then, of course, I would wonder who I was talking to and why, so I made a conscious effort to stop praying. But when I did, instead of feeling released and reassured, I merely felt even more abandoned, hurt and alone. I discovered that without God, it no longer mattered what I thought or how I felt. Depressed at my own inability to erase or evacuate God, I resigned myself to believing and soon realized that I was actually talking to Him more than I had done when I was a radical Christian. Mind you, before you become too impressed by the irrepressible depth of my innate spirituality, it was neither polite nor pretty. I prayed like a drunk mumbling at the mirror, and many of my words to God were self-pitying, disjointed and insolent. I'd given up trying to impress Him and, as a result, my prayers were becoming more honest than they had been in years.

## Psalms of Disorientation

Many of the psalms, I now know, bristle with disgruntled prayers like these. They are filled with expressions of grief, lament, anger and even doubt. The Old Testament scholar Walter Brueggemann calls them "psalms of disorientation." Bono compares them to the blues. "It's in his despair," he says, "that the psalmist really reveals the nature of his special relationship with God. Honesty, even to the point of anger: 'How long, Lord? Wilt Thou hide Thyself forever?' (Psalm 89)."[2]

In Gethsemane and on the cross, Jesus also prayed with stark honesty: "If it is possible, may this cup be taken from me . . . I thirst . . . Why have you forsaken me?" (Matt. 26:39; John 19:28; Matt. 27:46). Meanwhile, the descriptions of the disciples' behavior during this same period are honest to the point of embarrassment. Take a look at Peter: He sleeps when Jesus needs him most, he cuts a guy's ear off, he gets scared and denies being a disciple, he's nowhere to be seen at the crucifixion, and he doesn't believe the women when they say they've seen the risen Lord. This is the great apostle of the Christian Church: Peter, depicted in a thousand stained-glass windows;

Peter, author of entire chunks of the Bible; Peter, who walked on water and first called Jesus the Son of God; Peter, from whom the Roman Catholic Church proudly traces the papal succession. In telling Mark these stories for inclusion in his Gospel, Peter refused to play the superhero and made it okay for you and me to handle Gethsemane badly. He permits us to struggle and fail and get it wrong.

## Honest to God

Jesus once told a funny story to reassure us that God really does respond to honesty in prayer. It's the one about a Pharisee and a dirty, rotten tax man who both went to pray at the Temple one day. The Pharisee prayed with smug self-confidence, but "the tax man, slumped in the shadows, his face in his hands, not daring to look up, said, 'God, give mercy. Forgive me, a sinner.' Jesus commented, 'This tax man, not the other, went home made right with God. If you walk around with your nose in the air, you're going to end up flat on your face, but if you're content to be simply yourself, you will become more than yourself'" (Luke 18:13-14, *THE MESSAGE*).

When we open our hearts to be honest with God in prayer, He hears us and steps through the door to be with us, totally unfazed by the mess of our interior world. The thing that keeps God out of our lives is not our sin. It is our compulsion to pretend, to cover up our nakedness with fig leaves, to climb sycamore trees in order to see without being seen. And when we do, He will sometimes look up laughing and invite Himself to tea.

I found a prayer on the Internet that is so painfully honest that I can't even reprint most of it in a respectable Christian book like this! Cecily Kellogg, who wrote the prayer, and her partner Charlie had been trying to start a family for more than three years when she informed readers on her blog, "We finally got pregnant on our first IVF cycle, only to lose our twin boys (and nearly me) at 22 weeks . . ." Grieving the loss of her babies, Cecily was advised to try telling God how she felt. Here, then, are a few censored highlights of the honest prayer that Cecily prayed on January 23, 2005:

Dear God,

I really don't know how to talk to you anymore, but I've been told that I should try . . . Ever since you took the boys from me, I've been on emotional lockdown . . . Why would I let you back into my heart when you treated me so badly? How could you abandon me that way? This letter to you is only an exercise, an attempt to make contact. But be careful if you show up. I can scream, and scream loud, and I have some things to say to you. If you were standing before me, I'd hit you. I want to tell you to go away, to leave me alone. In truth, I want to beg you to stay. Because even with my beloved standing here with me, my amazing friends, my internet support team—I have never felt so *** alone. So stay here, you ***. Stay here and make this better. Because it hurts so *** much.

Cecily

What are we to make of a prayer like that? It certainly wouldn't fit well in many church services. It's not just the swear words. It's also the sentiments expressed: being angry at God, calling Him names, telling Him to go away, asking Him to come close, and even threatening to hit Him!

I believe that the parable of the Pharisee and the tax man answers any concerns we might have about the acceptability to God of Cecily's prayer. In fact, the Bible as a whole—the psalms of disorientation, the lamentation and despair—speaks a moving "amen" to the honest heart of Cecily's blog to God.

Fifteen months after writing that angry prayer, another entry appeared on Cecily's blog. Having tracked her progress, I could hardly believe the news. On April 4, 2006, in an entry simply titled "Miracles," Cecily announced that the "spiritual angst over the loss of the boys" had led her to start attending a little church. Cecily is quite open about the fact that she was a former drug addict. Knowing this, her new pastor had done a wonderful thing: "At the start of Lent, my pastor asked me to 'bear witness' about how addiction is similar to what Jesus experienced while being lost in the wilderness." As a result of this fascinating exercise, Cecily had a half-hour conversation over chocolate cake with a 10-year-old girl whose mother was in prison for issues related to crack-addiction. Cecily writes:

> How grateful I am to feel like I have a tiny piece of the answer for her. I told T that we addicts and alcoholics have something inside us that is broken; that when we have a drink or a drug we can't stop because the broken thing inside us only feels fixed when we are drunk or high . . . That it isn't because we don't love the people in our lives, it's that the addiction is more powerful than we are. T listened carefully, asked lots of great questions, and seemed to relax a little with each of my answers.

Cecily then concludes with a statement so remarkable that I am sure God heard her angry prayer in 2005 and that He has been working in her life accordingly: "I swear to you," she writes, "it was worth every minute of pain and spiritual agony I suffered to be able to spend a half hour helping this girl. Really. I would have never been there to help if I hadn't lost the boys. How amazing is that?"

Cecily's positive attitude towards her own loss is remarkable—particularly when compared with the remorse expressed by Rabbi Kushner who, you may recall, said that he would happily have surrendered every good thing wrought in him by his son's disability, in order to go back to simply being "the father of a bright, happy boy." Perhaps this says more about the personality differences between Cecily Kellogg and Harold Kushner, or perhaps it's a matter of the comparative severity of their suffering (though who can measure such things?). However, both characters do acknowledge that goodness has somehow been worked in and through their lives through the excruciating circumstances of unanswered prayer. They both discovered how deeply redemptive it can be if our hurts can be harnessed for the care of others. The apostle Paul describes this principle in terms of comfort that rolls out from God to us, and thus, through us to others: "the God of all comfort . . . comforts us in all our troubles so that we can comfort those in any trouble with the comfort we ourselves have received from God" (2 Cor. 1:3-4).[3]

## When It All Ends in Tears

Gary, a friend of mine in Missouri, opened a 24-7 prayer room at his church. At first, Gary was uncertain about the congregation's ability to fill a week's worth of one-hour prayer slots night and day. But they kicked off anyway, and God showed up in such a remarkable way that the congregation didn't want to stop praying at the end of the week and continued non-stop for several *months!* God did so much in that one little prayer room that I could probably fill half a book just with the stories Gary has told me. It became such a holy season that several times I've seen Gary fill up with tears just talking about it. Other times, he just gets really excited and earnest and says things such as,

"God's wrecked my life, Pete." I tell him that it's not my fault, and then we just kind of grin at each other inanely.

About two-thirds of the way through that holy season of night-and-day prayer at Gary's church, one of the members came to him in a terrible state, saying, "I've spoiled it all. I'm so sorry but I've broken the prayer chain." Assuming that the member had just missed her prayer slot, Gary was about to tell her not to worry. But she continued, "Pastor Gary, I got to the room fine, but instead of praying I'm afraid that I just broke down in tears and cried my heart out the entire hour. I didn't say a single thing to God. Not a word. I just cried. I am so sorry."

When Gary heard this, he assured this dear lady that tears are the very best sort of prayer. "Even the Holy Spirit prays with groans that words cannot express," he told her. Eugene Peterson puts it beautifully: "History is lubricated by tears. Prayer, maybe most prayer, is accompanied by tears. All these tears are gathered up and absorbed in the tears of Jesus."[4]

## Learning to Lament

All too often, it is the Church that creates cultures in which people feel compelled to have it all together and, therefore, to pretend. In January 2005, a huge mudslide demolished 15 homes and killed 10 people in the coastal town of La Conchita, California. The world watched their TV screens in horror as one traumatized father, Jimmie Wallet, described how he went out to buy ice-cream for his wife and three kids and returned to find his home buried under 30 feet of mud, sand and debris.

Jimmie fell to his knees in the rain, screaming the names of his children and digging in a frenzy with his bare hands and his credit card. Rescue workers arrived, but Jimmie continued digging. At one point, he thought he heard the cry of his two-year-old daughter, Paloma. The mud was hardening like cement.

The workers unearthed a pink princess dress, a pair of shoes and shattered family photographs. But it was not until 36 hours later that the lifeless bodies of Jimmie's three children and his wife, Michelle, were pulled from the mud. Ten-year-old Hannah, six-year-old Raven and little Paloma appeared to have been sitting together on a couch, no doubt waiting for ice cream, when the house was crushed.

The neighboring town of Ventura was still mourning when I visited a few weeks later to see my friend Greg Russinger, who was leading a church there at that time. Greg had prepared an eloquent sermon for the Sunday after the mudslide about Abel's blood crying out to God from the ground. However, as he looked around at the faces of the congregation that day, it was evident to him that many of the people were struggling with profound questions of doubt and grief. In that moment, Greg knew that there could be no easy platitudes. No absolution for a so-called "act of God" that kills a wife and three kids, sparing the father for the price of ice cream.

Abandoning his sermon, Greg drew attention to the black paper with which he had covered the walls. Next, he invited a couple of men to go out into the street and gather some dust and mud. This was mixed with red paint, and members of the community were invited to use this blood-mud paste to express their emotions, questions and prayers all over the black paper in the sight of God. Chaos ensued. "Pain is not ordered or aesthetically pleasing," reflected Greg wryly. Some people just wept. Others could barely paint. Children seized brushes. Adults used their hands. Some people didn't participate. Some expressed images of hope. And all this time, the mud-blood paint just kept splattering off the paper and onto the floor, creating a mess.

At the end of this unconventional evening, a visitor thanked Greg for allowing him the opportunity to mourn, to be silent and to remain in the questions. He also said that he had attended another church that morning where the pastor—no doubt a well-meaning man—had attempted to explain away the pain of the week's tragedy, as if to defend God's reputation. The sermon, the man said, had culminated with a well-intentioned yet clumsy offering to "respond to the mudslides with an avalanche of financial blessing."

Where, I wonder, is the mystery and the mess of biblical spirituality? What place is there in our happy-clappy culture for the disturbing message of books such as Ecclesiastes, Lamentations and Job? Where are the moments in both our private and public meetings with God when the major key turns to the minor, when the soft rock anthems pay respect to the blues, and when those top melodies of pop praise finally give way to the scattered logic of jazz?

Although more than half of the psalms are laments to God, the vast majority of our contemporary worship songs are celebratory in tone (musically as well as lyrically), leaving little space for the expression of our deepest anxieties. I just conducted a little analysis of the lyrical content of the modern Psalter (the official top 50 contemporary worship songs being used in American and British churches at the time of this writing). I discovered that only 2 of these 50 songs mention the reality of human suffering, and not a single one of them expresses doubt!

No matter what Bono says, the words of Psalm 89 would not work well in a context of congregational singing (and anyway, even when we're hurting, it is still appropriate to praise God). Yet it is important that we learn to lament. Jesus Himself was overwhelmed with sorrow, wrestled and cried out to God, begged for another plan, and allowed His friends to see that this was how He felt. Five days earlier, His shoulders had slumped, His eyes had filled with tears, and He had mourned for Jerusalem while the crowds around Him partied and praised.

Lamenting is more than a technique for venting emotion. It is one of the fruits of a deepening spiritual life that has learned to stand naked before God without shame or pretence. In fact, long before Gethsemane, Jesus Himself had pronounced that those who mourn are blessed (see Matt. 5:4)! "Implicit in this statement," notes Walter Brueggemann, "is that those who do not mourn will not be comforted and those who do not face the endings will not receive the beginnings."[5] Honest lament can express a vibrant faith; one that has learned to embrace life's hardships as well as its joy and to lift everything—*everything*—to the Father in prayer. As the author Richard Foster says of the lament psalms, "They give us permission to shake our fist at God one moment and break into doxology the next."[6]

· · · ·

*To pray is to confess not the abundance but the exhaustion of one's verbal, intellectual, and spiritual resources. It is surrender . . .*
ALAN E. LEWIS

In 1842, an Irishman named Joseph Scriven graduated from Trinity College, Dublin, and promptly fell head over heels in love with a girl from his hometown. They got engaged and, with great excitement, planned their wedding and began dreaming about their future together as husband and wife.

The eve of their wedding arrived at last, and Joseph's fiancée saddled a horse to go and see him. Tragically, it was one of the last things she would ever do. A little later, Joseph saw his bride-to-be riding toward him, and he grinned. But suddenly, just as she was crossing the bridge over the river, her horse bucked and threw her like a rag-doll down into the river below. In blind panic, Joseph ran to the river, calling out her name. He plunged into the icy waters, but it was too late. His bride was already dead.

Heartbroken, Joseph emigrated to Canada, where eventually he fell in love again. In 1854, Joseph was due to marry Eliza Roche, but she fell ill and grew progressively worse. The wedding was repeatedly postponed until, three years later, Eliza died. Joseph Scriven would never again give his heart to another.

Back home in Ireland, Joseph's mother was deeply concerned for her heartbroken son, and he in turn was concerned for her. One night, Joseph penned a poem to comfort her, little knowing that it would become one of the best-loved songs of all time. Several years later, a friend found it in a drawer at Joseph's house and was deeply moved. "The Lord and I wrote it together," Joseph explained. That poem, forged out of so much disappointment and pain, continues to call millions of people in their own Gethsemanes to admit their grief, their trials and temptations, their sorrows and their every weakness to Jesus in the privilege of prayer:

> *What a friend we have in Jesus,*
> *All our sins and griefs to bear!*
> *What a privilege to carry*
> *Everything to God in prayer!*
> *O what peace we often forfeit,*
> *O what needless pain we bear,*
> *All because we do not carry*
> *Everything to God in prayer.*
>
> *Have we trials and temptations?*
> *Is there trouble anywhere?*
> *We should never be discouraged*
> *Take it to the Lord in prayer!*
> *Can we find a friend so faithful,*
> *Who will all our sorrows share?*
> *Jesus knows our every weakness*
> *Take it to the Lord in prayer!*[7]

Chapter Five

# A DARKER TRUST

*Yet not my will but your will be done.*
Jesus, Mark 14:36

Three days. That's all it would take for me to learn more about the meaning of these nine words—their power as well as their pain—than I had done in a lifetime of Good Friday sermons.

When I met Floyd McClung at a large conference in England, there was no indication that the towering American missionary's life was about to be turned upside down. Floyd is truly one of God's great adventurers. As a young man, he and his wife, Sally, followed the hippy trail across Europe through Istanbul to Afghanistan, where they settled in Kabul. In one of his books, he describes the city like this: "In all the world there was no country so rugged, so stark and frightening to Western eyes as Afghanistan. And all of that wild land was reflected in Kabul . . . The city virtually overflowed with sick, stranded, strung-out young people."[1]

For several years Floyd and Sally reached out to these people in Kabul before retracing their steps from Afghanistan to Amsterdam, where they based themselves in the city's infamous Red Light District, renting a building between a satanist church and a sex shop.

These days, Floyd lives in Cape Town, South Africa, and resembles a gigantic version of everyone's favorite grandpa. He's at least 6′ 6″ tall, with big hands like the roots of a giant old tree, a goatee that's almost white, smiling eyes, half-moon glasses that rest on the end of his nose, and shoulders that shake when he laughs. Many years before our meeting, Floyd had written a book called *The Father Heart of God* that had changed my life when I read it as a teenager and it was his knowledge of God's heart, shaped through such an extraordinary life, that was about to change me once again.

At the conference in England, it was late at night when Floyd received a devastating phone call from home. His daughter, Misha, was unconscious. She had been admitted to St. Joseph's Hospital in Washington State, expecting the routine arrival of her second child. At first, the labor had progressed normally, but then Misha had begun struggling for breath and had lost consciousness. Doctors would later diagnose an amniotic embolism. Some of the fluid in Misha's womb had leaked into her bloodstream, and from there it had leaked into her heart, causing cardio-respiratory collapse.

The shocking news was broken to Floyd that although his daughter had been rushed into surgery immediately, it had taken at least eight minutes to get a tube into her lungs so that she could breathe. Meanwhile, doctors had performed an emergency C-section to rescue the baby. Lionel, Misha's husband, had been told by a weeping nurse that his wife would not be coming home with him. Standing 5,000 miles away, Floyd listened in shock as he learned that his daughter, though breathing again, was being kept unconscious in a drug-induced coma.

The prognosis both for her and for his new little grandchild was frightening. She was suffering from the most dangerous and untreatable condition in obstetrics, a set of complications associated with an 86 percent mortality rate.[2] Misha, the doctors said, was unlikely to regain consciousness and was not exhibiting any signs of awareness, let alone awakeness. If she did come around,

Floyd was told that Misha would probably suffer long-term neurological damage as a result of the protracted period with insufficient oxygen. As for the new grandchild, it was a baby boy named Luke who seemed to be breathing normally but had probably been starved of oxygen for as long as 14 minutes.

Floyd's giant frame seemed to slump and crumple under the news. His only daughter, so bright and affectionate, was suddenly imprisoned in a coma, and if she ever woke up, she would probably be brain damaged. This should have been one of the happiest days of her life, but instead it was the worst and, possibly, the last. And what about little Luke, Floyd's beautiful new grandchild? Would he grow up without a mother? Would he grow up at all?

## Will Power

The next day, Floyd disappeared for a long time. We were all worried, and when eventually he reappeared, he looked older, pale and drawn. He said that he wanted to be with me because he knew that I had been through something similar with Samie. Unsure what else to say, I just asked Floyd where he'd been all day. He looked at me sadly and paused.

"Walking," he said eventually. "I've been walking. On the beach. I've been wrestling with God. Trying to pray for Misha."

He studied my face, and I got the impression that he was trying to decide whether to tell me any more. It felt awkward.

"Pete," he said softly, "Sally and I used to have a very good friend called Corrie ten Boom. You heard of her?" I nodded. I'd grown up with the tales of the sweet old Dutch lady who had rescued Jews from the Nazis before being imprisoned with her sister in a concentration camp.

"Pete, when Corrie was dying, she prayed an amazing prayer." Floyd was speaking quietly. "Corrie prayed that God would do whatever would bring the most glory to His name. She told Him that if it would bring Him glory to heal her so that she could continue her ministry, then, yes, she wanted to be healed. But she also told God that if it would bring Him greater glory if she died and went to be with Him, then she would surrender to that eventuality too."

Floyd paused, and I could see the strain on his face. "I went to the beach today because I realized that I needed to get myself to a place where I could pray that same prayer for Misha. I've been begging God for my daughter's life, as any father would. I've been reminding Him of the unfulfilled promises over her future. But I knew that I also had to give her back to God. If it's somehow going to bring God more glory to take Misha home . . ." Floyd's voice trailed away. He was sallow. Everything seemed gray, and his hair was scruffy from the wind on the beach. The atmosphere in the room seemed heavy with a great and exhausting sadness. I guess you might say that it felt holy.

Facing the possibility of losing his daughter and his new grandson, Floyd had wrestled and wept until eventually he could relinquish his will to the will of God. I suspect that it was the most painful thing he had ever prayed.

Just a year earlier, I had been in a similar situation when I faced the strong possibility that Samie was going to die or suffer some form of brain damage. But my response had not been like Floyd's. Back then, I had told God angrily that I would fight Him for her life. I told Him I didn't care what His will was. I wasn't going to let Him take my wife without a fight. In my Gethsemane, I yelled, "Abba, Father, take this cup from me," and with that I had pretty much slammed the door. But Floyd, in his darkest hour, had wrestled until he could pray the second bit too: "Not my will but Your will be done."

"Okay," said Floyd, interrupting my reverie before I could say something stupid. "I don't want to talk about it anymore.

Let's eat!" So we went out and ate curry, and we did not talk anymore that night about the fearful thing haunting the shadows of our minds.

## Memories of Easter

The next day I mobilized as many of the 24-7 prayer networks as possible to pray for Misha, Lionel and baby Luke. Within a few hours, thousands of people had received a text message on their cell phones asking them to cry out to God for this desperate situation.

Having done all I could do, I marveled at Floyd's inner strength as he continued to minister at various seminars and in endless conversations. But it was clear from the strain on his face and from the way he clutched my cell phone that it was not an easy fortitude. On the fifth day, doctors decided to withdraw the drugs that were cocooning Misha in her comatose state. It was the moment of truth, when we would all have to face the likelihood of massive neurological damage.

And it was that night, with the lives of his daughter and grandson lying in the balance on the other side of the world, that Floyd was scheduled to address several thousand people. He strode out on the platform and, with a peculiar kind of defiance, abandoned the proscribed text in order to proclaim the message of God's eternal goodness and undying love.

He preached passionately and ministered tenderly to the crowd, describing the broken heart of the Father. And all the while I knew that his own father's heart was breaking for a girl in a coma 5,000 miles away. I don't know what reserves Floyd drew from to preach that message that night, but the pain was etched on his face and emblazoned on the large video screens. Many people responded to Floyd's message, and when at last he came down from the platform, he was emotionally spent.

Anxious for the latest news of Misha and Luke, Floyd turned on the cell phone I'd lent him. Standing there with his big hand wrapped round that tiny phone, fresh from preaching one of the most painful messages of his life, Floyd received a shock.

It seemed that a miracle had taken place.

It was the best possible news. Not only had Misha come around from her coma, she was also showing no signs of any lasting neurological problems. In fact, a CAT scan two days later would reveal a perfectly healthy, undamaged brain. The only indication of the extreme trauma her brain had endured appeared to be a temporary loss of short-term memory. Doctors had also run the usual tests on little baby Luke and—although 81 percent of babies in his situation do not live—Luke was showing every sign of having come through the ordeal as a healthy newborn child. The prayers of people all around the world had, it seemed, been answered.

The medical staff was so amazed by Misha's and Luke's combined recoveries that they set about calculating the statistical probabilities. They worked out that the likelihood of Misha and Luke both surviving an amniotic embolism without brain damage were about 1 in 1.2 million. "No one we've talked to in the medical field knows of any case in which both the mother and her baby have survived an amniotic embolism without severe neurological damage to one or both of them," said Floyd in amazement a few weeks later. However, the trauma left its mark in that to this day, Misha has virtually no recollection of her time in the hospital. "Easter," said Lionel poignantly, referring to the day before Misha had gone into labor, "Easter is where her memory stops."

## Triple Miracle

I saw Floyd again seven months after those terrible-wonderful days. As he sat at my kitchen table, he showed me beautiful pictures of Misha and Lionel, smiling and happy with both their children. Then he passed me another photograph. This one showed baby Luke, just two days old, lying asleep on his unconscious mother's chest. There were wires and tubes coming out of her. It was a photograph, he told me, that they had been advised to take so that Luke would have at least one record of having been with his mother.

"It seems like we had a triple miracle," Floyd said as I stared at the picture and tried to compute what had happened. "First, Misha is alive! Second, she has all her mental faculties. And third, little Luke lived and is also healthy and well." He looked up and smiled.

A few days after Misha's miracle, Floyd sent out an e-mail to all those who had prayed for his family, explaining exactly what had happened. He was not only concerned to give the glory to God for a triple miracle but also to care for those still wrestling with their own unanswered prayers:

> Many people prayed and God intervened because of those prayers. But God doesn't always answer our prayers the way we want Him to . . . Every promise He speaks will come to pass if we obey Him, but some of them are fulfilled in heaven, not on earth . . . God spared Misha's life for one reason above all others: It will bring Him more glory for her to be here longer.

The miracles of Misha's healing testify to the power of prayer. But so too does the hidden testimony of Floyd's willingness to surrender to the will of God in his darkest hour, even if it meant the greatest pain any father can be asked to endure.

### "Yet . . ."

The power to choose God's will instead of one's own personal preferences is, according to Scripture, the defining human opportunity. In the Garden of Eden, our ancestors first prayed the tragic prayer that we have been praying ever since: "Not Your will . . ." they said to God, greedily eyeing the fruit of knowledge and power, "Not Your will but our will be done." In that one cataclysmic moment of decision, lust and craving corrupted the human psyche, passing from heart to heart through the placenta from one generation to the next.

And so, in another garden, another Adam must make another choice that will reverse the one made at the dawn of human history. Every human instinct of survival cries out against what Jesus knows He must do; every rational argument insists on self-preservation. And subtler voices, too: the promise that a single prayer could even now summon "more than twelve legions of angels" to his side (Matt. 26:53), the dark prospect of becoming a sin offering, and the most terrifying prospect of all—separation from God Himself. No wonder Jesus cries, "Father take this cup from me." Surely, on hearing the cry, there are tears in the Father's eyes, and His hand moves immediately to do just that.

"*Yet . . .*" and on that single word from Jesus, I imagine traffic screaming to a halt and birds falling from the sky. The Father's hand pauses by the cup, heaven falls silent in suspense, hell jeers, drooling with lust for blood and power, too stupid to understand its own undoing. "Yet not my will"—and perhaps the screams of delight in hell were so loud when they heard these four words from the lips of the one whose will had tormented them for so long that they never even heard the final five words at all—"but your will be done."

A little later, during His arrest, Jesus would tell the guards, "This is your hour, when darkness reigns" (Luke 22:53). In surrendering to the will of God and the satanic onslaught to come, Jesus showed us that the way to overcome the world—the way to subvert the reign of darkness—is sometimes not to stand and fight but rather to submit like a lamb being led to the slaughter (see Isa. 53:7). In the words of the great Welsh poet Dylan Thomas, when our lives are enveloped by darkness, our duty may not always be to "Rage, rage against the dying of the light" but rather to "Go gentle into that good night."[3]

## Bribery of the Infinite

The apostle Paul challenges us to follow Christ's example radically by offering ourselves to God as "living sacrifices" (Rom. 12:1). In part, this means saying yes to God's will, even when it's painful to do so. This could sound rather masochistic and morbid, but in fact, as counseling professionals tell us, acceptance is ultimately a healthier response to suffering than denial or defiance. In 1969, Elisabeth Kubler-Ross described the Five Stages of Grief typically displayed by her terminally ill patients in coming to terms with their diagnoses. Although we now know that not everyone goes through all these stages in exactly this order, it's a process that applies to all forms of trauma and, significantly, should culminate with an attitude of acceptance:

1. Denial: *I don't believe it. This can't be happening to me.*
2. Anger: *I don't deserve this. God, it's not fair.*
3. Bargaining: *Please, God/doctor, if you heal me, I'll do anything for you.*
4. Depression: *What's the point? My situation is hopeless.*
5. Acceptance: *I need to get on and make the most of life within these limitations.*

Coming to terms with God's will may sometimes take us through similar stages of grief. The process by which we arrive at a place of Godly acceptance often involves various emotional responses that are both messy and confusing. When you talk to people with an amazing attitude toward suffering, you invariably discover that they have not always been so joyful or brave. Even the Son of God wrestled for a protracted period before He reached the necessary place of acceptance, praying, "Your will be done."

The Five Stages of Grief help explain why we may initially get angry with God, raging against the apparent unfairness of His will (this, as I have already confessed, was my reaction to Samie's diagnosis once the initial shock had worn off). At other stages, we may seek to bargain with God, repenting of our sin, trying to be a better person, fasting and making all sorts of promises to try to persuade Him to change His mind. One writer calls this "bribery of the infinite."[4]

Having vented our anger and having failed to bribe God, we really only have two choices left: depression or acceptance. Thus, we see that Floyd's agonizing prayer of acceptance, in which he released Misha to God's will, was actually (in clinical terms) a healthy human response to a grievous situation beyond his control. Ultimately, peace lies in accepting that God knows best—a stage that Samie finally reached the night before her surgery while writing her goodbye letters to those she loved.

You may already be wondering whether some of your unanswered prayers have, in fact, been answered. Maybe God has simply been replying to your prayers with a loving but firm no. I don't suggest this lightly. It may well be the most painful possibility you have ever had to consider, and it may also seem to fly in the face of everything you know of God's heart and will.

As we all know, it can be incredibly difficult to discern what God wants in any given situation. Embarrassingly, I would probably have prayed passionately against the plot to crucify Jesus. The prospect of His death would surely have seemed demonically wrong and utterly opposed to the purposes of God in every way. There are Bible verses that I could have quoted to prove that my prayers were in line with God's will. What's more, common sense would surely have railed against the termination of Christ's ministry at a time when it was proving more fruitful than ever before. The apostle Peter took this understandable, even obvious, position and tried to talk Jesus out of the cross, but when he did, Jesus rebuked him in the strongest possible terms for resisting the will of God! Of course, a few days later, the ultimate example of unanswered prayer would become the greatest miracle of all time.

As we mature in Christ, we begin to understand that God's logic is rarely ours and that His path to joy is often marked by suffering. The world is full of people prepared to trust God for promotion, prosperity, healing and popularity, and this is good, because God loves to give good gifts to His children. It's certainly better to trust God for these things than to trust in ourselves for them. But as we mature spiritually, God asks us to trust Him in the hard times as well. It's a lesson I learned from the life and death of a delightful old lady called Barbara Fisher.

## Faith for Dying

Barbara and Terry Fisher had been missionaries in Zambia for most of their lives until they retired to a little bungalow by the sea in England. I would sometimes visit the Fishers for tea, and whenever I did, they would regale me with amazing stories about times when they lost all their possessions or nearly died in two-seater planes or witnessed incredible miracles. I would always come away from tea with the Fishers inspired and refreshed in my faith.

Then one day, news came that Barbara had been diagnosed with a form of cancer. The disease advanced very quickly through her body, and she was soon admitted to a hospice. I didn't visit for several weeks, until Terry grabbed me one Sunday at church and said reproachfully, "Hey, why haven't you been to see us recently?" The truthful answer was that I felt nervous. I didn't know what I would say to Barbara now that she was dying.

For the next few weeks, whenever I bumped into Terry, he would bully me good-naturedly to come and see him and his dying wife, and I would always say that yes, I very much hoped to pop in. But, of course, I never got around to it. Eventually, Terry confronted me outright. He placed his hands on my shoulders and looked me in the eyes. "Pete Greig," he said firmly, "you're scared of seeing Barbara dying, aren't you?" I tried to deny it, but Terry knew me too well.

"Pete, when Barbara's diagnosis first came through, we asked God, as we always do, how we were supposed to pray, and He told us a very upsetting thing. God said that He wasn't going to heal Barbara this time."

"I'm sorry, Terry," I said, staring at my shoes. "You're right. I haven't known what to say."

"I understand," said Terry kindly, as if I were the one in need of comfort. "Pete, many times in our lives Barbara and I have needed to exercise faith. Faith for healing in the face of sickness. Faith for finances when we had no food in the cupboard or when we lost everything. Faith for guidance. But this time, God has asked us to trust Him in a different way: to have faith not for healing but for dying. The challenge she's facing is to die *well*, to die faithfully, to die peacefully, to trust God and to love God in the most frightening days of her life. And that's why she appreciates it," Terry prodded me with a boney missionary finger, "when young guns like you take time to go round and talk to her."

A few days later I ventured into the hospice, where I found Barbara looking pale and old. We talked about all sorts of things and then, after a few minutes, Barbara came right out and told me she was dying. It was obvious of course, but such things are seldom voiced, and it was actually quite a relief to hear it said. Then, speaking quietly, Barbara let me in on a secret: A few nights earlier she had heard quite distinctly the sound of a distant trumpet. "It was calling me home," she whispered gently, "home to Jesus!"

When Barbara said "Jesus," she smiled without meaning to smile. After that, we prayed a bit, and then I said goodbye. Thanks to Terry, it was, I think, a good goodbye, and I left feeling as if I'd been *entrusted* with something. Barbara died soon after, and I want you to know that she died full of faith in Jesus and that there was a trumpet sounding out there somewhere, calling her home. Somehow—and it makes me smile even now—Barbara Fisher had even managed to use her dying for the glory of God.

There is faith for life, and then there is a darker faith for death. There is faith for miracles, but also for pain. There is faith for God's will when it's our will too, but there is also the grace to trust God when His will is not what we would choose. I don't pretend it is any easier for us than it was for Christ to exercise this darker trust. It may be one of the most painful prayers of our life—as it was for Floyd on the beach that day—but it may also be one of the most powerful.

I am ashamed to admit that, in my Gethsemane, I failed to relinquish control. It's something I've subsequently had to pray about, and I can only tell you that I have sensed the Father's love and grace. I guess that Jesus, more than anyone else in heaven and on Earth, understands how hard it is for a human being to surrender to the Father's will. I do not feel condemned by my own petulance, but I do feel humbled, provoked and inspired by those friends of God who manage to choose His will instead of their own—even when every part of their heart and soul is screaming no! In the lives of people such as Floyd McClung, Corrie ten Boom, Barbara Fisher and, ultimately, in Jesus, we see that the power of prayer is really that of sacrifice.

• • • •

And so we come to the end of Christ's 21-word prayer in Gethsemane. Jesus has been, perhaps unconsciously, following the form of His own "Our Father" prayer, the one He gave to His disciples to teach them how to pray. Instead of "Our Father, who art in heaven," He has said, "Abba, Father, everything is possible for you." He has made Himself an answer to His own prayer, replacing the request "Thy will be done on earth as it is in heaven" with the relinquishment of "not what I will but your will be done." Instead of "lead us not into temptation," Jesus has told the disciples to stay awake and pray so that they will not fall into sin.

The lines from the "Our Father" prayer that He leaves unmirrored are also significant because they are the lines He will pray the following day on the cross. In Gethsemane, Jesus does not say, "Give us this day our daily bread . . ." because He knows that He Himself is the bread that will soon be broken for many. Neither does He pray, "Forgive us our trespasses . . ." because He, the one who needed no forgiveness, will cry out instead, "Father, forgive them." Most painfully, He does not pray, "deliver us from evil" because He is about to deliver Himself to hell. The words of the Lord's Prayer—or this abbreviated version of it that Jesus uses on Maundy Thursday—are worth repeating and exploring several times a day, especially when we are seeking to walk through our own Gethsemane in darker trust.

## The Oil of Suffering

Gethsemane means "The Oil Press" and, as I'm sure you know, olive oil was one of the great resources of the ancient world. Back then, it was not only used in cooking (as it is today) but also as a fuel—a *source of light*—that was burned in lamps in every home and as a *source of health*, used in various medicinal treatments of the time. In fact, in the Qur'an, Muhammad lists no fewer than 70 conditions that he says should be treated with olive oil. The Israelites also used olive oil *in worship*, pouring a fresh measure each day into the seven cups of the golden menorah that was kept burning continually at the heart of Jewish life. Furthermore, olive oil was used for *anointing the kings of Israel.* As such, it had particular resonance for Jesus in Gethsemane, because the very word "Christ" means "anointed one," referring to this Jewish custom of touching the forehead of a prince with olive oil.

This unparalleled resource—important for cooking food, lighting homes, curing diseases, maintaining worship and anointing kings—could only be acquired by crushing the fruit of the olive tree to a pulp. Without intense pressure and the destruction of something good, there could be nothing better.

It's easy to see the potency of these images for Jesus, who endured such pressure that night in Gethsemane to become the everlasting Light of the World, the Healer of Nations and the anointed King of kings. Precious oil can flow in our lives too from the crushing experiences we endure. We see this in the resilient faith expressed in the rich tradition of African-American spirituals born out of slavery and in Joseph Scriven's broken-hearted hymn, which has brought comfort and strength to millions of people. We see the oil press at work in Floyd McClung, who surrendered his daughter and grandson to God's glory. We see it in Barbara Fisher, who found faith to die well as the trumpet called her home. We even see it in the Holocaust survivors, who somehow found faith through the horror of the concentration camps.

We may not see any such beauty in our own lives, and perhaps this is good. But we know that there is an anointing—an authority—that can only come to us through the darker trust of unanswered prayer. It is an illumination both in us and through us that can only come through suffering; a healing that we can only minister when we have ourselves been wounded. Ultimately, we know that there is a sevenfold worship more precious to God than any other: the offering of a broken heart and a crushed spirit that prays, "Abba, Father, everything is possible for You. Take this cup from me. Yet not what I will, but what You will."

## Prayer

*Oh yes, fix me, Jesus, fix me.*
*Fix me so that I can walk on*
*a little while longer.*
*Fix me so that I can pray on*
*just a little bit harder.*
*Fix me so that I can sing on*
*just a little bit louder.*
*Fix me so that I can go on*
*despite the pain,*
*the fear, the doubt, and yes, the anger,*
*I ask not that you take this cross from me,*
*only that you give me the strength*
*to continue carrying it onward 'til my dying day.*
*Oh, fix me, Jesus, fix me.*

AFRICAN-AMERICAN SPIRITUAL[5]

Good Friday

# WHY

## AREN'T MY PRAYERS BEING ANSWERED?

*My God, my God,
why have you forsaken me?*
MATTHEW 27:46

What an alarming question for God to ask God. And there is no immediate answer. No word from heaven. No miracle. No sign except the darkness itself in the middle of the afternoon. In this moment, Jesus legitimized for all time the need we have for explanation. He also demonstrated that the explanation may not come when we think we need it most. Although we will never suffer in the way Jesus did on that day, there are Good Friday seasons in all our lives when pain, disappointment, confusion or a sense of spiritual abandonment cause us to ask God the ultimate question, "Why?"

## Chapter Six

# WONDERING WHY

*My God, why?*
JESUS, MATTHEW 27:46

Hospital orderlies, dressed in white, had taken Samie down to the operating room. We'd said our goodbyes and now, somewhere in Southampton General Hospital, a surgeon was preparing to conduct his third operation of the day. There was nothing more I could do. Samie's life was in the hands of God and an Irish brain surgeon named Liam Gray. Quite a team.

Dreading the hours of uncertainty, I left the hospital and ended up, as if in some parallel reality, sitting in a TGIF restaurant. There I waited for the surgeon's call and watched waitresses serving people ice cream sundaes and cocktails with glittery umbrellas. There was Saturday afternoon football on the television and, at regular intervals, a gaggle of waitresses would erupt from the kitchen carrying a cake covered in sparklers to sing Happy Birthday to a wide-eyed child or a mortified teenager.

This, I concluded, is the absurd world we leave behind when we die. It's not like the movies where people die magnificently at the opera, or in a high-speed car-chase, or even with a particularly profound last word on their lips. Instead, on my final day, checkout girls will still be swiping groceries, bleeping in time with the hospital monitors on the other side of town, and someone, somewhere, will probably be blowing out candles on a cake in a TGIF restaurant.

At last, the call came through from the hospital. "Hello? Mr. Greig?" a man with an Irish accent said. A girl walked past carrying a strawberry daiquiri and a side of ribs.

"Yes," I said, rising inexplicably to attention. "This is me."

"Are you doing okay?" he asked.

"Yes, not too bad, thanks," I lied. In the background, the waiters were beginning to sing "Happy Birthday."

"Samantha's come through the procedure very well. There was enormous pressure in her skull, but you'll be glad to hear that we got the tumor out."

"She seems," the surgeon continued, "to have full mobility, but it'll be a while before we know if her speech is intact."

I sat down, realizing that I hadn't breathed since the start of the call. "But, she's definitely . . . erm . . . *alive?*" I spluttered, wishing I knew a more medical way of asking the ultimate question.

"Oh yes," came the voice. "Your wife's going to be just fine."

"Thank you," I said. "Thank you." Waves of relief and gratitude were sweeping around the room. The place was buzzing and swirling like a candy-striped fairground. "Thank you, Dr. Gray"

"Goodbye, Mr. Greig."

The call had taken almost exactly as long as it takes to sing "Happy Birthday."

. . . .

The recovery was inevitably slow, painful and riddled with complications, but Samie had indeed survived with her mobility, speech and sense of humor intact. Our prayer had been answered through the genius of human dexterity, so we must face the likelihood that had Samie been born 100 years ago or in a less developed part of the world, she would have died.

This was a disconcerting thought, and yet God's hand had been evident in so many of the details. For instance, preoperative scans had indicated the closure of a particular vein in Samie's head on which the tumor was growing. Dr. Gray told us, in that lilting Irish accent, that he had therefore fully intended to remove the dead section of vein. However, an unexpected moment of intuition held his knife at bay. "I don't know why," he told us later, "but I just had a hunch that I shouldn't cut the vein, even though I knew it was dead." This intuitive restraint proved momentous when post-operative scans revealed that the vein had reopened as soon as the pressure of the tumor was removed.

"What would have happened if you'd cut it?" Samie asked nervously.

"Oh, paralysis," the doctor said matter-of-factly in the sort of way only an Irish brain surgeon can. "Paralysis, loss of speech or death. Pretty lucky, eh?"

We weren't so sure it was luck.

When the bandages were finally removed from Samie's head, her hair was blood red and dreadlocked, framing a face that appeared to have endured five rounds with Mike Tyson. I thought she looked fantastic! Slowly, she was recovering, and it was dawning on us that our dreams had come true. I busied myself redecorating our house to welcome Samie home, and some dear friends even bought us a new double bed. Recalling the icon of St. Martin frolicking on the beach, I also decided to book us a holiday in the sun. We were giddy with the possibilities of beginning life together again—this time as a family of four.

For the time being, the great danger of the tumor had been defeated, but it had left its mark and, a few days before our holiday in the sun, just as we were beginning to relax, the epilepsy returned with a vengeance.

Within a matter of months, terrifying fits were coming every two or three days, scarcely leaving Samie enough time to recover from one to the next. Even going to sleep was not restful for Samie, because she would often wake with the shooting jolts of another seizure kicking in. We tried to conceal all this from the children, but it wasn't always possible. Sometimes the convulsions didn't stop, and Samie's body would spiral into a dangerous cycle called *status epilepticus* in which every seizure triggered another one. Our neighbors got used to the mobile disco appearing outside the house.

Alongside the shame, pain, dullness and humiliating dependency, there was also the long shadow of fear. Samie admitted to me one day that she had once discovered the twisted body of a young woman who had died during an epileptic episode. Of course, it had always been a distressing memory, but now it became an image that haunted every seizure.

I tell all of this to you because for me, it has been the relentless battle with Samie's epilepsy during the past six years rather than the initial diagnosis of her tumor that has provoked me to address the painful reality of unanswered prayer. Why doesn't God heal her? Is the problem my unbelief? Is it a matter of spiritual warfare? Is it simply the Fall? Why doesn't Jesus do what He did 2,000 years ago? Is it His will for Samie to suffer? Why would He want such a thing? I wouldn't wish seizures on my worst enemy. It's not as though another assault on my wife's body is going to further world peace or even deepen our faith in a way that the previous 10 seizures did not.

Meanwhile, doctors have done what they can. They have put Samie on the highest possible doses of various anticonvulsant drugs, which have helped reduce the frequency of her fits to a manageable level. For this we are grateful, but the trade-off is that the drugs leave her feeling mentally dull and exhausted most of the time. Samie has had to give up her driving license and gets described as "handicapped," "epileptic" and, on one occasion, the cruelest label of all: "invalid," which literally means "a person or thing that is not deemed valid or valued." *Why*, we often still wonder, *doesn't God just heal her?*

## Then . . .

One night as I sat slumped on the sofa trying to come to terms with the effects of yet another seizure, God seemed to whisper five words in my ear: "I know how you feel."

Whether or not I had imagined the voice, it had an immediate impact on me. I replied angrily out loud, "No, You don't!" I was in no mood to be patronized. Especially not by God, who'd just let me down once again. "How can You pretend to know how I feel? If You knew how this felt, You'd stop these seizures!" Tears were scalding my cheeks. "When did You ever see the face You love more than any other contorted demonically, blue and gasping for air? When did You ever have to sit there whispering the stupidest prayers that were ever prayed, feeling totally and utterly helpless? God, I don't think You have any idea how it feels to be one flesh with someone and to watch that person spasm and writhe as if her bones were breaking. When did You ever experience all that?"

Silence.

Brushing away the tears, my gaze settled on a familiar postcard on the shelf above the fireplace, just a little to the left, beneath the mirror. It was Salvador Dali's depiction of the crucifixion—Christ of Saint John of the Cross. God knew where I was looking because He waited a moment before whispering just five more words: "That's how I felt then."

••••

*Happy are those who know what sorrow means, for they will be given courage and comfort!*
MATTHEW 5:4, *PHILLIPS*

Through our relatively moderate suffering, Samie and I have learned to cherish life with dimensions of gratitude that we could never have known without all the pain. How can we not thank God for doctors, nurses and anticonvulsing drugs, for our gorgeous children, and for the kindness of family and the miracles God does in other situations? The journey of life proves itself more wonderful and more terrifying than we could ever have anticipated.

This, then, is the context for many of my why questions. Yours will be different. I'm acutely aware that many people's experiences of chronic illnesses do not have the relatively happy outcome of Samie's. Perhaps your struggle is far more severe than ours. Or perhaps your questions don't relate to illness at all but rather to your sexuality, or to the death of a dream, or to a loved one who is far from God. Whatever your question, we're going to turn now to look for biblical answers to the intellectual problems of unanswered prayer. To do this, we're going to focus on three particular areas: (1) *God's world* and the way it seems to work, (2) *God's will* and the way it interacts with human free will, and (3) *God's war* and the cosmic struggle between good and evil.

Chapter Seven

# GOD'S WORLD

*Then Miss Watson she took me in the closet and prayed,*
*but nothing come of it. She told me to pray every day, and*
*whatever I asked for I would get it. But it warn't so. I tried it.*
*Once I got a fish-line, but no hooks. It warn't any good to me*
*without hooks. I tried for the hooks three or four times, but*
*somehow I couldn't make it work. By and by, one day, I asked*
*Miss Watson to try for me, but she said I was a fool.*
*She never told me why, and I couldn't make it out no way.*
*I set down one time back in the woods, and had a long think*
*about it . . . No, says I to my self, there ain't nothing in it.*

MARK TWAIN, *The Adventures of Huckleberry Finn*

Our problems with unanswered prayer can be relatively minor,
like Huckleberry Finn's prayer regarding a fishing line, or they
can be matters of life and death. Some requests matter more
than others in the degree of their consequence. So, as we turn
now to search God's world for clues to the problems of unanswered prayer, we might as well start with the ones that are
marginally easier to explain.

## Common Sense and Inconsequential Prayers

C. S. Lewis says of God, "You may attribute miracles to Him,
but not nonsense."[1] If we were to stop and think about some of
the things we say when we pray, we would realize that they are

meaningless or just plain stupid. In chapter 4, I described my
prayer for a gas station while driving home from watching
*Schindler's List.* It's the sort of prayer we've all muttered from
time to time, so let's think about it for a second.

What did I actually expect God to do? Was He supposed to
drop an entire filling station, staffed by angelic attendants, on a
cow field just before I rounded the bend? Maybe some people can
believe in that sort of miracle, but I'm still struggling to trust
God for the healing of an occasional headache or the patience to
keep my temper. I guess I could imagine God supernaturally pro-
pelling my car a couple of extra miles to a non-angelic Texaco
with nothing but fumes in my tank. In purely scientific terms,
this would not be any less impossible than the materialization of
a supernatural filling station, but it involves far less divine inter-
ference with the world, and—as we shall see—God seeks to intervene as little as possible.

Huckleberry Finn may have light-heartedly given up on
prayer merely because he received a fishing line without any
hooks, but I'm not going to lose my faith if I have to walk a few
miles with a gas can. *Schindler's List* is still far more likely to
cause me to do that. Some prayers are just inconsequential, and
when a person defies 2,000 years of Christian experience on the
basis of a fishing hook, a broken-down car or a flunked exam,
it's a fair bet that he or she wasn't really serious about God in
the first place!

---

### Why Unanswered Prayer?
#### #1: Common Sense
Some prayers aren't answered because
they're just plain stupid!

## Contradictory Prayers

We must also apply common sense to our more meaningful prayers. There are 6.6 billion people on Earth, which means that, at this very moment, many millions of prayers are rising simultaneously to the throne of God. Experience assures us that many thousands of these prayers are contradicting one another.

There is the semi-serious prayer of a football fan longing for his team to win the game, while at the other end of the stadium a man in different colors is earnestly praying for his team to win as well. There is the prayer of a bride for sunshine on her wedding day, while the neighboring farmer surveys his crops and prays for rain. There are prayers for deliverance from Israeli oppression and prayers for protection from suicide bombers. There are prayers in the West for economic recovery, while the developing world prays and cries and bleeds and dies for a fairer distribution of the world's wealth.

Last week, I boarded a train at the station behind my house and waited for it to leave. I was running late for a meeting, and so I sat there watching the platform clock, praying that the driver would get a move on so that I wouldn't miss my connecting train. Just then, I noticed a red-faced man running across the platform and, as the conductor's whistle blew, he clambered into my compartment. "Thank God it was late," the man murmured, mopping his brow.

*Whose prayers,* I wondered, *does God answer at such times?* In this case, perhaps He preferred to answer neither of us directly, knowing that it would be best for the system as a whole—and for the thousands of people who will get on and off that train that day—if the timetable was simply allowed to take its natural course. Is it not more likely that in the vast majority of situations, God hears our prayers sympathetically and meets with us in our need but very deliberately allows life to proceed as normal?

But let's think about the idea of God's stopping the train for that red-faced man or speeding it up for me. If we believe that an infinite number of these relatively tiny events are being determined minute by minute by the explicit intervention of a micro-managing God in answer to millions of human prayers, something very disconcerting happens to our theology: Prayer stops being a powerful submission to the sovereign wisdom of God, and God Himself starts to look like a cosmic version of one of those bright, flashing pinball machines, frenetically flicking around train timetables, weather-fronts, football scores and world markets at the behest of His creatures.

Now, it would suit me very nicely to be able to control trains through the power of prayer, but it might not suit the red-faced man. And if God, being fair, were to give the red-faced man the same power over locomotives as me, what would happen when our requests contradicted? Surely, it's more likely and more pleasant to assume that the angelic realm generally respects train timetables, that the outcome of football matches has not been predestined, and that brides will continue to discover that rain cannot dampen the joy of a wedding day.

Whenever God looks down on two drivers circling a crowded parking lot and both are praying for a space (and verily He alone knoweth there to be but a single remaining vacancy), are we to believe that the Lord of all the earth continually intervenes to show crass favoritism to one driver over the other? Isn't it far more likely that He watches as the car closest to the remaining grail-like space happens to discover it? Then, if that lucky driver should see fit to thank Him for the space, so much the better!

Why, then, should we bother praying about the small things of our lives?

First, we should pray about them simply because we can. It's a privilege to be heard by God when we tell Him what's troubling us, and it's natural for us to ask for His help. Conversation is the mark of any loving, living relationship—especially conversation about trivial matters![2]

Second, God will sometimes surprise us by answering one of our tiny prayers in a supernatural way—perhaps because He understands that it is not a tiny prayer at all but has major implications, unbeknownst to us, for the rest of our lives. Suppose those two drivers praying for that one parking space are doing so in a hospital parking lot. Suppose also that the driver who is naturally about to find the space because he happens to be closest to it is a man who has arrived early for a job interview while the other driver is about to have a heart attack on his way to a routine appointment. In such a situation, I have no problem believing that God might intervene and answer the prayer of the second man, because his trivial prayer is, unknown to him, not trivial at all. Our lives are full of such "coincidences," which, as Christians, we believe are not coincidences at all but moments when God kindly interfered with the mundane details of an ordinary day to protect or to provide.

Third, praying about the tiny things of our lives opens our eyes to the hidden myriad of God's daily blessings, which then enables us to live with greater gratitude. People who don't pray for stupid things such as parking spaces only get to thank God when sensible things happen—which means that they live less grateful lives! Maybe this is why we are told to pray for our daily bread even though we may live in a nation where food rarely requires supernatural provision. If we ask God for bread, we can be grateful for it when it comes.

One of the great champions of such gratitude was the writer G. K. Chesterton, whose work brims over with delight at what he calls the Great Minimum of life—its lamp posts and daisies and chance encounters. The wonder of such everyday miracles seemed so lavish to Chesterton that any added joy in life appears almost superfluous. Such gratitude for little things has always marked those who pray ridiculously and continuously about the details of life. They believe that God is intimately concerned about them and, as a result, they continually thank Him for the things that everyone else takes for granted. They receive the smallest pleasures as answers to prayer.

Since all good things come from God, it hardly matters whether He gives them to us through supernatural intervention or simply through the natural order of cause and effect. If the infinite complexities of life's patterns conspire to give us a sunny wedding day or a train just when we need it, let's give thanks to God! However, conversely, when trains and rain clouds fail to submit to our prayers, we should thank God anyway that one or more of our 6.6 billion neighbors has been blessed instead of us with the train, or the weather, or the parking space they needed.

---

### Why Unanswered Prayer?
#### #2: Contradiction
Some prayers aren't answered because they contradict other prayers.

---

## Complexity and Creation

None of the scenarios mentioned so far has been particularly disturbing. It makes sense that prayers for things such as fishing tackle, gas stations and parking spaces are just too inconsequential to be worth losing any sleep over. We can also understand why contradictory prayers must generally remain unanswered. But common sense must now be applied to a much less comfortable possibility: the idea that miracles must, by definition, be rare—much rarer than we would like them to be and rarer by far than a lot of preachers would lead us to expect.

This is not what we want to hear. We would all rather believe that every prayer for healing could work, that every car hurtling toward a child could brake in time, that every marriage could be restored and that every prodigal might return to the Lord. However, we know that God has intricately established certain governing principles (laws of nature) that make life work, and that they do so most of the time with almost infinite complexity and exquisite harmony.

Later, we will explore the devastating effect of human free will and the Fall on this fragile system, but for now let us remember—as contemporary scholars such as N. T. Wright remind us—that this delicate and infinitely complex world is our home. We are called to rule it, but we are also part of it, and therefore we are subject to its laws. Christians cannot switch off gravity when a brick is hurtling toward their toes or when a plane is tumbling from the skies. We know from bitter experience how uncommon miracles in such situations are, and now, we can perhaps begin to better understand that they are rare for the sake of the greater good.

*That God can and does, on occasions, modify the behavior of matter and produce what we call miracles is part of Christian faith; but the very conception of a common, and therefore stable, world demands that these occasions should be extremely rare.*

C. S. Lewis[3]

If God did miracles all the time, continually interfering with the governing principles of life on Earth in answer to every single one of our prayers, far from creating a cornucopia of greater happiness, the effects would, in fact, be devastating. One man's miracle could make misery for millions of his fellows. Let me give an example.

One day, Jesus and His friends were crossing the Sea of Galilee when a sudden storm blew up. The disciples, several of whom were seasoned fishermen in these very waters, believed that they were in grave danger of drowning. Jesus, however, simply "rebuked the wind and the raging waters; the storm subsided, and all was calm" (Luke 8:24). No wonder the disciples spoke in amazement, "Who is this?" (v. 25) until a few verses later when Peter answered, "[You are] the Christ of God!" (9:20).

Around the world today, many people in different situations will pray earnestly for Jesus to quell dangerous storms just as He did that night on Galilee. A hurricane may be threatening to destroy their livelihood. Force-10 gales and mountainous seas may be about to drown them. Dark thunderclouds may be gathering ominously, threatening to spoil the long-awaited church barbecue event.

However, most of these prayers will not "work" for a very important reason: The storms against which we may sometimes pray are vital to the wellbeing of millions of people. Storms are the air-conditioning system of the earth, keeping the climate— and thus the ecosystem—delicately in balance. Without storms, the Tropics would become significantly hotter, gradually causing desertification, and the Arctic would become far colder. Crucial winds would die down and lightning would become trapped in the clouds, making air travel treacherous to the point of impossibility.

These would be just a few of the dire consequences that would occur if every prayer against every storm in every part of the world were to be answered today. Can God control weather systems? Of course! God is sovereign and omnipotent. He sent rain on Noah, drought on Ahab and peace that day on Galilee. Meteorological miracles do take place (I described one in the Introduction to this book). But if God were to calm every storm (or even most storms), the balance of creation would be thrown off-kilter with devastating implications. And so, although it is sad, there may well today be crops destroyed, ships that sink, and church barbecues spoiled by the rain. Reluctantly, perhaps, God may say no to many prayers for the sake of the majority.

Occasionally today, in what probably amounts to "merely" a few thousand situations spread between 6.6 billion lives, Christ will unleash His power, intervening miraculously in the weather, or in a medical prognosis, or in a financial crisis in answer to prayer. However, as C. S. Lewis explains, "The very conception of a common, and therefore stable, world demands that these occasions should be extremely rare."[4]

> ### Why Unanswered Prayer?
> ### #3: The Laws of Nature
> Some prayers aren't answered because they would be detrimental to the world and to the lives of others.

## Chaos and the Fall

At least once a year, I try to go surfing for a weekend of hilarity with a bunch of guys. This time away, which has come to be known as "The Board Meeting," always follows the same primal format of food, drink and freezing seas. Some of the boys are pretty good at surfing, but I'm just happy to throw myself around in the gray cold ocean like a sock in the wash, screaming at seagulls and laughing at the impossibility of the most uncoordinated man in the world managing to ride the waves by standing on a piece of fiber-glass for any more than about three seconds.

The "Members of the Board" are an eclectic mix of eccentric characters. There's a Polish priest; a social-worker with an irrational fear of fish; a gay filmmaker; a very un-gay policeman; my old friend Alex, who speaks like a member of the Royal Family, a graphic designer who met Jesus after smoking enormous quantities of pot; and an entrepreneur called Matt, who was once ranked eighteenth on the U.K. surf scene (which sounds pretty good until you remember that there can surely only be about 20 people in Britain who possess their own surfboards).

I drove home from the most recent Board Meeting with my good buddy Mike, a guy who looks so much like Buzz Lightyear that he could (and, in my opinion, should) make a fortune at children's parties. More important, Mike is almost certainly the nicest person to exist since Jesus. I'm sure you know some nice people, but I guarantee you that Mike could out-nice them all, *and he wouldn't even know that he had done it.*

In spite of his niceness, Mike and his wife, Jo, have not had an easy ride over the past few years. Their daughter Lucy was born with a profound physical disability, which means that she will never walk. In three years, her little body has endured four major operations. Mike and Jo were only beginning to come to terms with the emotional and practical challenges of this situation when the leaders of their church had a disagreement that gradually led to their community falling apart.

Understandably, Mike and Jo felt sad and angry, unsure even whom to blame. Around this time, Mike's hips began aching and, at the age of just 32, he was diagnosed with degenerative arthritis. To make matters worse, Mike is an outdoor "pursuits" instructor whose job involves hiking, cycling, climbing, canoeing and sailing. What would this diagnosis mean for his career and their future? On top of all these difficulties, I knew that Mike and Jo were desperate to relocate and had been praying like crazy (without success) for their house to sell.

"How on earth do you cope with it all?" I asked Mike as we drove slalom through the rain down the narrow, winding lanes of Dorset.

"With what?" he asked.

"You know . . . the church, the house, Lucy's condition, the arthritis . . ."

"Oh that," he laughed. "Erm . . . I'm not sure that I do cope!"

"Yeah, but how do you make sense of it all, Mike? Where does it leave you and God?"

He went quiet. The wipers swept rain from the windshield. And then Mike, looking more like Buzz Lightyear than ever before, cleared his throat and said something very simple and very profound: "I guess I've realized that life is fundamentally tough."

I chuckled and Mike drove on in silence. "I guess," he continued eventually, speaking slowly as if he were laboriously pulling thoughts from a swamp, "I guess I used to think that . . . that I had some kind of divine right to happiness. I mean, obviously I knew there was going to be the occasional rough patch but . . . well, to be honest with you . . . these days I find it easier to just accept that life's tough—like they did hundreds of years ago—than to feel sort of hard done as if I've been robbed. Why blame God for stuff that's just the reality of life on a messed-up planet? Am I making any sense, Pete?"

I nodded. I knew exactly what he meant. Some words aren't cheap.

The rain roared and hissed on the road and the wipers kept time. Mike nodded toward the large white beak protruding over the front of the car. "We've got surf canoes and painkillers and combustion engines and all kinds of good stuff," he continued. "But I reckon that for most people, sooner or later, just getting out of bed in the morning becomes unbelievably difficult. And when things are sort of ticking along nicely in life as they sometimes do . . . you really need to treasure those times, because they're not normal."

As we drove on through the rain, I thought about Mike's words and remembered a good friend in America who had just lost his job and now had no income for his four children. I thought about him, and I thought about Samie's epilepsy . . .

*Lay down this book and reflect for five minutes on the fact that all the great religions were first preached, and long practiced, in a world without chloroform.*

C. S. LEWIS[5]

For me, there is something liberating and even cheering in Mike's morose pragmatism. Maybe life is just very hard, and that's okay. "Each day," says Jesus, "has enough trouble of its own" (Matt. 6:34, *NASB*). He of all people was realistic about how tough life can be. The apostle Peter was equally phlegmatic when writing to the saints who, due to persecution, were scattered across Asia Minor, saying, "Do not be surprised at the painful trial you are suffering, as though something strange were happening to you" (1 Pet. 4:12).

Perhaps we should accept what older people and poorer people and many of those with disabilities already know: Things are probably going to be very difficult today and just as hard tomorrow, too. Maybe by adjusting our expectations we can reduce the sense of disappointment, isolation and unfairness riding on the back of unanswered prayer. With a business-as-usual approach to life's trials, the good times can become surprising and delightful. It will be our blessings more than our sufferings that provoke us to ask God, "Why?"

Imagine two sets of people living together in the same grand, old, dilapidated building. Half of them think it's an expensive hotel, and they are bitterly disappointed. The other half think it's a prison, and they are pleasantly surprised![6] Ironically, it is when we finally accept the fact that life is not a five-star hotel and lay down our indignation at the way we are being treated that we begin to find hope. As long as we rage against the heavens, we will remain impoverished in our pain. But when we allow our eyes to fall to the mire, we may then discover a wealth of little epiphanies glimmering in puddles at our feet. When G. K. Chesterton finally gave up trying to be optimistic about the world and accepted that it was fallen, far from feeling depressed, his heart "sang for joy like a bird in spring."[7]

In Alexander Solzhenitsyn's classic novel *One Day in the Life of Ivan Denisovitch,* the hero's code of survival in a "special" camp is to accept horror as normative. The novel, which Solzhenitsyn considered his best, follows a prisoner called Shukov through a typical terrible day. It begins with him waking up sick and then being forced to clean the guardhouse for being late to work in sub-zero temperatures. However, by accepting such conditions as natural and unalterable, Shukov is able to climb into bed at the end of the day fully content and counting his blessings:

> They hadn't put him in the cells; they hadn't sent his squad to the settlement; he'd swiped a bowl of kasha at dinner; the squad leader had fixed the rates well; he'd built a wall and enjoyed doing it; he'd smuggled that bit of hacksaw blade through; he'd earned a favor from Tsezar that evening; he'd bought tobacco. And he hadn't fallen ill. He got over it.[8]

Shukov was serving 10 years of forced labor, surrounded by death, in one of the harshest environments on Earth as a prisoner of one of the most oppressive regimes in world history. Yet he was able to climb into bed that night contentedly grateful for "a day without a dark cloud. Almost a happy day."[9]

In spite of all the advances in technology and increased life expectancy, there is an extraordinary fragility to our generation. We collapse easily, our marriages fall apart, and we are quick to take offence. In our celebrity-obsessed world that is cosseted away from death and anaesthetized against pain, we need to be reminded that it's normal to have problems, get sick, experience financial challenges and face relational breakdown. Jesus promises us, "You will have trouble" (John 16:33), but not many of us stick that verse on the fridge. Instead, when we encounter setbacks, we feel betrayed. We ask, "why me?" as if such things should not beset a follower of Christ. As if we should be immune from the diseases that afflict our neighbors.

One of the problems, ironically, can be prayer. In prayer we set our hopes high and call it faith and pray for the perfect spouse, healthy children, successful careers and serene families. We don't just wish for these things but actually train ourselves to expect them! We fear the worst if we should ever lower our sights. Yet this is false faith. The apostle Paul longed not just "to know Christ and the power of his resurrection" but also "the fellowship of sharing in his sufferings" (Phil. 3:10). The Christian witness, and our ultimate hope, is not merely a miraculous succession of miraculous escapes from all human affliction. Rather it is the joy of a deepening relationship with the "man of sorrows familiar with suffering" (Isa. 53:3) who loves us and lives in us.

I'm not suggesting that we should pray for hard times but rather that when such times come, we should feel a little less outrage and a lot more hope because Jesus, who went through similar struggles, predicted that we would have them and promised to be with us in the midst of them.

> **Why Unanswered Prayer?**
> **#4: Life Is Tough**
> Some prayers aren't answered because creation is
> "subjected to frustration" and has not yet been fully
> "liberated from its bondage to decay" (Rom. 8:20-21).
> Tragically, life in such an environment is inevitably
> going to be acutely difficult at times.

## Faith and the Fall

The name "Israel" literally describes one who contends, or fights or wrestles with God. Like Jacob, we question, we wrestle, we doubt, we believe and we fight. At times there is, therefore, a certain bloody-minded defiance about the Judeo-Christian determination to trust and delight in God irrespective of circumstance. "Though he slay me," cries Job, "yet will I hope in him!" (Job 13:15). Do you hear the defiance? This is the fighting talk of a faith forged in the fires of struggle.

This same irrepressibility is evident in the defiance of Shadrach, Meshach and Abednego. When they are commanded by King Nebuchadnezzar to worship a grotesque golden idol on pain of death, they respond with indomitable courage:

> O Nebuchadnezzar, we do not need to defend ourselves before you in this matter. If we are thrown into the blazing furnace, the God we serve is able to save us from it, and he will rescue us from your hand, O king. But even if he does not, we want you to know, O king, that we will not serve your gods or worship the image of gold you have set up (Dan. 3:16-18).

The paradox of faith is encapsulated in this rousing speech. On one hand, the three young men assert that "the God we serve *is able* to save." What's more, they believe that God is not just able but also *willing* to intervene miraculously on their behalf, declaring, "*he will* rescue us from your hand." But on the other hand, having made these unequivocal statements of faith, they add, "*but even if he does not* . . . we will not serve your gods."

In the first part of their speech, we see that Shadrach, Meshach and Abednego have faith for a miracle, and this is impressive. But then we see that they also have faith of a deeper kind altogether—faith to endure suffering should the miracle not happen.

· · · ·

A few months after his father had been diagnosed with lung cancer, a guy I will call Kevin started coming to church and heard a message about God's power to answer prayer that ignited hope in him for his ailing dad. His best friend had recently become a follower of Jesus, and it didn't take Kevin long to do the same.

From the start, most of his prayers and most of his hopes understandably revolved around his dad's worsening condition, and he learned quickly to cry out to God for healing. One day, Kevin's sister, who was not a Christian, was driving alone in her car when she heard an audible voice telling her that their dad was indeed going to make a miraculous recovery. Bolstered by such a remarkable encouragement, we joined with Kevin in earnest prayer for his father. God had spoken, and we prayed with faith! Yet even though there was the occasional remission (for which we were always quick to thank God), the bitter truth of the matter was that overall, Kevin's dad's condition was getting steadily worse.

With a heavy heart, I sat down with Kevin one day to ask him the "what if" question. What if his dad died? How would he cope? Where would it leave his faith if all these prayers and his sister's mysterious experience all came to nothing? Kevin told me that he understood there were no guarantees of healing. He assured me if his father died, it wouldn't cause him to give up on Christianity—although he admitted that he would "have some big questions."

A few months later, Kevin's father passed away, and within weeks so did Kevin's belief in God. It was painful to watch his grief and disappointment turn to bitterness and uninterest. Like Shadrach, Meshach and Abednego, Kevin had a defiant faith in the possibility of divine intervention, but unlike them, Kevin's faith in God was shackled to that possibility. In prayer, he was simply not prepared to take no for an answer. I think I can understand Kevin's desperation for a miracle and his sense of desolation when his prayers made no notable difference and his father died. However, it seems desperately sad that when Kevin lost his father, he also lost faith in his heavenly Father just when he needed Him more than ever before.

Looking back, I realize that we failed to lay the correct doctrinal foundations in Kevin's life as a new believer. Superficially, he certainly looked like a zealous young Christian who desired to live for God. But when the floods came, he crumbled. His foundation was made of sand.

Many people are shattered when their prayers are not answered. Often, they begin to doubt God. Sometimes we patch these people up with a few words of comfort or even counseling and some bland comments about God moving in mysterious ways when what they really need is biblical teaching about what it means to be a Christian. Perhaps when they became Christians, they were told that God was going to make all their problems disappear, or perhaps they just assumed this, as Kevin did. But in fact, the Bible itself teaches that "we share in his sufferings in order that we may also share in his glory" (Rom. 8:17), and Jesus actually tells us to expect the very opposite of an easy life, as we have seen (see John 16:33).

What did Barbara Fisher, Floyd McClung and my friend Mike have that Kevin did not? They had a correct understanding of the integral place of suffering in Christian experience.

---

### Why Unanswered Prayer?
### #5: Doctrine
Some prayers aren't answered the way we think they should be because our understanding and expectations of God are wrong.

---

Living as we do in the space between the Fall and the resurrection, acknowledging both the terrible afflictions of life and the miracle-working power of prayer, the story of Shadrach, Meshach and Abednego reminds us to believe in God even more than we believe in miracles. Like these three men, we trust that the God we serve is able to save us. We insist on the possibility of miracles. But to such faith we add faithfulness so that even if our brave words fall flat—even if our prayers are not answered and we are plunged into the fiery furnace of suffering—we will still trust God.

I can think of no better contemporary example of such defiant faith than a quiet Scottish lady called Margaret Lee. Margaret was fair-skinned and shy, gentle yet determined and, though her face was often serious, she always had twinkling eyes. Three years ago, out of the blue, Margaret was diagnosed with throat cancer. The multiplying cells in her esophagus were gradually strangling Margaret, so the doctors introduced a tube into her throat to enable her to swallow. Terrifyingly, this tube also began to constrict under the cancerous pressure, but Margaret chose not to have another one inserted. "I'm not scared of dying," she whispered. "But I do get scared about the implications once my throat finally closes up."

Many people went to visit Margaret, and when they did, they would often express great sadness for her predicament. "You've had such a very tough life," they would say, "and now this . . ." as if "this" (by which they meant cancer of the throat) was the worst thing imaginable. Margaret soon got so used to this well-meaning assessment of her situation that she wrote her standard response on a piece of scrap paper. I think it's probably one of the most courageous declarations of faith in Jesus that I have ever seen:

> This is not the worst thing to ever happen! Cancer is so limited. It cannot cripple love, shatter hope, corrode faith, eat away peace, destroy confidence, kill friendship, shut out memories, silence courage, quench the Spirit or lessen the power of Jesus.

Isn't that extraordinary? Cancer was killing Margaret, and yet she was able to list its many limitations. She could barely speak or swallow, her body was emaciated and the pain was insistent, but the cancer had not—and could not—consume Margaret Lee. To all outward appearances, she had become a grim testament to the corruption of nature and the limitations of Christ's power. Yet in reality, her life and her death bore eloquent witness to the power of prayer for those who believe.

"I must ask, very gently," writes Francis Schaeffer, "how much thought does [our identification with Christ] provoke? Is it not true that our prayers for ourselves are almost entirely aimed at getting rid of the negative at any cost rather than praying that the negatives be faced in the proper attitude?"[10] With Margaret Lee, we see someone whose identification with Christ (His suffering and His resurrection) meant that she "no longer aimed at getting rid of the negative at any cost" and instead sought grace to face cancer with a deeply Christian attitude.

Margaret's body was buried in a meadow on a hillside in the Scottish Borders. Around her grave stood those whose lives had been changed by her courageous and consistent witness. Like Shadrach, Meshach and Abednego, Margaret knew that God can and does work miracles in answer to prayer. But unlike Kevin, she was also prepared to trust Him if the miracle did not materialize.

We cannot remove Gethsemane and Golgotha from the reality of life in Christ. Preachers who say that it is always God's will to heal simply have no theology of suffering. They are in grave danger of becoming what Paul calls "enemies of the cross . . . [whose] mind is on earthly things" (Phil. 3:18-19). In his exposition of Ephesians 6, the renowned English preacher Dr. Martyn Lloyd-Jones describes the problem as follows:

> If you believe that "healing is in the atonement"—that it is never God's will that any of his children should be ill, and that no Christian should ever die from a disease . . . if you believe that and then find yourself, or someone who is dear to you, dying of some incurable disease, you will be miserable and unhappy. Probably you will be told by certain people, "There is something wrong with your faith" . . . You will be depressed in your spiritual life. Such a person's condition is due to error or heresy concerning a primary central doctrine. He or she has insinuated something into the Christian faith that does not truly belong to it.[11]

Let's be absolutely clear: While suffering is part and parcel of the Christian life, God hates it as much as we do. He hates Samie's seizures. He hates what happened to Margaret Lee, Kevin's father and what nearly happened to Misha and Luke McClung. We should not be surprised when trials come, but neither should we pretend to enjoy them. "God will not befriend our death," wrote theologian Alan Lewis as he was dying of cancer, adding that one glimpse of Christ's agony on the cross exposes "how perfect, uncompromising and implacable is God's hatred of death's curse and all it does to us."[12]

There is no indication to suggest that there was sickness in the Garden of Eden before the Fall. Neither is there any evidence in the life of Christ that sickness is ever God's desire unless it is to bring glory to the Father (see John 9:3). The book of Revelation anticipates a time when the dwelling place of God will be with men so that "there will be no more death or mourning or crying or pain" (21:4). But until that day, we live in the gap between the Fall and the coming redemption of all things. And so, we still sometimes may get sick, our businesses may fall foul of world markets, our homes may be flooded, and so on.

Of course, occasionally, a miracle breaks in: The storm calms, the train leaves early, an anonymous gift comes through the door, the blind man sees, the fishing line comes with hooks. And when these things happen, we are granted a tantalizing foretaste of the new creation in which all things will conspire with unbounded complexity to perpetuate beauty and harmony for the glory of God.

· · · ·

In seeking to make sense of our unanswered prayers, we have looked at God's world and the expectations that we may reasonably have within it. In particular, we have seen that:

- Some prayers are either meaningless or inconsequential, like Huckleberry Finn's for fishing tackle and mine for a gas station (though we should not necessarily stop praying for such things);
- Many prayers are contradictory, such as my prayer for the train to leave on time;
- Some prayers must be taken in the context of the natural order and the fact that miracles are necessarily rare;
- Many prayers are thwarted by the ongoing chaos of the Fall and the fact that praying people are not immune to its corruption even though they can be victorious in Christ, like Margaret Lee who bravely catalogued the limitations of the disease that was killing her body; and
- Some prayers are unanswered because we're asking the wrong thing of God based on an unbiblical set of expectations.

Having identified these logical, environmental and practical parameters within which we pray, we will now turn our attention to some of the spiritual dynamics by which we may interact and occasionally rearrange these parameters through faith, perseverance and spiritual warfare. But first, we must turn our attention from God's world to make sense of God's will.

Chapter Eight

# GOD'S WILL

*We shall come one day to a heaven where we shall gratefully know that God's great refusals were sometimes the true answers to our truest prayers.*

P.T. Forsythe, *The Soul of Prayer*[1]

In the last chapter, we looked at factors in *God's world* that thwart our prayers. As we continue to ask why there is unanswered prayer, we turn now to look at the most important issue of all: the way *God's will* interacts with human free will to determine the outcome of our prayers. We'll do this by exploring the inward and outward dimensions of God's will, including (1) God's will for our lives, and (2) God's will versus free will.

. . . .

## God's Will for Our Lives

The first time I really fell in love was at the age of 10. Now, I know you may be thinking that this was a little premature, but you have to trust me—this was the real thing. I was attending a boys-only private school in the English countryside, replete with a mahogany-paneled dining room, a deputy headmaster who wore bow ties, and a sports program that included rugby (American football without the padding) and cricket (a game that can last up to three days and, at its best, manages to incorporate mealtimes).

My friend, whose father was an ophthalmologist, would sometimes come to school with a small pot in his pocket containing a single floating eye. He'd shake the pot and we'd gather around excitedly to see who the eyeball ended up staring at. I learned Latin at the age of eight, French from a retired colonel with a gray walrus moustache, and English from a man who carried a peregrine falcon around on his wrist. The British don't do many things well, but we remain world class at eccentricity.

This school was the backdrop to the whole falling-in-love-at-the-age-of-10 thing; otherwise, I'd hesitate to tell you about it for fear of losing your sympathy as a man of the people. Of course, my pseudo-Marxist friends despise me for having attended a school like this, but what choice did I have? At the time, I wasn't allowed to choose my own underpants let alone a school in the inner city and a government for the people. So, yes, this was my school until the age of 11. I admit it and I do remember it affectionately.

It was in my third year that the school decided to go co-educational. Just two brave girls turned up at the start of the next semester. One of them (we shall call her Annie) inevitably found herself the focal point for more than a hundred prepubescent boys' fascination.

It's hard to convey the startling impression that Annie made on the school. The best I can do is to use the analogy of my friend Malcolm who was once asked to play guitar in front of 20,000 people in a remote part of Nigeria. Everything went fine for Malc until it got dark and the spotlight came on. At that point, it quickly became clear to him that, as the only white face under the only bright light within hundreds of square miles, it had been a bad idea to wear a white shirt that night. The spotlight lit Malc like a human lighthouse, attracting swarms of ravenous insects to converge on his shirt from the four corners of Africa. To make matters worse, they invaded his nostrils and even his mouth whenever he opened it to sing. And so, as dusk turned to night, 20,000 Nigerians watched in amazement as the white guy from England slowly turned black before their very eyes. I like to imagine that Malc had become a guitar-playing version of that mad beekeeper man on the Discovery Channel, who attempts to talk nonchalantly to the camera while covered in a second skin of swarming bees.

Back at my school in the English countryside, there was a similar effect as the spotlight fell on Annie. Clouds of swarming boys found themselves mysteriously drawn from the four corners of the playground to congregate like idiots around Annie's brilliant glow. I wasn't one of the really confident kids who could just swoop in on a girl like Annie and shamelessly share gum. I've always been at least one rung down the ladder of cool—the awkward guy mumbling on the fringes and trying not to stare too much. I was never a stalker or anything like that, just in case you're worrying, but I do have a little sympathy for the lovesick geeks who rifle through rubbish bins outside the home of the oblivious blonde from summer camp. Maybe I shouldn't have told you that.

Gum or no gum, I was head-over-heels in love with Annie. When she was in the room, I could hardly breathe. I even sent her an anonymous Valentine's card. In hindsight, she probably had her own personal postal delivery truck on the 14th of February that year, but I hoped and I prayed that we might one day have something special. Night after night I asked God to make her like me the way I liked her. I was 10 years old, and I had never prayed about anything so persistently and passionately (and ridiculously) in all my life. Looking back, it's easy to patronize these prayers, but maybe, just maybe, you can remember how it felt. How real it was. How desperately it mattered.

Several years later, I met Annie once more, and she still did not seem interested in me. Those 10-year-old prayers remained unanswered. But as I looked at her, it was as though that beautiful butterfly that had once fluttered daintily around our school, enchanting the hearts of a hundred mesmerized boys, had somehow undergone a metamorphosis backward into a cute but clomping caterpillar. Perhaps it sounds callous, but I remember thanking God from the very bottom of my heart for ignoring those passionate early prayers for a girlfriend.

**God's Will Is Best**
Sometimes we have to admit that God really does know the best for our lives. Annie reminds me that God is, by definition, bigger than my understanding and desires. He is big enough to think up the entire universe while maintaining personal knowledge of more than six billion people simultaneously. This is a very serious level of multitasking. Every second, five babies are born into the world, and God is there tracking each choice they will make every second of every day of their lives. In that same second, two people will die, and we believe that He knows them too.

It does make sense, therefore, that we won't be able to understand everything that such a big God does or does not do. "Our life," says Annie Dillard, "is a faint tracing on the surface of mystery."[2] How tragic it would be if our destiny were limited to the projections of human logic and the meager possibilities created by our own temporal imagination. What could possibly be worse than the prospect of our every prayer being answered so that "god" became little more than the name for our personal power source.

I've got a theory that this is why the wives of so many world leaders get into astrology and all sorts of weird New Age stuff. Maybe it's just the media, but many intelligent, powerful and otherwise rational women have been discovered consulting the stars or clutching crystals or tracing the energy lines of their governmental abode. My theory is this: These women are terrorized, subconsciously, by the notion that world peace lies in the hands of a man who can't remember the name of the cat and passes wind in his sleep. Their own sense of security necessitates the belief that there is a higher intelligence pulling the strings of power than that of the man struggling to put together a simple piece of furniture in the garage.

Well, the good news for these women—the good news for all of us—is that there really is a God who governs the affairs of men and to whom we owe allegiance. "My thoughts are not your thoughts," He reminds us when we don't understand the way our lives are turning out. "Neither are your ways my ways," He adds, which means that He doesn't necessarily do everything we pray (Isa. 55:8-9).

As I gaze at Samie and remember Annie, I know for sure that sometimes God denies my prayers because He has something even better for me. I breathe an easy amen to God's promise through Jeremiah: "I know the plans I have for you . . . plans to prosper you and not to harm you, plans to give you hope and a future" (Jer. 29:11). My heart rises to pray with Thomas á Kempis: "O Lord, you know what is best for me. Give what you will, how much you will and when you will."

It's easy to acknowledge that the Lord knows best with regard to a childhood crush. But most situations of unanswered prayer are far more perplexing and—let's be honest—more painful as well. Last week I asked my friend Emily if she had any experience of unanswered prayer. Immediately, she described the long, protracted, ongoing frustrations of her husband's work situation. Matt had been trying to find the right job for several years and they were now utterly demoralized and heavily in debt. "I've prayed and prayed but nothing seems to shift," she said wearily.

That was last week, but yesterday I found Emily in the kitchen crying tears of joy. At last, after all these years, Matt had been offered a fantastic job that was ideally suited to his skills in specialist recruitment. He is excited. Their finances are going to be okay. "The only downside," said Emily after several minutes of rejoicing, "is that the kids are really going to miss him. They've become so used to having him around during the week."

Why had there been such a delay in answering Emily's prayers? There is no simple explanation, but one aspect of God's goodness is surely revealed in the amount of time that Matt has been able to spend at home during this testing period, simply being a very good dad at a key time in the development of his children. An immediate answer to Emily's prayers would have, among other things, reduced Matt's involvement with his children. In the words of the Scottish author P. T. Forsythe, "We shall come one day to a heaven where we shall gratefully know that God's great refusals were sometimes the true answers to our truest prayers."

---

### *Why Unanswered Prayer?*
### #6: God's Best
Some prayers aren't answered because God has got something even better for us.

---

### God's Will Versus Our Will: Motivation in Prayer
After five fruitless years of solitary missionary work among the Lisu people of China's mountainous southwest territories, James O. Fraser couldn't understand why his prayers were not being answered. He had abandoned a promising career in Scotland and left behind all the people he loved and

every creature comfort in radical obedience to Christ's Great Commission, and yet his preaching was falling on deaf ears—and so, it seemed, were his prayers. Why had Jesus sent him to go and make disciples of the Lisu people, only to deny him in this way?

Gradually, Fraser realized that his priorities, which had seemed so righteous, were subtly wrong. "Unanswered prayers," he wrote, "have taught me to seek the Lord's will instead of my own."[3] When our prayers over a protracted period of time fail to bring any sort of breakthrough, we may need to ask whether we are really pursuing the Lord's will in the Lord's way or merely our own ambition.

Fraser subtly reorientated his prayers, no longer presuming to know God's will and God's way in every situation, but took the time to ask *how* he should pray. Slowly, his ministry became more fruitful. Then, after eight years of hard work, breakthrough came and many of the Lisu were swept into the Kingdom in a matter of months, as if a dam had broken (more on this later).

The breakthrough came not because the content of Fraser's prayers had changed—his longing had always been for the salvation of the Lisu people—but rather because the heart behind his prayers had changed significantly. Fraser discovered the hard way that in prayer, it's always more important *why* we pray than *how* we pray and *what* we say.

I guess everyone prays selfishly sometimes. I like the story about the ambitious mother who sidled up to Jesus one day and asked if her two boys, James and John, could have the top jobs in His coming Kingdom! I remember as a kid praying frantically that I would get a bike with drop handlebars, that I would pass my exams even though I hadn't studied and, on another occasion, that my parents wouldn't find out about my school detention. The apostle James explains very simply that one reason for unanswered prayer is selfish motivation: "When you ask, you do not receive, because you ask with wrong motives, that you may spend what you get on your pleasures" (Jas. 4:3).

Jesus never actually promised to answer our prayers uncondibionally. It is God's prayers in our mouths that are guaranteed to work. The apostle John puts it like this: "This is the confidence we have in approaching God: that if we ask anything *according to his will*, he hears us. And if we know that he hears us—whatever we ask—we know that we have what we asked of him" (1 John 5:14-15, emphasis added). It is when we pray "according to his will" that God hears and acts, which means that miracles happen only when our prayers harmonize with God's broad desires for our lives.

On my first date with Samie, I gave her a book about the legendary Irish soccer player George Best. Looking back, I now realize that this wasn't the most romantic gesture in the world and that although it was thoughtful on my part, it was also misguided, because no one could be less interested in football than my wife! Likewise, as we get to know God, we discover what He likes, what He dreams and what His will is. This is a powerful discovery, because it unlocks our ability to pray in His name—not just about big issues but also about the subtle dilemmas of daily life. The incredible promise of Jesus is that such prayers, prayed in His name, are guaranteed to work: "My Father will give you whatever you ask in my name" (John 16:23).

> ### *Why Unanswered Prayer?*
> #### #7: Motive
> Some prayers (even spiritual-sounding ones) aren't answered because they are, in fact, selfishly motivated.

## God's Will Is Relationship

The Hasidic masters tell an old rabbinic story to explain why God often delays the granting of our heart's desires:

> There is a king who has two sons. Each of them comes to receive his gift from the royal table. The first son appears at his father's doorway, and as soon as he is seen, his request is granted. The father holds this son in low esteem, and is annoyed by his presence. The king orders that the gifts be handed to his son at the door so that he will not approach the table. Then the king's beloved son appears. The father takes great pleasure in this son's arrival and does not want him to leave too quickly. For this reason the king delays granting his request, hoping that the son will then draw near to him. The son comes closer, he feels the father's love so deeply that he does not hesitate to stretch forth his own hand to the royal table.[4]

The Father's deepest desire for our lives is that we would "dwell in his courts" and thereby come into a more fulfilling relationship with Him. By holding back blessings from our lives, God beguiles us to tarry in His presence. Both royal sons in the story were loved and received gifts of equal value. But contrary to appearances, the son whose desires were not immediately gratified was, in fact, the most blessed. In God's kingdom, happiness is not marked out primarily by popularity, fat bank accounts or clean bills of health but rather by proximity to the Father. "Blessed are those you choose and bring near to live in your courts!" cries the psalmist (Ps. 65:4). "If you *abide* in Me," says Jesus, "and if My words abide in you, ask whatever you wish, and it will be done for you" (John 15:7, *NASB*, emphasis added).

For many months now, Samie and I have been seeking God's guidance about the possibility of a major geographical relocation. For us it is a very big decision—one of the biggest of our lives—and we desperately need God's counsel. But after more than 12 months of prayer, occasional days of fasting and numerous conversations with friends, Samie and I are still not sure what God is saying. This decision is getting urgent now, and whatever we end up doing will affect our friendships, our budgeting, our children's education and our ministry at large. However, although there have been occasional whispers from the Holy Spirit, there's been nothing unmistakable, nothing clear, nothing that warrants pulling our kids out of school.

The weird thing, however, is that God *has* spoken to us during this year with crystal clarity about lesser issues—some of which we've hardly bothered even praying about! Why does God speak clearly about peripherals but remain silent on the issue with which we most need His help? My answer—call it a hunch—is that God is *enjoying* the way we are wrestling with Him in prayer through this process. To put it another way, He may consider our wondering and questioning more important than the relatively simple act of supplying us with an answer. Whatever the reason, I can't begin to tell you how frustrating this is for us!

As a result of God's silence on this perplexing matter, Samie and I are praying harder, we are searching our souls more diligently, and we are tuning our ears to the slightest whisper from heaven in a way we would not normally do. In short, we are drawing nearer to God precisely because of our unanswered prayer. To paraphrase the rabbinic parable, "The father is taking great pleasure in our presence and does not want us to leave too quickly. For this reason the king is delaying granting our request, hoping that we will then draw near to him."

There is no doubt at all that the people with the deepest and most dynamic relationships with God are those who also suffer the silences of unanswered prayer. No saint ever basked perpetually in God's abundant provision. It is pain and frustration that spur us on to pursue a deeper life in God. "Afflictions quicken us to prayer," observed John Newton, the former slave ship captain best known for writing the hymn "Amazing Grace." "Experience testifies that a long course of ease and prosperity, without painful changes, has an unhappy tendency to make us cold and formal in our secret worship; but troubles rouse our spirits, and constrain us to call upon the Lord in good earnest, when we feel a need of that help which we only can have from him."[5] By allowing us to go through hard times, God needles our souls to prayer. "The outer need kindles the inner," says P. T. Forsythe, "and we find that the complete answer to prayer is the Answerer."[6]

God's great aim has always been, and will forever be, relationship with us. Sometimes, He may deprive us of *something* in order to draw us to *Someone*. And when we reciprocate—when we decide that we want Him more than we want His stuff—the most amazing thing happens. We are rewired and our requests are either altered as we grow to know and to prefer what He wants for us, or they are simply answered because, in seeking first the kingdom of God, "all these things" are given to us as well (Matt 6:33).

> *Why Unanswered Prayer?*
> **#8: Relationship**
> Some prayers aren't answered because God Himself is a greater answer than the thing we are asking for and He wants to use our sense of need to draw us into a deeper relationship with Himself.

. . . .

It goes without saying that I would never, ever have volunteered to go through the things we have experienced over these past few years. If, at any point, I could have flicked a switch to cure Samie, I would have done it without a second thought. I still would. However, having had the choice made for us (by God, by Eve and by the serpent—they all played a part), I would not want to go back to being the carefree person I was. God has changed me. He has rewired me. I think He has made me more sensitive. He blew a half-time whistle on my life and made me realize that I had many of my priorities wrong.

And so I'm comforted by the story of those wise old Hasidic masters and their outrageous idea that God might be withholding healing, not because Samie and I are so bad at praying, but rather because we are so precious to Him and He likes our asking and enjoys our presence. But I must go further. There is something solemn I must tell you (and this may well have been the hardest line to write in this entire book): I have come to believe that if Samie had been spared her brain tumor and we'd never been forced to face the possibility of her early death, we would thereby have missed out on God's best for our lives.

There, I've said it. I've thought about it a great deal and I mean it. God's best has somehow been drawn from the worst pain we could ever have imagined. I continue to hate Samie's illness, but I love Samie more because of it. God has shown Himself to be bigger than that fierce tumor. Bigger than a misfiring brain, too. Bigger than nights of fear. Bigger than my inability to comprehend. Is He bigger than dying as well? Well, I know what I'm *supposed* to say here, but on that one I guess we'll just have to wait and see . . .

## God's Will Versus Free Will

*Try to exclude the possibility of suffering which the order*
*of nature and the existence of free will involves, and you*
*find that you have excluded life itself.*

C. S. LEWIS[7]

There's an old joke about a man who believed utterly in God's control of every single event in his life. One day, he fell down the stairs and, lying in a bruised heap at the bottom, muttered, "Thank God, I've got that over with!"

The Bible, I believe, has a very different understanding of God's sovereignty, depicting the Almighty as one who continually chooses to limit His own power. We've already seen how God chooses to respect the laws of nature (which He Himself put in place for the good of all) and in His love does not continually override the order of creation in answer to every prayer. God also chooses (for reasons we shall now explore) not to override the free will that He has given to humanity. In the next chapter (about spiritual warfare), we will examine the free will of God's angelic realm, which remains partially in rebellion against its Creator.

In God's dealings with His creation, He prefers not to assert His dominion unilaterally but rather to respect the laws of nature and the choices of His creatures. We see this willingness to relinquish control ultimately expressed in Jesus. Here, we believe, is the omnipotent God becoming an incontinent baby. The second chapter of Paul's letter to the Philippians traces this startling process of God's self-limitation from the courts of heaven through the indignity of birth, the humility of servanthood and death at the hands of His creatures, even death on a cross. I believe that we will fail completely to understand the dynamics of prayer and the reasons for unanswered prayer unless we first understand God's determination to respect the free will of humanity.

On at least three occasions, Jesus Himself experienced unanswered prayer, but only one of these prayers remains unanswered to this day:

1. In Gethsemane, He prayed that the cup of suffering and separation would be taken from Him, but it was not. At least, not immediately.

2. On the cross, He asked, "Why have you forsaken me?" and there was no answer. The answer would come, but not for two days.

3. A third prayer of Christ has remained unanswered for 2,000 years: "I pray . . ." He said to the Father, "that all of them may be one . . . so that the world may believe that you have sent me" (John 17:20-21). That high priestly prayer for Christian unity, which He revealed as a key to God's mission on Earth, remains violently unfulfilled to this day. Why? Because unlike the other two prayers, this particular longing of God is dependent on voluntary human obedience. In our determination to divide and our refusal to forgive one another, we (mere humans) deny Jesus an answer to His cherished prayer for unity.

God could, by definition, enforce His agenda, but He has chosen instead to allow His creatures, in the words of Blaise Pascal, "the dignity of causality." God's sovereignty does not require Him to bully His creation into resentful submission. He is the Lord of lords, but His kingdom is not a dictatorship. Instead, He prays, He beguiles, He loves, He listens, He lays

Himself down. It is Satan who manipulates, dominates and rapes. God's nature is to entice our hearts with gentleness and infinite subtlety, dignifying our lives continually with choice.

In chapter 5, I described the miraculous deliverance of Misha McClung and her baby, Luke. But what I haven't told you is that two weeks before Luke's birth, Misha had a terrible dream in which she was in a wheelchair and somehow not all there mentally. Chillingly, Luke was also missing from the dream. What are we to make of such a dream? Are we to see this premonition as a word from God—a harrowing reminder of what might have been if His people had not intervened in prayer?

## A Tale of Two Trees

When I asked Samie to marry me, it was a terrifying moment. I knew that she could say one single-syllable word and dash all my dreams, or say another and make them all come true. My future hung on her choice. Had I decided to avoid the risk of disappointment, grabbing Samie by the hair with one hand while beating my chest in triumph with the other and declaring, *"You shall be mine,"* then my actions toward her might have been regarded as less than loving! Love always permits choice, and allowing choice takes terrifying risks.

> *You are free to eat from any tree in the garden; but you must not*
> *eat from the tree of the knowledge of good and evil.*
> GENESIS 2:16

Right at the heart of the creation story, we see God establishing this principle of free will by planting a tree from which Adam and Eve were not to eat. In so doing, we understand that God created for them the dangerous possibility of disobedience in order to create the higher possibility of voluntary submission.

His selfless desire was to allow them to participate in His own intimate Trinitarian relationship of mutual surrender and infinite dependency.[8] We struggle to describe in mere words or pictures the wonder of this possibility. Perhaps the intimacy experienced by lovers surrendering mutually to one another's affections in sexual intercourse gives us the merest glimpse of the intimacy for which we have been created—an intimacy that is attainable only through complete and mutual self-sacrifice.

God made humanity to share in the very exquisite relationship of mutual self-sacrifice that exists at the heart of His being. He did not create a fleet of personal robots that are carefully programmed to do the right thing at any given moment in a predetermined and hermetically sealed universe. He made us with the divine capacity for creativity, generosity, restraint and relationship, knowing that these treasures are only available to those who possess the ultimate power of self-determination.

There has never been a greater risk than the one God took in choosing to create humanity with this ability to love and be loved. As Barbara Brown Taylor writes in her book *When God Is Silent*, "The most dangerous word God ever says is 'Adam'."[9] What a risk He took! When Adam and Eve elected to exploit the possibility of disobedience, the consequences were inevitably cataclysmic. Eve was persuaded by the serpent to doubt two things: the *truthfulness of God's word*, ("you will not surely die") and the *goodness of God's intentions* ("God knows that when you eat of it your eyes will be opened, and you will be like God").

At that moment, by choosing to doubt God's word and God's intentions, Eve created the psychic space within the universe for disbelief in God's truth and love—which is His very nature. Into this space, created by the notional absence of love, came the actual possibility of hatred and selfishness. In the same way, by entertaining the previously unthinkable idea of God as anything less than love and truth, Adam and Eve—who had been created by God's love and His word—inevitably divorced themselves from their only source of identity and being.

Earth-shattering sin came into the world through that simple choice of our forefathers and, as we have seen, it took another simple yet cataclysmic choice—this time from Jesus, praying, "not my will but yours"—to bring about salvation. And how do we enter into that salvation today? By making our own simple choice to believe! We stand between two trees. In the Garden of Eden grows the tree of aspiration and acquisition that promises knowledge yet produces death. And in the Garden of Gethsemane grows the tree of self-sacrifice that promises death yet produces life. No one will suicidally eat the fruit that promises death unless first they trust that the One who says, "when you eat of it you will surely die" (Gen. 2:17) is also "the resurrection and the life," and thus that "he who believes in me will live, even though he dies" (John 11:25).

Lodged in the reality of human free will, we recognize terrible danger yet also the highest potential in the universe. I believe that it is this potential that is unlocked in Christian prayer. When Jesus promised miracles to those who pray in accordance with the will of God, He was not so much laying down a condition as making an observation. When a human being, by the power of God's grace, expresses a desire that is rooted not in his or her own selfishness ("my will") but rather in God's plan for creation ("Thy will"), such a posture reverses the bias of the Fall in that individual's own life and reestablishes a little piece of Eden, through him or her, on Earth.

However, the very power of human choice that can release the purposes of God in prayer can also be used to resist God's will. That's what happened in the Garden of Eden, and it's happening still, thwarting God's purposes, at least for the time being. Let me tell you how this important principle first made sense to me.

## Going for a Fistful of Converts

I once took part in an intensive outreach program that targeted an unsuspecting village near London. During a two-week period, we offered every single person in the community multiple opportunities to hear about Jesus. The locals hardly knew what had hit them (and, sadly, it probably did feel to them a bit like being "hit") as an alien invasion of grinning evangelists seized control of their village, armed only with Bibles and breath-fresheners.

We did pretty much everything imaginable to proclaim Christ to them. We washed their windshields at traffic lights, we knocked on their doors, we took lessons for their kids in school, we offered to dig their gardens, we bought clipboards and conducted surveys in the shopping center, we played Beatles covers for the men in the pub, we sang "Danny Boy" to their grandparents in the local care-home, and a guy named Steve even escaped from a straight-jacket hanging upside down from a crane. Everyone in town knew about our mission, and quite a few people seemed really interested in Jesus Christ. One night, an entire scout troop raised their hands and said yes, they would like to invite Jesus into their hearts. When that happened, the scout leader—who'd been smirking at the back—was so surprised he almost fell off his chair.

Looking back on those two surreal weeks of my life, I have some pretty big questions. For one thing, I suspect that we alienated more people than we attracted. I also doubt that there has been much long-term impact, because the whole thing was so unsustainable. I'm ashamed to admit that in our hearts, we were probably more interested in trading the gospel for the price of a hand raised and a prayer prayed than we were in the actual thoughts and lives of the people to whom we were talking. With hindsight, I can see that our approach was more like the team from *Ocean's Eleven* raiding a casino in Las Vegas as quickly as possible than it was like Jesus and the Twelve interacting together for three years, telling stories, healing the sick and weeping over the crowds. Jesus never reduced the gospel to a neat equation, preferring instead to preach in pictures and act out prophecies without explanation; and as for numbers, He often tried to dissuade the crowds from following Him!

However, although it would be easy to trash our hit-and-run approach to evangelism, there were also many positives. Looking back, I'm attracted, for instance, to the sheer passion and willingness we had back then to get out there and do something—anything—to break the bullet-proof glass and share the good news about Jesus Christ. What's more, although the entire enterprise was socially inept and a little fanatical, the results were surprisingly good. Within two weeks, more than 100 people in that small community made some kind of profession of faith in Jesus. It would be patronizing to these people to conclude that none of them knew what they were doing or that there was no depth or sincerity to their prayers.

At the start of the mission, I was encouraged by the leaders to set "faith targets" regarding the number of people I expected to lead to the Lord during the coming days. By clenching every muscle in my body, I could just about imagine five people becoming Christians, and I obediently began praying for that to happen. All in all, the mission got off to a pretty good start, and before long, the team lounge was reverberating with exciting reports of people "praying the prayer" in all sorts of strange locations. Everyone seemed to have morphed into mini-Billy Grahams, but not me. I prayed and prayed for my five conversions, but it just didn't happen. After an exhausting week, I returned home encouraged by what God had done but secretly very disappointed that I hadn't led a single person to Christ.

Sitting with my mentor, Roger—a man with a long, blonde ponytail and one of the huskiest voices this side of Springfield—

I poured out my frustration. I told him about washing windshields and digging gardens, about "Danny Boy" and scout troops. Then I told him about my earnest prayer for five people. I said that I felt like a failure and that I couldn't understand why God had let me down. Roger gazed at me with a wry smile and leaned back in his seat. I was about to learn a lesson I would never forget.

"You can set all the faith targets you like, Pete," he croaked, "but ultimately, the issue of who responds to the gospel is in God's hands." I looked surprised, so Roger continued. "If it were that simple, He'd just zap everyone into His kingdom by lunchtime, but it's not His call. The decision to accept or reject Christ sits fairly and squarely with every individual, and no one else can make that choice for them—not even God."

Roger was warming to his theme. "Obviously, praying does help and evangelism is essential, but from the moment Eve took a munch on that apple—or whatever fruit it was—God has been paying the price for the choices we make. Satan cannot override a person's free will, and God will not." Roger took a sip of his coffee and chuckled. "Sadly, Pete, it appears that God is not about to change His mind about human free will just to fit in with your shopping list."

> *Why Unanswered Prayer?*
> **#9: Free Will**
> Some prayers aren't answered because
> God will not force a person to do something
> that he or she does not want to do.

## Under the Influence

Roger had been right—my prayer list had been a shopping list. But although his wise counsel had answered my immediate question, it had also provoked others such as, Why bother praying for anyone to become a Christian (or to do anything, for that matter) if God will never override a person's free will?

*Power is nothing without control.*

Many of our questions concerning unanswered prayer can be attributed to the fact that we mistakenly expect it to work like a Pirelli tire, exerting power through absolute control. However, as we shall see, God's power is about *influence* rather than *control.*

In the Western world, power tends to be seen as a mechanism, a force that makes a person, an animal or a thing do a particular activity that they would not otherwise have done. Mechanically, this makes sense. When a hammer hits a nail, the nail has little choice but to move. When a spark plug creates a tiny explosion in a four-stroke combustion engine, the piston has little choice but to rocket away, turning the camshaft and thus the wheels of the car. The control exercised by mechanical power is almost absolute. We often wish that prayer worked in the same manner. But, of course, it doesn't.

In asking God for five converts within a seven-day period, I was expecting prayer to work mechanically. All I had to do, I thought, was press all the right buttons to see targets met and bewildered converts delivered to the door of the church singing the "Hallelujah Chorus." However, God doesn't exercise His power mechanically to control people's lives in answer to prayer. He works relationally with us and through us. According to the New Testament, godly power is supremely revealed in Jesus (see Col. 1:15) and in the cross (see 1 Cor. 1:22-24). Jesus opposes all those forceful, mechanically controlled depictions of power with which we are so familiar. Instead, He redefines power as a by-product of gentleness, of sacrifice and even of suffering.

When we stop to examine the world around us, we quickly realize that most of the truly effective manifestations of power are—because they flow from God—systems of influence rather than control. For instance, we know that prison (which functions as a classic control mechanism) solves little, while education and counseling (which are models of influence) are much more effective in dealing with the root problems of criminality. Similarly, if a parent has to continually use physical force to make a child obey, we know that the parent's authority is not strong, but weak. In this book, I am unashamedly seeking to influence your thinking, but I am not trying to control you or force you to agree with me. And, of course, no writer would want to do that, because it's only when the reader's free will is respected and engaged that anything lasting can be sown.

Ultimately, it is the power of influence that shapes and changes lives. When we begin to see prayer-power as a model of relational influence within people's lives rather than an impersonal control-mechanism over them, we begin to sense the importance of perseverance in prayer and of allowing the Holy Spirit to guide the way we pray for a person or community over a protracted period of time.

> ### *Why Unanswered Prayer?*
> ### #10: Influence
> Some of our prayers aren't yet answered because they are working gradually and not as an impersonal mechanism of forced control.

### When a Burglary Is an Answer to Prayer

A lady I used to know prayed for years that her husband would become a Christian, but he just wasn't interested. She left tracts on the coffee table, dropped unsubtle hints in the conversation, and invited him to endless meetings, but he was a self-sufficient businessman who felt no need for God.

As the years went by, the wife began to despair and her prayers became little more than wishful thinking. Then one day when she was away with the kids, their family home was burglarized. Her husband came home alone to find the place trashed and many valuables missing. Alone in that ransacked house, years of self-sufficiency crumbled and he knelt, at last, to surrender his independence. I don't think God sent the burglars to rob that home (although He did clearly permit them to do it), but that couple now look back on their burglary as an answer to prayer that came at just the right time!

If the power of prayer worked through control, that woman's husband would surely have been compelled into the Kingdom many years earlier in response to her insistent asking and fasting. After all, her prayers had undoubtedly been in line with God's will for her husband's life. But in fact, he was perfectly able to resist the power of her prayers consistently over many years. Gradually, however, a much subtler shift had taken place through a restrained supernatural process interacting respectfully with his free will. Imperceptibly, his prejudices had been dismantled through a relational combination of prayer, patience and consistent witness. This is why, when at last the circumstances of life conspired to confront him with his own need, his response was at last to capitulate to Christ, whose "unhurrying chase, and unperturbèd pace" had overtaken his ambition and won his heart at last.

*Still with unhurrying chase,*
*And unperturbèd pace,*
*Deliberate speed, majestic instancy,*
*Came on the following Feet,*
*And a Voice above their beat—*
*"Naught shelters thee, who wilt not shelter Me."*

FRANCIS THOMPSON[10]

## The Subtle Spirit

We can't change people's minds in prayer as if they were remote-control cars or computers waiting to be hacked. But maybe we can influence their circumstances so as to soften their hearts. In prayer, we appeal to the gentleness of Christ's nature as well as His power and engage with the complex free will of people He loves. That's why prayers for people generally work slowly, like water seeping silently into the tiny cracks of a vast boulder. For a long time, nothing may appear to have changed. Our prayers, resembling mere dribbles of water, appear to be of an entirely different nature than the substance of the rock. But then there comes the first great freeze of winter—some circumstance beyond human control—and overnight, as if by magic, as if struck by lightning, that vast boulder splits open.

In prayer, we may partner with God to influence a person's environment and experiences (and if the person's free will is already inclined toward God, our prayers will effect a change much more quickly than in those whose hearts are hard). However, we cannot make a person do anything that he or she doesn't want to do. To use the analogy of a restaurant, prayer helps to present people with the menu, and perhaps it can even help make them hungry (here we have the supernatural dimension). Yet because prayer is not a control mechanism, it cannot force the food into their mouths. Frustratingly, it's up to them to order and eat. Only then will they "taste and see that the Lord is good" (Ps. 34:8).

. . . .

In this chapter, I've explored the relationship between God's will and our will, suggesting various reasons for unanswered prayers:

- Perhaps God has something better for us
- Perhaps our motives in prayer are selfish
- Perhaps God is allowing us to struggle awhile in order to draw us into a deeper relationship with Himself
- Perhaps a positive answer to our prayer would violate someone's free will
- Perhaps God is answering our prayer subtly and slowly through the power of influence rather than control

We are discovering that there are reasons for many of our struggles, both in the complex and fallen nature of *God's world* and in the benevolent complexity of *God's will*. However, as we continue to ask the great question of why our prayers go unanswered, we shall turn our attention next to the conflict that is raging between *God's world* and *God's will*: the vicious reality of *God's war* . . .

---

### Prayer of Surrender

*Afresh I seek thee, Lead me—once more I pray—*
*Even should it be against my will, thy way.*
*Let me not feel thee foreign any hour,*
*Or shrink from thee as an estranged power.*
*Through doubt, through faith, through bliss, through stark dismay,*
*Through sunshine, wind, or snow, or fog, or shower,*
*Draw me to thee who art my only day.*

GEORGE MacDONALD[11]

---

## Chapter Nine

# GOD'S WAR

*For our struggle is not against flesh and blood . . .*
THE APOSTLE PAUL, EPHESIANS 6:12

It was a golden afternoon and the dark shadows of trees straggled out lazily across the road ahead like discarded stockings. In the back of the van, Hudson and Danny were jabbering away excitedly with our friends Paul and Rachel. Our spirits were high, because we were on our way to spend the weekend beside the Lake of the Ozarks in Missouri, where wooded hills slope down to hundreds of secluded creeks and gullies. How could we possibly have foreseen, on such a beautiful afternoon, that God was about to grant us a dramatic insight into the reality of the spiritual battle of our lives?

I looked across at Samie. She had her feet up on the dashboard and was humming along to Coldplay. She smiled, and I remember pointing out a picturesque white church that was coming up on the left. It had some kind of poster out front. As I did so, Samie's humming suddenly stopped and the look of panic on her face told me everything I needed to know. "Not now, Lord," she murmured.

I swung the van into the parking lot of the church and screeched to a halt in a cloud of dust. I signaled to Paul and Rachel, who grasped the situation immediately and hurried the kids, screaming with delight, to a convenient play area. Turning my attention to Samie, I pushed back her seat, wedged a sweater carefully behind her head and removed the rings from her fingers. Sure enough, the seizure kicked in and I began counting her through a breathing exercise we use to reduce pain.

"Breathe in. Breathe out. And one. And two." The seizure was advancing rapidly. "Breathe in . . ." Samie's right hand was contorting. "Breathe out . . ." Spasms were marching up her arm. "And one . . ." When it reaches her head, things can go crazy. "And two . . ." I tried to stay calm. "Breathe in . . ." The seizure was moving too fast. "Breathe out . . ." With rising panic, I made a calculation . . . "And one . . ." We were at least a hundred miles from the nearest hospital. "And two . . ."

"*P-p-pray*," Samie gasped through clenched teeth, and so I did. I stopped counting and started asking God to intervene. It had never made any noticeable difference before, but what else could I do? Where else could we turn out here in the middle of nowhere? As I prayed, my gaze fell on the religious poster outside the church. It was the sort of thing I'd seen on hundreds of similar notice boards: Christ wearing the crown of thorns, and underneath something about "the blood of the Lamb."

More out of desperation than inspiration, I took the prompt and focused my prayers on the power of Jesus' blood. That's when the most remarkable thing happened: The frenzy in Samie's arm halted its advance. Then, as I continued to pray, I watched as the spasms began to retreat back down toward her hand. I could hardly believe what I was seeing. With mounting faith, I continued to pray, and soon the convulsions reached her hand and seemed to subside altogether.

I gulped and let out a sigh. What had just happened? Had I imagined it? Reeling, I glanced across the parking lot at the kids playing on the swings. However, almost as soon as my prayers lapsed, the seizure started again. Great defibrillating jolts began to shudder up Samie's arm, relentlessly progressing toward her body like a wave about to break. "Don't stop! Keep praying," she begged, and so, of course, I did. But this time I prayed with vigor and rising faith. This time I was really calling out to God, declaring that Samie was a new creation and that she had been made whole by the wounds of Christ. I claimed the power of the blood of the Lamb. I declared and claimed and prayed pretty much anything I could think of declaring and claiming and praying. I probably sounded like an old-time gospel preacher. And as I did all this declaring, claiming, praying stuff, the seizure once again seemed to obey. The shaking just halted and then, as before, it reversed back down into Samie's wrist and out of her body.

I sat there staring at Samie's hand as if it was the eighth wonder of the world, daring it to start shaking again. But instead, her fingers relaxed, her breathing became easier and there was peace. Samie looked at me with a mixture of delight and denial. Had we really just won a battle against her epilepsy?

The kids were still on the swings, and above their heads the leaves of the trees seemed to be shimmering in the sunlight like shoals of fish swirling in the turquoise sky. Inside the van, Samie and I sat silently blinking at each other, still trying to make sense of what had just happened. You would really have to go through hundreds of seizures, praying each time without success, to have any idea how stunned we were by what had just transpired. Then, in a low voice, Samie told me something equally bewildering: During the seizure, she had, for the first time ever, experienced the presence of Jesus actually with her in the pain.

I gazed across at the poster—so religiously clichéd and yet, suddenly, so relevant and profound to me. This was the very first time we had seen any impact on Samie's condition physiologically through prayer. What's more, in some mystical way that she found hard to put into words, Samie had also encountered

Jesus in the midst of it all. After years of ineffectual praying, this incident had given us a dramatic insight into some of the spiritual dynamics at work behind the grim neurological realities of Samie's condition.

Since that time in the parking lot, prayer has only made that kind of difference to a seizure on one other occasion. But these two interventions have been enough to renew our faith in the supernatural power of prayer to impact our personal situation. We have also been prompted to remember that there really is a battle going on when we pray.

I've heard people say that God answers every prayer in one of three ways: "yes," "no" or "not yet." But when I prayed for Samie's healing in the van that day, it wasn't as simple as that. On this occasion, God said yes, Satan said no, and the resulting conflict was dramatic.

## The Fight of Your Life

The Bible exhorts us to understand spiritual warfare so that we can take a stand against Satan's varied onslaughts in many different ways. We are called to persevere in prayer, to fast, to debate intelligently, and to resist afflictions practically, whether in acts of civil disobedience against an institutionalized injustice or simply by taking our medicine when we are sick because we believe Jesus would like us to get better. Sometimes, submission to God involves meek acceptance of suffering; but at other times, we should get angry about our unanswered prayers and fight! Why? Because Christians do not believe that all suffering is God's will. We know that the terrors and tragedies screaming from today's newspapers cannot possibly reflect the heart of a loving Father at work in His world. Instead, we believe something so surprising that it would be almost impossible to accept if it wasn't so blatantly true: The

Almighty God does not always gets His way on Earth—even though He is the Almighty God!

Jesus taught us to pray to the Father, "Your Kingdom come, Your will be done," precisely because it isn't a foregone conclusion. We are told that Jesus lives to intercede for us (see Heb. 7:25), while the Holy Spirit prays for us in "groans that words cannot express" (Rom. 8:26), presumably because there are things God longs for that have not yet happened. It is also the Father's desire that "everyone come to repentance" (2 Pet. 3:9), and yet people manifestly do not.

How on earth are we to make sense of such an extraordinary state of affairs in which the omnipotent God is not getting His way? The Bible points back to the devastating consequences of the Fall, but it also explains that we are currently caught up in a cosmic rebellion between angels and demons and ultimately between God Himself and "that ancient serpent called the devil, or Satan, who leads the whole world astray" (Rev. 12:9). Such apocalyptic ideas may not sit comfortably with our supposedly sophisticated modern sensibilities, but there is no doubting the biblical position.

History is moving toward a day of *shalom* when God's yes and God's no will be unopposed and undefeated. John of Patmos was granted an insight into that amazing moment:

> *I heard a loud voice in heaven say:*
> *"Now have come the salvation and the power*
> *and the kingdom of our God,*
> *and the authority of his Christ.*
> *For the accuser of our brothers,*
> *who accuses them before our God day and night,*
> *has been hurled down.*
> *They overcame him by the blood of the Lamb."*
> REVELATION 12:10-12

## Dark Powers in a New World

Of course, secular humanists laugh at the very notion of a cosmic battle featuring angels and demons. More disturbingly, there are skeptical voices within the Christian tradition—not just among twentieth-century liberals, but also among twenty-first-century leaders. I attended one gathering of contemporary church practitioners at which a speaker admitted that he did not believe in the existence of demons.

I appreciated his honesty in voicing what many people believe secretly, but I could not (and still cannot) see how such a position can be reconciled with a biblical worldview, let alone the witness of the world Church and many of my own experiences.

One of his hearers challenged the speaker's skepticism with an unusual question: "Where do you live?"

"Orange County, California," he replied, adding, "I've lived there all my life."

"Nice place!" she said with a grin. "That's probably why you don't believe in demons. I'd imagine that all the demons are very well camouflaged in an affluent, respectable place like Orange County!" She invited the speaker (who was starting to look a little uncomfortable) to visit her in one of North America's poorest inner-city neighborhoods. "You'll soon encounter the reality of demonic oppression where I live," she chuckled, and went on to describe one of her own hair-raising encounters with a demonized individual.

We shouldn't be surprised that some people are skeptical about the idea of a cosmic battle between good and evil. Social scientists such as Max Weber and theologians such as Rudolf Bultmann have taught us to regard belief in angels and demons as primitive and to rationalize away all references to such things from the Gospels. I read one commentary that went to great lengths to purge Mark's Gospel of miracles. This was done in a well-intentioned attempt to make the Bible more culturally relevant to a scientific age.

However, the commentator had to resort to extraordinary measures to demythologize the text in this way, which occasionally became quite absurd. For instance, referring to the incident in which Jesus cast demons out of the man known as "Legion" and into the herd of pigs (see Mark 5:1-17), this writer actually tried to cast the demons out of the story itself by suggesting that Jesus must have shouted so loudly that those 2,000 pigs all panicked and drowned themselves! What's more, this episode of shouting and mass pig suicide was somehow supposed to have cured the afflicted man's psychosis.

Such unnecessary mental acrobatics would seem, to the majority of people in the world, like a form of madness in itself. For those in the non-Western world, the reality of angels, demons and miracles has never gone away. And for those in the West, there are signs that such beliefs are coming back.

During the Second World War, Walter Lippmann, the American journalist whose parents had been German-Jewish immigrants, admitted that "the modern skeptical world has been taught for some two hundred years a conception of human nature in which the reality of evil, so well-known to ages of faith, has been discounted."[1] However, as Lippmann witnessed the horrors of the Second World War (even as we may regard the contemporary atrocities of apartheid, Rwanda, Columbine, 9/11 and Iraq), he reluctantly accepted the reality of evil in the human soul: "We shall have to recover this forgotten but essential truth."[2]

The evidence of evil at work in our world is, of course, manifold. A riot-policeman once described to me the terrifying sensation of violence coming down a street in waves several seconds before the rioters themselves physically appeared around a corner. As I write these words, a man is on trial for the rape of a baby. A woman has just been imprisoned for deliberately passing the AIDS virus on to a number of sexual partners.[3] Walter Lippmann is right: We need to rediscover the essential truth of the reality of evil in our world and, as Christians, we must also work out how on earth to take our stand against such evil in prayer:

> For our struggle is not against flesh and blood, but against the rulers, against the authorities, against the powers of this dark world and against the spiritual forces of evil in the heavenly realms (Eph. 6:11-12).

## A Biblical Worldview

About six centuries before Paul wrote these words, the biblical hero Daniel had an extraordinary encounter with an angel while praying one day. It's a story that teaches us much about the relationship between unanswered prayer and spiritual warfare. "Since the first day that you set your mind to gain understanding and to humble yourself before your God," the angel told Daniel, "your words were heard, and I have come in response to them. But the Prince of the Persian kingdom resisted me twenty-one days. Then Michael, one of the chief princes, came to help me" (Dan. 10:12-13). This encounter provides a fascinating insight into the battle that goes on when we pray and also into the time lapse that may require our perseverance in prayer.

We see this same battle repeatedly at work in the life of Jesus, whose public ministry began with an intense 40-day season of spiritual warfare in the wilderness and was punctuated by strange encounters with screaming demons. He told stories about heaven and hell and even saw Satan falling from heaven like lightning. When we read the text objectively, the Jesus of the Gospels begins to look like the kind of apocalyptic mystic

who would not fit at all well in the lecture halls of most sem-
inaries, let alone the polished pulpit of an average Sunday
morning sermon.

## Materialists and Magicians

Of course, for all His mysticism, Jesus was not spooky. In fact, we
know that He was immensely popular (see Matt. 14:13), could be
witty (see 19:24), and was often very practical (see 21:2). A life
modeled on Christ will therefore combine a sober recognition of
the demonic realm with an earthy dose of good humor and
common sense. The story is told of a famous preacher who woke
in the night to see a terrifying demonic manifestation at the end
of his bed. "Oh," he said, "it's only you," and went back to sleep.
"There are two equal and opposite errors into which our race
can fall about the devils," observed C. S. Lewis. "One is to disbe-
lieve in their existence. The other is to believe, and to feel an
excessive and unhealthy interest in them. They themselves are
equally pleased by both errors, and hail a materialist or a magician with the same delight."[4]

Martin Luther once poked fun at the extremism of many of
his contemporaries, saying that they resembled drunken peas-
ants who fall off a donkey and then remount only to slide off
the other side. When it comes to spiritual warfare, the key is to
stay balanced and avoid swinging wildly between extremes. On
one side of the donkey (so to speak), there are many today who
take Satan and demons far too seriously, spending more of
their time thinking, talking and praying about complicated
spiritual infrastructures and intercessory technologies than
they do in simply talking to the Lord Jesus Himself and absorb-
ing His Word. The New Testament scholar N. T. Wright helpfully reminds us that "because of what Jesus did on the cross,
the powers and authorities are a beaten, defeated lot, so that

[no one] who belongs to Jesus need be overawed by them again."[5] On the other side of the donkey, there are those who have given up believing in anything so primitive or uncomfortable as demons and spiritual warfare. But this is neither intellectually necessary nor consistent with the biblical worldview.

## The Call to Stand

The passage of Scripture quoted more often than any other in relation to spiritual warfare is Ephesians 6:11-18, and yet it is almost entirely about spiritual resistance rather than attack. In these eight verses, the apostle Paul tells the Ephesians no fewer than four times simply to stand their ground!

> Put on the full armor of God so that you can *take your stand* against the devil's schemes . . . so that when the day of evil comes, you may be able to *stand your ground*, and after you have done everything, to *stand. Stand* firm then (emphasis added).

Paul's emphasis here is on courageous resistance. There is no license in the text for that common kind of macho militancy that continually (and unwisely) picks fights with the devil in prayer. Both the apostles Peter and Jude warn against rebuking the demonic realm in prayer. Jude teaches that "even the archangel Michael, when he was disputing with the devil . . . *did not dare* to bring a slanderous accusation against him, but said, 'The Lord rebuke you!'" (Jude 9, emphasis added). If the archangel Michael did not dare to rebuke the devil but instead prayed that the Lord would do it, how much more should we beware arrogance and even discourtesy in spiritual warfare. In his book *Needless Casualties of War*, John Paul Jackson cautions us thus:

Courtesy is the hallmark of God's Kingdom. Discourtesy is the trademark of Satan's. When contending with the devil, Jesus spoke firmly but with the utmost respect. He did not revile when answering Satan's temptations. Nor did Jesus speak rudely, disrespectfully, or call Satan demeaning names. Rather, Jesus simply quoted Scripture to rebuke the devil.[6]

There is a place for aggression against the enemy, using the "sword of the Spirit, which is the word of God" (Eph. 6:17), but that is the only piece of military hardware Paul lists with which we can mount an attack. No spears. No flaming arrows. No battering rams. Just the Word of God (this was also Christ's approach against Satan in the wilderness). A balanced posture in spiritual warfare will predominantly consist of standing firm against Satan and, when we must attack, simply wielding the Word of God.

On one occasion, Jesus informs Peter that Satan has requested to "sift him" like wheat. "I have prayed for you, Simon," He says, "that your faith may not fail" (Luke 22:31). When Satan is sifting your life—tempting, attacking and attempting to undermine your faith—sometimes instead of delivering you immediately from evil, Jesus will intercede for you in the midst of your trials. Indeed, the mere fact that you are reading this now and still standing in spite of so many trials may well be an answer to Christ's prayers "that your faith may not fail."

We've seen that God doesn't always get His way and that the Bible explains this strange state of affairs in terms of ongoing spiritual warfare. It is entirely possible, therefore, that some of our prayers currently remain unanswered because of direct satanic resistance. Our lives may also be attracting specific spiritual attacks because of the stand we are taking for Jesus, and if this is the case, there may be some encouragement in understanding that it is not God who is letting us down. "When God's people are called upon to pass through severe sufferings and tribulation," says the theologian George Ladd, "they should remember that God has not abandoned them, but that their sufferings are due to the fact that they no longer belong to This Age and therefore are the object of its hostility."[7]

As objects of hostility, our call is to stand firm, never doubting the reality of the battle raging against our lives nor the victory that is ours to come. There is much we could say about this, but we will look in particular at what it means to stand against the devil's schemes with *courage, faith, perseverance* and *integrity*.

## Standing with Courage

*Be strong and courageous. Do not be terrified; do not be discouraged, for the Lord your God will be with you wherever you go.*
JOSHUA 1:9

"It is finished!" cried Jesus on the cross, and with that triumphant shout He gave up His soul. He knew that the terrible price had been paid! Sin had been defeated! Satan had been overcome! Yet sin multiplies. Tsunamis and earthquakes ravage nations. Apostasy abounds. My friend Andy keeps praying for an end to his wife's diabetes, but it steadily gets worse. So did Jesus get it wrong?

The opening sequences of Steven Spielberg's film *Saving Private Ryan* are widely considered to be some of the most disturbing in cinema history. For 30 minutes, we are bombarded with graphic depictions of the battle for Omaha beach on June 6, 1944. The official record of the 1st Infantry Division states, "Within ten minutes of the ramps being lowered, [the leading] company had become inert, leaderless and almost incapable of action. Every officer and sergeant had been killed or wounded.

. . . It had become a struggle for survival and rescue."[8]

More than 3,000 young men were killed in a few hours on that day. It was a bloody massacre. And yet, as we watch the surf turning red on the sand, we are witnessing a battle being won, not lost. It was victory for sure, but victory at a terrible price.

The battle between God's kingdom and Satan's tyranny rages all around us, but the Bible insists that we are watching a battle being won, not lost. Our Christian faith celebrates the fact that Satan is a defeated foe, but we know from bitter experience that his death throes are lethally protracted until the return of Christ. "He is filled with fury, because He knows that his time is short" (Rev. 12:12). The biblical scholar Chuck Lowe puts it graphically:

> Like a wounded and cornered animal, Satan thrashes around desperately with the aim of injuring as many of his enemy as possible, before his own destruction . . . So the defeat of Satan does not mean the end of trouble for the church. To the contrary, it signals an escalation and intensification of opposition and persecution. But the end is in sight, and those who endure to the end shall be victorious even if, in the mean time, they become victims.[9]

Tragically, there are many "victorious victims" as we endure the death throes of Satan and anticipate the renewal of all things. We all experience battles with temptation, sickness, injustice and every mutation of selfishness. But the Bible assures us that *God's will* and *God's world* will eventually harmonize, because Jesus has secured the eventual outcome of *God's war* and will return to vanquish Satan and his demons forever (see Rev. 12:12-17). In the meantime, we experience the ebb and flow of battle, celebrating victories and enduring set backs valiantly "as soldiers of Christ" (2 Tim. 2:3).

Long before the members of the 1st Infantry Division bled and died on Omaha beach, the unofficial motto of the battalion was, "No mission too difficult, No sacrifice too great." There is absolutely no point in pretending that our mission in Christ will be anything but difficult or that the sacrifices required of us will be anything but great. Our Commander in Chief Himself insists that we will overcome Satan only through sacrifice (see Matt. 5:10-12; Rev. 12:11). This may mean persecution and even martyrdom, but for most of us it rarely feels or looks heroic. Instead, it takes the mundane form of a daily struggle, sacrificing ourselves not just once but repeatedly (see Rom. 12:1), preferring others, holding our tongues when we want to criticize, and trusting God when we feel like quitting. As we pay the price of obedience, we can be sure that every unanswered prayer, every short-term loss, plays its part in the long-term certainty of victory in Christ. It's just that we never realized that winning could sometimes hurt like hell.

> *Why Unanswered Prayer?*
> **#11: Satanic Opposition**
> Some prayers aren't answered because God's will is being directly contested by "the spiritual forces of evil in the heavenly realms" (Eph. 6:12). Perseverance, faith and aggressive use of the Word of God become vital in winning through.

### Standing in Faith

*If you believe, you will receive whatever you ask for in prayer.*
MATTHEW 21:22

The disciples knew all about unanswered prayer. One day, they attempted to kick a demon out of a guy and, rather embarrassingly, it didn't work. When Jesus returned from His prayer time, they asked Him why the demon hadn't shifted. He came back with the fascinating reply: "Because you have so little faith" (Matt. 17:20). In Mark's Gospel, Jesus adds, "This kind can come out only by prayer" (9:29). Faith, it seems, is the fundamental ingredient of all effective prayer. How then are we to get more of the stuff?

The first and most important thing to say is that faith is a gift from God and not something we work up. As a kid, I tried desperately to make myself believe again in Father Christmas after discovering a Santa outfit in my mum's cupboard. But you can't make yourself believe something by gritting your teeth and pretending! Likewise, I have a friend who, due to his outrageous comments and loud personality, seemed to me to be utterly untrustworthy the first time I met him. However, as I got to know him, I discovered that he was, in fact, the most loyal and trustworthy friend I could wish for. By getting to know him, I have inevitably come to trust him.

Faith in God comes from getting to know God's faithfulness. It is a gift He gives to us when we spend time in His presence. It is a reflection of His character in our lives. Faith is not, as many people seem to believe, a transactional commodity we earn. Nor is it a spiritual currency with which we can acquire divine healing, provision or success. It is a relational posture of trust that enables us to receive the will of God in a way that others can't. Faith is a pair of open hands.

How, then, are we to open our hands to receive more faith? Libraries are filled with books attempting to answer this question. So, for the purposes of this book, I will simply offer a list of 10 practical keys that have helped me unlock the revelations of God's faithfulness in my own life.

## 1. Keys to Faith: Prayer and Worship

The key to Jesus' ministry was surely the many hours He spent in prayer, because, as He Himself said, "The Son can do nothing by himself; he can do only what he sees his Father doing" (John 5:19). It was undoubtedly because Jesus took time away from the crowds to refocus on the Father's presence and priorities that He found fresh faith, insight and power. On one occasion, He returned from His prayer time walking on water. After another time with God, He appointed His disciples. In Gethsemane, as we have seen, He found the greatest faith of all.

It's natural to make requests to God, and He invites us to do precisely this. But to grow in faith, we must also give time as we pray to wait, listen, watch and worship. We must consciously take our eyes off ourselves and our long lists of problems and fix them instead on God. Faith grows by focusing on God's goodness and greatness and it shrivels when we obsess about our problems. For this reason, it's a good idea to develop a rhythm in prayer, an easy ebb and flow between petition (asking God to do things) and thanksgiving (celebrating the things He has already done). No matter how many unanswered prayers we struggle with, there will always be blessings for which we can be grateful and in which we can discern the faithfulness and goodness of God.

The apostle Paul advises us to bring our "shopping lists" before God with grateful hearts: "In everything," he says, "by prayer and petition, with thanksgiving, present your requests to God" (Phil. 4:6). In my relationship with Samie, it's when we stop talking about problems and practicalities and take time instead to celebrate one another's company with leisurely dinners, trips to the cinema, walks in the country and surprises that our relationship actually grows. In the same way, faith grows as we learn to relax in God's presence, taking our eyes off ourselves and celebrating His goodness in all things. The Danish philosopher Sören Kierkegaard puts it beautifully: "Teach me, O God, not to torture myself, not to make a martyr out of myself through stifling reflection, but rather teach me to breathe deeply in faith."

### 2. Keys to Faith: Fellowship

While personal prayer is vital to any deepening faith, there are certain aspects of God's character that can only be absorbed, explored and enjoyed by leaving the cloister and engaging in community. Theologian Richard Lovelace suggests that a person cannot be more filled with the Holy Spirit than his or her community is. The words and lives of godly people invariably prove contagious, and we come away from time in their presence feeling stronger in our convictions. They help us (as we help them) to become "sure of what we hope for and certain of what we do not see" (Heb. 11:1).

One of these people for me was an old lady (who has since died) named Pearl Lavers. She was always, it seemed, full of joy and hope in spite of all sorts of afflictions. On our wedding day, the weather was terrible. It poured with rain! But Pearl came bounding up to me, saying, "Isn't it *wonderful*? How *marvelous to have rain, today of all days!*" I didn't know how to respond. "My dear, don't you realize?" she said quivering with excitement. "In Scripture rain is always a sign of the Lord's favor, and for you," she indicated the dark torrents cascading down the windows, "for you He's made it absolutely bucket down!" People like Pearl are good for faith!

Even if you don't have the benefit of such remarkable friends, you can still train yourself to speak and think positively rather than cynically, and by doing this, you can stir up a more expectant culture amongst your friends. You can also find inspiration in the many biographies of heroes of the faith, and by doing that, you may keep fellowship with those who have gone before you and allow their lives to increase your faith.

### 3. Keys to Faith: Fasting

The discipline of fasting can focus your prayers in the way a magnifying glass can focus sunlight to start a fire. If you're struggling to get a breakthrough in a particular area through prayer, it's well worth considering some form of bodily self-denial. This could mean going without food, sex, entertainment or other luxuries for a limited period of time (Daniel even fasted body lotion for three weeks!). In *God's Chosen Fast,* one of the best books on this important discipline, Arthur Wallis says, "When exercised with a pure heart, and a right motive, fasting may provide us with a key to unlock doors where other keys have failed."[10]

### 4. Keys to Faith: Start Small
Right now, if you haven't got the faith to walk into a hospital ward and pray for the sick, you might want to start with a prayer for a friend's headache. Try to pray at an appropriate level for the amount of faith God has given you right now. Start small and build up. Jesus said that we only need faith the size of a mustard seed! Elsewhere, He is seen coaching the disciples toward greater spiritual authority (see Matt. 15:29; Mark 9:29; Luke 10:4; 22:36). When God first asked me to trust Him for financial provision, it was for relatively small amounts of money (although at the time it was terrifying!). Over the years, as He has proved Himself faithful, my faith has grown. Now I find that I am able to trust God for the large sums of money required to resource an international organization—a level of faith that would have crushed me 15 years ago.

### 5. Keys to Faith: Impulsiveness
Sometimes God will give you a particular burst of faith for something, and when this happens, it's important to act straight away. It might be during worship or some less obvious moment, but you suddenly have a conviction not only that God *can* do the thing but also that He *will* do it if you ask Him. Seize the moment to pray for that thing. The New Testament is full of

words such as "immediately" and "suddenly." There is often a sense of urgency and immediacy in the movements of the Spirit.

### 6. Keys to Faith: Adventure

Martin Luther defines faith as "a living, daring confidence in God's grace."[11] We can afford to live with daring confidence because God's grace covers our mistakes and blesses us unconditionally. Luther might have paraphrased Hebrews 11:6 to say, "Without daring confidence, it is impossible to please God."

I have often experienced the smile of God due to the risks I have taken in His name. In fact, with hindsight I can see that without exception, the biggest blessings of my life have been the result of taking some terrifying step of faith into the unknown. Perhaps this is why of all Brennan Manning's writings, the quote to which I turn more frequently than any other describes faith as a movement into uncertainty:

> The way of trust is a movement into obscurity, into the
> undefined, into ambiguity, not into some pre-determined,
> clearly delineated plan for the future. The next step dis-
> closes itself only out of discernment of God acting in . . .
> the present moment. The reality of naked trust is the life
> of a pilgrim who leaves what is nailed down, obvious and
> secure, and walks into the unknown without any rational
> explanation to justify the decision or guarantee the
> future. Why? Because God has signaled the movement
> and offered his presence and his promise.[12]

### 7. Keys to Faith: Bible Study

Whenever we are sure of God's will, we can pray with absolute faith and confidence. Our guidebook is, of course, the Bible, through which God builds our faith by revealing to us both His promises and His person in Jesus.

God's will is not, I suspect, nearly as difficult to understand as we tend to assume. When we are befuddled by a situation, it is more likely to be because creation is infinitely complex or because Satan is deliberately confusing us than because God is concealing His will. The Father has revealed His heart fully in Jesus, "For God was pleased to have all his fullness dwell in him" (Col. 1:19). The apostle Paul says that "God's invisible qualities—his eternal power and divine nature—have been *clearly* seen, being understood from what has been made, so that men are without excuse" (Rom. 1:20, emphasis added). The ubiquitous *What Would Jesus Do?* question remains an excellent, if simplistic, premise for guidance and prayer because it is Jesus who made the will of the Father clear for all time (see John 14:9).

I sometimes hear people offering up long prayers that begin, "If it is your will . . ." They then go on to request something that God has promised in Scripture. But because God has already revealed that it is His will, we need to stop wishing and seek Him with absolute assurance that He will be true to His word. It is guaranteed by the promise of God.

Sometimes I have used the "if it is your will" clause as a sort of spiritual disclaimer—an excuse for my lack of faith. If I am praying for the conversion of a friend, I know that God hears my prayers because His heart is that none should perish. There will be elements of warfare necessary, my friend's free will (which God will not defile) might stubbornly resist God's advances, and I will need to await God's timing, but I can be absolutely sure that I am praying in accordance with His will. Similarly, if I am praying for someone to receive the Holy Spirit, I can know that He has promised to give the Spirit more readily than a father gives bread to his child. And so, I can pray with a faith rooted firmly in the evidence of God's Word.

## 8. Keys to Faith: Pilgrimage

One of the benefits of a pilgrimage—whether it's to a special place of ancient or personal significance or to a context of renewal like an annual retreat or a particular conference—is that it can release faith and enable us to gain a new perspective on old situations. Faith is also easier in certain environments, a phenomenon that even seems to have affected Jesus when He couldn't manage many miracles in His hometown because of the unbelieving atmosphere (see Mark 6:5).

## 9. Keys to Faith: Journaling

By making time to record experiences, insights, poems, frustrations, myths and stories over many generations, the people of Israel wrote the Bible. In the contemporary world, maintaining a journal or a blog can be a useful way of recording God's work in the different seasons of our lives, and it can therefore be a great way of growing in faith. My journals are covered in doodles, Bible studies, late-night depressive rants, terrible poetry and ticket stubs. They are also populated with random lists—things to do before I die, music and books I want to buy, bizarre places I hope to visit, things God has said to me, the fixtures for Portsmouth Football Club. I am often reminded of God's faithfulness by returning to things I have journaled in the past.

## 10. Keys to Faith: Listening to God

The apostle Paul said, "Faith comes through hearing" (Rom. 10:17). It is vital, therefore, to learn to listen to God, turning our ears to hear His voice in order to grow in faith, and then proceeding with increasing confidence in His will.

Professor Dallas Willard shares a refreshingly practical method of listening for God. "Personally," he says, "I find it works best if, after I ask for God to speak to me . . . I devote the next hour or so to some kind of activity that neither engrosses my attention with other things nor allows me to be intensely focused on the matter in question. Housework, gardening, driving about on errands, or paying bills will do. I have learned not to worry about whether or not this is going to work. I know that it does not have to work but I am sure that it will work if God has something he really wants me to know or do. This is ultimately because I am sure of how great and good he is."[13]

> ### *Why Unanswered Prayer?*
> ### #12: Faith
> Some prayers aren't answered because we just don't believe they will be. However, faith grows as we get to know God.

## Standing with Perseverance

*Be joyful in hope, patient in affliction, faithful in prayer.*
ROMANS 12:12

It was June 9, 1978, and Bob Specas was almost ready for the moment he'd been dreaming of all his life. This was the day he hoped to enter the history books by breaking the world record for domino toppling. For days he'd been carefully erecting thousands of small black rectangles in a vast pattern, knowing that he would have to bring down 100,000 dominoes to claim the title. By June 9, Specas was almost ready for the big moment, and the media had gathered to broadcast the historic event. Specas had just placed his 97,499th domino carefully in line—2,501 to go—when a careless cameraman happened to drop his press badge. The badge nudged a single domino, and

Bob Specas watched helplessly as a hissing, writhing snake of others fell in perfect succession.

Prayer can be a lot like domino toppling, because while some prayers get answered the very first time you ask, most take months or even years of faithful asking before there is any kind of breakthrough. Day after day, you say essentially the same thing to God, and sometimes you wonder if it's ever going to make a difference. Then, one day, you pray the same thing you have prayed countless times before and, in a matter of minutes, it triggers the fulfillment of years of faithful prayer.

Two of Jesus' parables specifically emphasize the importance of persevering in prayer. He told His disciples the parable about the persistent widow explicitly "to show them that they should always pray and not give up" (Luke 18:1). Modern-day disciples probably need to hear this even more than His original audience, living as we do in a frenetic world of instant everything. We hate to wait for anything.

The great preacher D. L. Moody is said to have carried a list of the names of 100 non-Christians for whom He prayed all his life. Over the years, his prayers for many of these people were answered and, whenever one of them became a Christian, Moody would cross their name off the list. It is a tribute to the power of perseverance in prayer that, by the time of his death, no fewer than 96 of those 100 people on Moody's list had become followers of Jesus. What's more, the remaining 4 gave their lives to Jesus at Moody's funeral.

If an angel was to appear right now and tell you that your very next prayer would bring the breakthrough you've been longing for, I guarantee you'd be on your knees in a flash! How would you respond if that angel told you to pray daily for a year and that a miracle would take place instantly on the 365th time? Would you do it? Probably! We have no idea how long it's going to take, but Jesus Himself has already told us not to give up.

The apostle Paul says that "suffering produces perseverance; perseverance, character; and character, hope" (Rom. 5:3-4). By requiring us to persevere, our unanswered prayers can therefore do more to shape our characters and nurture our faith than the instant gratification of wall-to-wall miracles. God Himself may sometimes deliberately delay answering a prayer in order to teach us an important lesson or shape our character

The word "immediately" is attached to most of the miracle accounts in the Gospels. But not all! In some situations there was a deliberate time delay, during which Jesus invariably sought to teach His disciples an important lesson. For instance, have you ever noticed that in Matthew's Gospel, before Jesus calmed the storm, He first took time to rebuke His disciples? "'You of little faith,' he said, 'why are you so afraid?'" (8:28). Only then did He get up and calm the waves. Jesus clearly wanted to teach them something in and through the trauma, without rushing immediately to answer their prayers for help. It was important that they suffered a little while longer. However, Jesus also had things to show the disciples by delivering them from the trauma, and so, when the time was right and the lesson had been learned, He calmed the storm.

On another occasion Jesus responded so slowly to the appeal from Jairus to come and save his daughter's life that, by the time He arrived, it was too late. She had died. But Jesus used the situation to glorify God even more by raising her from the dead.

When four men lowered the quadriplegic man down through a hole in the roof, Jesus revealed how different His priorities are by ignoring the man's most obvious physical need in order to forgive his sins.

When we ask Jesus for a miracle but there is no immediate answer, sometimes it is because Jesus wants to teach us other lessons or deal with deeper issues in our lives. By persevering in prayer we prove that we are willing to wait faithfully and to surrender consistently to the priorities of Christ for our lives.

A wonderful example of perseverance in prayer is the Scottish pioneer missionary James Fraser (mentioned in chapter 9) who went to China and gave his life to a primitive mountain people called the Lisu.

The first few years were very hard. Fraser often found himself sleeping on the mud and dealing with almost constant discouragements. His first hard-won converts invariably renounced Jesus and reverted to idol worship. Worse still, the majority of the Lisu people were apathetic toward the gospel message that Fraser had given up everything to bring them. After five years of sacrifice, hard work and prayer, the impact of Fraser's work was so small that he became deeply depressed. In his journal, Fraser dared to voice the very question with which we are wrestling in this book: "Does God answer prayer? Does He know and care?"[14]

It was not until Fraser had become almost suicidal with despair that he realized why his prayers were not being answered. It was not, as he had assumed, that God was ignoring or denying his requests but rather that God's will was being resisted by the forces of Satan. It was this revelation of the spiritual forces ranged against him that galvanized Fraser to persevere with fresh vigor:

> The opposition will not be overcome by reasoning or by pleading, but by (chiefly) steady, persistent prayer . . .
> I am now setting my face like flint: if the work seems to fail, then *pray;* if services fall flat, then *pray still more;* if months slip by with little or no result, then *pray still more and get others helping you.*[15]

James Fraser died of cerebral malaria just before the outbreak of the Second World War, leaving a small group of Lisu Christians to endure severe persecution first from the Japanese and later from the Communists. But in spite of all these trials, by 1990 the Communist's own official statistics acknowledged that 90 percent of the Lisu people were Christians. "Here then we see God's way of success in our work," wrote Fraser years earlier, "a trinity of prayer, faith and patience."[16]

---

### *Why Unanswered Prayer?*
### #13: Perseverance
Some prayers just haven't been answered—yet!
Whether your prayers are being resisted by
mysterious spiritual forces, by stubborn people
or even by God Himself, don't give up!
Keep stacking dominos.

---

## Standing with Integrity

*Then the Lord said to Moses:*
*"Quit praying and get the people moving! Forward, march!"*
EXODUS 14:15, *TLB*

We've seen that Satan can oppose our prayers even when they are in line with the will of God and that we are therefore called to stand against him in prayer with courage, faith and perseverance. Finally, we must understand the vital relationship between what we pray and the way we live our lives day to day.

Saint Augustine said that "It is by true piety that men of God cast out the hostile power of the air which opposes godliness; . . . and they overcome all the temptations of the adversary by praying, not to him, but to their own God against him."[17]

When Floyd and Sally McClung (mentioned in chapter 5) situated their mission to the Red Light District of Amsterdam between a sex shop and a satanist church, they chose not to spend their time praying against the evil establishments on each side of them. Instead, they pursued Augustine's "true piety" by worshiping Jesus and seeking to live out His holiness day to day. This nonconfrontational approach proved to be an effective strategy. After a few years of standing their ground in persevering prayer, a fire destroyed the satanist church. As for the sex shop, today it is the home of a Chinese church.

Integrity and prayer are a powerful combination. We all know people who walk closely with Jesus and whose prayers seem to carry exceptional weight before God. The apostle James talks about this phenomenon when he links honesty and transparency with healing and increased power in prayer. "Confess your sins to each other and pray for each other so that you may be healed," he says, before adding, "The prayer of a righteous [person] is powerful and effective" (Jas. 5:16). When our relationship with God is right, says James, our prayers will be more powerful and effective, particularly in the realm of healing.

This biblical principal of confession is embedded in Alcoholics Anonymous's Twelve Steps Program. In the fifth step, which is often considered the most painful and yet the most vital, we are invited to "Admit to God, to ourselves, and to another human being the exact nature of our wrongs."

God never promises to answer the prayers of a person who is not living in an honest relationship with Him (although, in His grace, He sometimes does!). "If I had cherished sin in my heart," reflects the psalmist, "the Lord would not have listened" (Ps. 66:18). If we want our prayers to be heard by God, we cannot afford to "cherish sin" but should confess it that we might be made whole.

· · · ·

Standing with integrity involves personal transparency and radical honesty, but it also means living out the implications of our prayers in very practical ways. An old Russian proverb says, "Pray to God, but row for the shore!" In the sixteenth century, the Council of Trent said the same thing: "God giving you the grace commands you to do what you can and to pray for what you cannot." Isn't that refreshingly practical? Of course, there will always be areas in which we are truly helpless to effect a change and for which we need supernatural intervention. But there will be many other aspects of life in which God may call us to become an answer to our own prayers by changing the way we live. In such situations, our prayers may be unanswered not because of God's unwillingness to act but because of ours. Conversely, miracles often occur when we allow God to turn us into an answer to prayer.

For instance, my friend Kelly prayed so hard for a community of drug dealers and prostitutes in Mexico that eventually she became an answer to her own prayers and relocated from Tulsa, Oklahoma, to live among them. As a result, her prayers are now being dramatically answered in a way that they would not have been if she'd stayed home praying. At least one prostitute and one drug dealer have come to know Jesus in the past year thanks to Kelly's willingness to live out her prayers with integrity.

*So let God work his will in you.*
*Yell a loud no to the Devil and watch him scamper.*
*Say a quiet yes to God and he'll be there*
*in no time. Quit dabbling in sin. Purify your inner life.*
JAMES 4:7, *THE MESSAGE*

> **Why Unanswered Prayer?**
> **#14: Sin**
> Some prayers aren't answered because of
> areas of disobedience in our lives. Are there hidden
> sins we need to confess or actions we need to take
> in order to lend power to our prayers?

## Justice

The prophet Isaiah tells us that another reason for unanswered prayer—one we rarely consider—is personal injustice and disregard of the poor. He describes the way the Israelites were fasting and persevering in prayer: "Day after day they seek me out; they seem eager to know my ways" (Isa. 58:2). Yet their prayers were unanswered, and they demanded to know why. "'Why have we fasted,' they say, 'and you have not seen it? Why have we humbled ourselves, and you have not noticed?'" God responds to this question in no uncertain terms, pointing to their lifestyles and specifically naming their fighting, their lax hospitality, their malicious gossip and their disregard for the poor.

> *Is not this the kind of fast I have chosen . . .*
> *to share your food with the hungry*
> *and to provide the poor wanderer with shelter—*
> *when you see the naked, to clothe him,*
> *and not to turn away from your own flesh and blood?*
> *Then your light will break forth like the dawn,*
> *and your healing will quickly appear . . .*
> *Then you will call, and the Lord will answer;*
> *you will cry for help, and he will say: Here am I.*
> ISAIAH 58:5,7,9

Perhaps one of the reasons why there are so many fewer miracles in affluent Western churches than in poorer countries is that we are more liable to the kinds of injustices listed by Isaiah. However, as we actively engage with the needs of the poor, our prayers will become more powerful because, as God promised the Israelites, "then your healing will quickly appear . . . then you will call and the Lord will answer."

---

*Why Unanswered Prayer?*
**#15: Justice**
Some prayers aren't answered because
of our disregard for the needs of others in our
communities and in other nations too.

---

## Finally, Stand . . .

*Don't get too daring. Satan has had thousands of years of practice and we do not know 100th part of what he knows.*
MARTIN LUTHER[18]

This chapter has been all about taking a stand against Satan's death throes with courage, faith, perseverance and an integrated lifestyle. Some people advocate "binding" spiritual principalities, mapping territorial strongholds in prayer and generally taking the fight to the enemy. I'm not opposed to these activities at certain times, but I am convinced that our primary order is not to attack the enemy but rather to stand against him resolutely in faith.

*Standing*, far from being passive, can have powerful results because the devil is a coward who relies on fear to do much of his work. "Resist the devil," says the apostle James—and I can imagine him saying it with a slightly dismissive shrug—"and he will flee from you" (Jas. 4:7).

### Help Me to Stand

Lord,
help me to stand today.
Temptations and trials abound.
When life hurts,
I get confused, dishonest, suspicious and critical.
*I put on the belt of truth.*
When life hurts,
my relationships suffer—especially my
relationship with You.
*I put on the breastplate of righteousness.*
When life hurts,
I either get really lazy or I make myself really busy.
*I put on the shoes of the gospel.*
When life hurts,
I let down my guard and leave myself exposed.
*I take up the shield of faith.*
When life hurts,
my thinking gets negative and I question everything.
*I put on the helmet of salvation.*
When life hurts,
I'm a coward.
*I take hold of the sword of the Word.*
Lord, it doesn't feel very finished down here.
I don't feel very finished.
See me kneeling.
Help me stand.

• • • •

In this section, I've proposed 15 reasons for unanswered prayer. Five were derived from an analysis of God's world (see chapter 8), five from an understanding of God's will (see chapter 9), and the other five from the present consequences of God's war (see chapter 10). I hope that one or more of these 15 explanations has helped you make a little sense of your situation. But maybe there isn't any easy answer to the questions you're asking. With that in mind, I want to finish this section with an excerpt from C. S. Lewis's *Screwtape Letters* in which a senior demon writes to his nephew about the times when people can no longer sense God's presence and His purposes have stopped making sense:

> Sooner or later [God] withdraws, if not in fact, at least from their conscious experience . . . He leaves the [human] to stand up on its own legs—to carry out from the will alone duties which have lost all relish. . . . Our cause is never in more danger than when a human—no longer desiring but still intending to do [God's] will—looks round upon a universe from which every trace of Him seems to have vanished, and asks why he has been forsaken, and still obeys.[19]

There will always be unanswered prayers that defy explanation and agonizing times when God will inexplicably withdraw from our conscious experience and leave us to "carry out from the will alone duties which have lost all relish." During such confusing seasons of life, there is nothing more powerful than our faithfulness expressed in perseverance. As C. S. Lewis says, Satan's cause "is never in more danger than when a human—no longer desiring but still intending to do [God's] will—looks round upon a universe from which every trace of Him seems to have vanished, and asks why he has been forsaken, and still obeys."

And speaking of a universe from which every trace of God seems to have vanished, we turn now to explore Holy Saturday, surely one of the most fascinating and important days in human history.

# WHERE

## IS GOD WHEN HEAVEN IS SILENT?

*They have taken away my Lord,*
*and I do not know where they have laid him.*
JOHN 20:13, *ESV*

Holy Saturday fascinates me. The Bible tells us almost nothing about this mysterious day sandwiched between crucifixion and resurrection when God allowed the whole of creation to live without answers. It's a day of confusion and silence. Roman Catholics and many Anglicans strip their altars bare—back to the bones—on Holy Saturday. I guess it's the one day in the entire year when the Church has nothing to say. And yet, although we know so little about it, Holy Saturday seems to me to describe the place in which many of us live our lives: waiting for God or speak. We know that Jesus died for us yesterday. We trust that there may be miracles tomorrow. But what of today—this eternal Sabbath when heaven is silent? Where, we wonder, is God now?

## Chapter Ten

# EXPLORING THE SILENCE

*The question and the cry "Oh, where?" melt into
tears of a thousand streams
and deluge the world with the flood of the assurance "I am!"*

RABINDRANATH TAGORE, *GITANJAL*[1]

No one really talks about Holy Saturday, yet if we stop and think about it, it's where most of us live most of our lives. Holy Saturday is the no-man's land between questions and answers, prayers and miracles. It's where we wait—with a peculiar mixture of faith and despair—whenever God is silent or life doesn't make sense.

As we turn to explore the silence of God, we are compelled to address the problem of unanswered prayer more literally than we have done so far, examining the times when God simply doesn't reply to us when we pray. It's not that He's saying "yes," "no" or "not yet" to our prayers; it's that He's not saying anything at all. We pray and pray but God remains silent. We ask for help and He appears to ignore us. We try to make sense of our situation and there is no explanation, no revelation, no intimation that God even cares. We may wonder if He's there at all. This experience of God's silence, or even His absence, is not uncommon in the Christian life—especially among those God uses most powerfully. It is an experience both epitomized and legitimized by the silence of God on Holy Saturday.

*What happened today on earth?*
*There is a great silence.*
*A great silence, and stillness,*
*a great silence because the King sleeps.*
(ANCIENT HOMILY FOR HOLY SATURDAY)

## A God Who Speaks and Does Not Speak

The Bible opens with the voice of God: He speaks and life begins. It closes with "What sounded like the roar of a great multitude in heaven shouting: 'hallelujah'" (Rev. 19:1). In between these two cataclysmic moments, the story hinges on the Word of God spoken in Jesus. The Bible is a book about a God who speaks! But it does not portray Him as one who speaks incessantly to His people (or to anyone else for that matter). Instead, we often endure Holy Saturdays in which God's word is muted and His presence is veiled.

In the wake of his wife's death, C. S. Lewis experienced this sense of God's silence and began to wonder, *Where is God?*

> When you are happy, so happy that you have no sense of needing Him, so happy that you are tempted to feel His claims upon you as an interruption, if you remember yourself and turn to Him with gratitude and praise, you will be—or so it feels—welcomed with open arms. But go to Him when your need is desperate, when all other help is vain, and what do you find? A door slammed in your face, and a sound of bolting and double bolting on the inside. After that, silence. You may as well turn away. The longer you wait, the more emphatic the silence will become. There are no lights in the windows. It might be an empty house. Was it ever inhabited? It seemed so once. And that seeming was as

strong as this. What can this mean? Why is He so present a commander in our time of prosperity and so very
absent a help in time of trouble?[2]

Human beings can endure extreme pain and many years of
unanswered prayer provided they know God is present in the
midst of it all and can say with the psalmist, "Even though I
walk through the valley of the shadow of death . . . you are
with me; your rod and your staff, they comfort me" (Ps. 23:4).
We may not understand our suffering at such times, but at
least we have the comfort of knowing God's presence in the
pain. But sometimes, instead of the reassurances of God's word
in the darkness, we only hear the "bolting and double bolting"
of the door and "after that, silence."

As slaves in Egypt, the Israelites cried out to the God of
their Fathers. Yet it would be 430 years before He spoke, saying,
"I have heard them crying out because of their slave drivers, and
I am concerned about their suffering" (Exod. 3:7). These forgotten people—who surely grew to question the dusty, old desert
legends of the Abrahamic Covenant—these were the people
who became the prime example in world history of what God
can do. But it took the best part of 430 years.

"This seemingly unending stretch of the experience of the
absence of God," writes Eugene Peterson, "is reproduced in
most of our lives and most of us don't know what to make of
it."[3] When a man like Peterson says something, you really have
to sit up and listen. Having spent decades studying every word
of the Bible forensically in its original language, including
seven and a half years working on his paraphrased translation
THE MESSAGE, Eugene Peterson understands the broad sweep
of Scripture far better than most. And from that privileged
position, he makes this extraordinary observation: "The story
in which God does his saving work, arises among a people

whose primary experience of God is his absence."[4]

The question that screams out from such a startling and depressing statement is simple and personal: Why?

## Why Is God Absent?

At the end of Hudson's first year at school, his report proposed an interesting objective for future success: *Aim for next year: To reduce overall dependency on adult supervision.* Reducing dependency on supervision is a spiritual process, too. God is committed to helping us mature, and to do this, He sometimes withdraws from our conscious experience by deliberately making Himself less obvious and less immediately available and by allowing some of our prayers to remain unanswered.

When the prayers of an entire nation were rejected and Jerusalem was destroyed by the Babylonians, Jeremiah observed of God, "You have covered yourself with a cloud so that no prayer can get through to you" (Lam. 3:44). Why does God wrap Himself in such a cloud? Why does He withdraw when we need Him? Has He become less concerned about our needs than He once was? No more than Hudson's teacher had become less concerned about his progress. No more than we, as Hudson's parents, will love him less as he needs us less and grows to maturity. But in our love we will, at times, withdraw and insist that he stand on his own two feet to face the challenges of life alone.

Hudson is currently learning to ride a bike. We've taken the stabilizers off his back wheel and, as a result, he's wobbling all over the place, endangering himself and anyone within about 20 feet. I run along the road holding him, but I've noticed that he doesn't really try to balance as long as he can feel my hands on his back and see me by his side. He just leans into me and the bike proceeds perilously at a 45-degree angle. So I've taken to running with my hand lightly on the back of his seat so that he can neither feel me nor see me. He hates this. Sometimes he gets cross with me for not doing it the way he wants me to do it. A number of times he's announced that he doesn't want to ride a stupid bike anyway. But I know he'll get there eventually.

The process is a little risky (though not nearly as treacherous as it seems to Hudson), but he's slowly learning an uncomfortable lesson as I withdraw my support. As long as he can feel me or see me, he will remain "dependent on adult supervision," which in this case means that he won't learn to ride a bike. It's in my love for Hudson that I'm allowing him to get some scrapes and bruises. It's actually because I care that I'm refusing to answer all of his cries for help.

If we can't see God in our situation right now and can't feel His hands on our life, we may feel scared, angry or helpless, or we may want to just quit. Where once we could lean on God and life seemed manageable with His help, now He seems to have abandoned us. But the Bible assures us that God hasn't left us, even when we can't feel His presence. Quite apart from the fact of His omnipresence, Jesus promised never to leave or forsake us. On the cross, He endured complete forsakenness so that we would not have to. The apostle Paul assures us that nothing can separate us from the love of God. The Bible leaves us in no doubt at all that when God is silent, He is not absent from His people—even if that's the way it *feels*. He is with us now as much as He ever was. He's no less involved in our lives than He was when we could hear His voice so clearly and could sense the joy of His smile. Instead, God has switched off for a while our ability to be conscious of His presence, and He has done this in order to reduce our dependency on outward things so that we may learn some vital lesson of life.

Martin Luther argued that God withdraws and falls silent in order to draw us into the deeper relationship with Him that is only possible when we move beyond merely outward experiences and purely rational understanding. If Luther is right, then the silence and unknowing of Holy Saturday are essential to growing deeper in our relationship with God. The silence of God is intentional. It is one of the great disciplines He puts on His children "that we may share in his holiness" (Heb. 12:11). Such seasons are often described as "the dark night of the soul," a technical term that comes from a work by the sixteenth-century mystic St. John of the Cross. In his usage, it means a very high degree of spiritual progress, one most of us will never see. However, the sense that prayer and Scripture have ceased to resonate and that our spiritual journey is heading for a dead-end is common to many Christians. It's different from boredom. We're not tempted to go back to frivolous pastimes. Something in us has changed and we are hungry for something that no earthly distraction can satisfy.

Sometimes God removes the stabilizers from our bicycle and His hands from our frightened lives. As we grow toward spiritual maturity, every believer is granted seasons of unanswered prayer when God is silent and may even appear absent from the world. At such times, we may be sure that God is weaning us off "adult supervision" but that He has not abandoned us altogether.

## The Miracle of Unanswered Prayer

It is one of the great ironies of life that our unanswered prayers can be used to craft the greatest answers to prayer that we will ever experience. When we first become followers of Jesus, we often enter a phase of spiritual infatuation not dissimilar to the overwhelming obsession of falling in love. There can be tears, fascination, joy and moments of deep intimacy. Our minds are full of God's wonder and our lifestyles naturally reprioritize around our new, all-consuming relationship with God. Infatuation can be a vital time in our early spiritual formation—launching us out with abandonment in passionate pursuit of Christ for the rest of our lives—but it cannot and should not be protracted.

Many studies have been conducted into the powerful and delightful chemical urges that occur when we fall in love. One recent report even compared human behavior at such times to a form of madness. If you've ever experienced it, it's not hard to see why! However, we know that infatuation, which appears so selfless, is in fact profoundly self-centered. You only have to listen to the words of every love song in the charts to realize that the emotion of infatuation is all about "how you make *me* feel," "what *I would like* to do to you" or "what *I want* from you." Such caricatures of love barely compare with what they may one day become: the beautiful sight of an elderly couple walking down the street holding hands.

Growing into maturity—whether it's in a romantic relationship, a child-parent relationship or in a relationship with God—always involves a steady process of recentering from our own priorities and preferences to those of the other. That's why our center of gravity shifts as we mature spiritually. We begin to pray that God would change our hearts and rewire our motivation. We long to become more like Jesus. We ask God to help us become more humble, more loving and more faithful.

It is in answer to these very prayers that God may decide to deny our requests and even withdraw a little from our lives. As long as it makes perfect sense to serve God and to live for Him, our faith can only mature so far. There's nothing very selfless or sacrificial in obeying God as long as it remains in our best interests to do so—enjoying His love, receiving miraculous provision, hearing His voice clearly, experiencing His reality in worship, gaining stimulating insights from the Bible, knowing God's comfort when we are hurting, and so on. Until these things are removed from our lives and we are left to stand alone without any reason for continuing except steadfast loyalty, we cannot truly mature from an us-centered relationship with God to a truly Christ-centered one. It isn't until the facts that once reinforced our beliefs are removed from our lives that we can truly "live by faith and not by sight" (2 Cor. 5:7).

## Rushing the Resurrection

Although seasons in our lives when God is silent may be important in our spiritual growth, they can also be deeply disturbing. As a result, we often attempt to solve the problem of God's silence with simplistic explanations of complex situations, lopsided applications of Scripture and platitudes of premature comfort. We are afraid to simply wait with the mess of problems unresolved until God Himself unmistakably intervenes, as He did on Easter Sunday. We are unwilling to admit, "I don't have a clue what God is doing or why this is happening." We may even suspect that it would be un-Christlike to cry out publicly, "My God, my God. Why have You forsaken me?" Why can't we wait with the mess and pain of Holy Saturday unresolved?

I went to the funeral of a friend named Simon who had died very suddenly of a heart attack, leaving behind a wife and four young children. It was unspeakably sad, especially as I watched his kids at the front of the church, pale as milk in their smartest clothes, trying to be so very brave and grown-up and *appropriate* for us all—trying to make their daddy proud. One of the daughters played a piece on the recorder. Another did a reading, and her voice hardly faltered. Then the pastor stood up and invited a band to lead us in a time of worship. We all sang songs and, to my surprise, some of the people in the front row started dancing. I know why they were doing it—they wanted to celebrate the fact that Simon was in heaven and that God was in charge.

In a way, I loved them for the sheer defiant absurdity of it all. But then I saw something that almost broke my heart. We were singing the song "Show Us Your Power, O Lord," which had—according to the service sheet—been one of Simon's favorites, when his seven-year-old daughter turned her head and stared at the coffin. "Show us your power, O Lord," we continued as she just kept staring at the coffin. It was a simple thing but, as I say, it almost broke my heart.

A number of eulogies followed, and everyone said lovely things about Simon. One of the speakers explained how intricately God's hand could be seen in the timing of Simon's death. We believed him—we *needed* to believe him—but it seemed to me that for the four little faces on the front row, the timing could not have been more wrong. Their father had been this inevitable presence in their lives. He had been forever. Theories of death and providence no longer applied. Streets should empty. The Disney Channel should come off the air.

In spite of all the singing, dancing and detailed assurances (or perhaps because of them), I drove away later thinking how very fragile our faith must be if we can't just remain sad, scared, confused and doubting for a while. In our fear of unknowing, we leapfrog Holy Saturday and rush the resurrection. We race disconcerted to make meaning and find beauty where there simply is none. Yet.

From dusk on Good Friday to dawn on Easter Sunday, God allowed the whole of creation to remain in a state of chaos and despair. Martin Luther dared to suggest, "After Good Friday"— and I imagine him whispering the words—"God's very self lay dead in the grave."[5] Is that possible? Can you imagine it? No one the disciples could look to for guidance? No basis for any hope? No meaning?

## When God Goes Missing

We know for sure that the family and friends of Jesus were terrified. John describes that they were gathered "with the door locked for fear of the Jews" (John 20:19), and the apocryphal Gospel of Peter says that the authorities were actively hunting Christ's followers down.[6] The disciples were scared, but they were also profoundly confused. Had they been cruelly misled for three years? Had Jesus been merely a prophet and not the Christ at all? What of all the miracles, all the proof? Hadn't He predicted something like this? But surely God would not permit His Son to be crucified?

For the disciples, these questions would all be answered within a matter of hours in the most glorious way. When we experience similar seasons of doubt and despair, we too may be sure that resurrection is on the way. However, the experience of God's absence is not one to be rushed over as if it has no value in the Christian life. Quite the contrary: Holy Saturday has been the experience of many of the greatest saints in history from St. John of the Cross to Mother Teresa.

When Mother Teresa died in Calcutta at the age of 87, her diaries were collected by Roman Catholic authorities and taken back to Rome. Many were shocked, however, when they read her words and discovered the extreme inner turmoil experienced by the nun and Nobel Peace Laureate who always seemed so confident of her faith. For instance, we now know that Mother Teresa wrote in 1958, "My smile is a great cloak that hides a multitude of pains . . . [People] think that my faith, my hope and my love are overflowing, and that my intimacy with God and union with His will fills my heart. If only they knew."[7]

In another letter, she wrote, "The damned of hell suffer eternal punishment because they experiment with the loss of God. In my own soul, I feel the terrible pain of this loss. I feel that God does not want me, that God is not God, and that God does not exist."[8] In response to such revelations, "*Il Messeggero,* Rome's popular daily newspaper, said: 'The real Mother Teresa was one who for one year had visions and who for the next fifty had doubts—until her death.'"[9]

Commenting on this, one priest described Mother Teresa's doubts as "a purification process," adding that it is also a part of sainthood.[10] It's an argument reflecting a long Christian tradition that regards the experience of God's absence not as an enemy of faith but rather as the very substance of greater faith and intimacy. Martin Luther goes so far as to call God "*absconditus Deus*"—literally, "the God who goes missing." The basis for this is Christ's own experience of forsakenness on the cross, a moment that speaks profoundly about the meaning of God's silence. "We want God to answer our prayers through powerful interventions," admits Tim Chester, "but in the cross we recognize by faith the presence of God in weakness . . . The silence remains silent, but we see in the cross the hidden God who is with us in our suffering."[11]

### Christ Became the Atheist

One of the most shattering stories told by Elie Wiesel about life in Auschwitz darkly communicates this truth of God's absence:

> One day when we came back from work, we saw three gallows rearing up in the assembly place . . . The SS seemed more preoccupied, more disturbed than usual. To hang a young boy in front of thousands of spectators was no light matter. The head of the camp read the verdict. All eyes were on the child. He was lividly pale, almost calm, biting his lips. The gallows threw its shadow over him . . . The three victims mounted together

onto the chairs. The three necks were placed at the same moment within the nooses.

Long live liberty! cried the two adults. But the child was silent.

Where is God? Where is He? someone behind me asked. At a sign from the head of the camp, the three chairs were tipped over. Total silence throughout the camp. On the horizon the sun was setting. Then the march past began. The two adults were no longer alive. Their tongues hung swollen, blue-tinged. But the third rope was still moving; being so light, the child was still alive.

For more than half an hour he stayed there, struggling between life and death, dying in slow agony under our eyes. And we had to look him full in the face. He was still alive as I passed in front of him. His tongue was still red, his eyes were not yet glazed. Behind me, I heard the same man asking: Where is God now? And I heard a voice within me answer him: Where is he? Here He is—He is hanging here on this gallows.[12]

Any other answer to this devastating question would surely be blasphemy.[13] We are left standing with Wiesel aghast, doubting God's love, His power or even His very existence. But, of course, even as we stand and doubt, it dawns uncomfortably on us that this scene of such evil—this scene that indicts our belief in God—also graphically depicts the very crux of our faith. The New Testament scholar Rudolf Bultmann says that when Christ cried out from the cross, "My God, my God, why have You forsaken me," it is possible that He was experiencing in that moment a total collapse of faith and meaning.[14] The philosopher Albert Camus said of Christ's suffering, "The agony would have been easy if it could have been supported by eternal hope.

But for God to be a man he had to despair."[15]

Jesus Christ may well have endured the same collapse, despair, doubt, rage and loneliness that Elie Wiesel did on that day in Auschwitz and that thousands have endured ever since. Raniero Cantalamessa, preacher to the papal household, makes this startling possibility explicit: "Christ," he says of that cry from the cross, "became the atheist, the one without God so that men might return to God."[16]

Is it really possible that at His moment of greatest need, Jesus did not suffer valiantly, defiantly and strategically but doubted His call and questioned the purpose of His imminent death and the message that He Himself had preached?

The previous day He had prayed, "Abba, Father, everything is possible for you." On Easter morning He would appear to Mary, and the tenderness of His love would shine as brightly as the evidence of His power. But in between these two acknowledgements of divine love and power, Jesus dies, and with Him dies our hope. Perhaps, therefore, we must point to the boy on the gallows and concur bleakly with Wiesel, saying, "There is God," sounding for all the world like bitter atheists (which, perhaps, at such times we all are). "There is love, dying for love," we say. "There, hanging like fly-bait, is the One for whom everything is possible."

> *No reason of man can justify God in a world like this. He must justify himself, and he did so in the cross of his Son.*
>
> P. T. FORSYTH[17]

## Via Negativa

The paradox of God's death in Christ and His presence in silence has been explored and experienced by many of the saints, including, as we have seen, Mother Teresa. It's an experience addressed by a school of thought known as *apophatic* or *negative* theology, which attempts to describe the nature of God by focusing on what God is *not* rather than what God is. Why? Because God must, by definition, confound human understanding—a reality we experience in so much suffering.

One of the foremost advocates of this inverted approach to faith was R. S. Thomas, perhaps the finest Christian poet of the twentieth century, who spent most of his life working as a priest in Wales. Ironically, because he lived and ministered in the shadow of the world-shaking Welsh revival, most of Thomas's work explored the experience of God's absence. In *Via Negativa*, he paints a picture of faith for those whose only experiences of God "are the echoes . . . the footprints he has just left":

> I never thought other than
> That God is that great absence
> In our lives, the empty silence
> Within, the place where we go
> Seeking, not in hope to
> Arrive or find. He keeps the interstices
> In our knowledge, the darkness
> Between stars. His are the echoes
> We follow, the footprints he has just
> Left.[18]

If that poem rings true for you, then chances are that you have a heightened sense of the transcendence and mystery of God—perhaps because of your own experiences of unanswered prayer. Negative theology has an important place in Christian spirituality, particularly for those seeking to walk with God through intense turmoil. It is, in many ways, the theology of Holy Saturday.

However, there are limitations to this highly mystical approach to faith. Although God is undoubtedly beyond our understanding, it is also important that we do not become too esoteric in the way we relate to Him, as the Gospels speak loud and clear of a God who can be known (even if not fully understood) in human terms. In Jesus, we are told, God has been fully revealed, so our faith does not need to be blind. St. Teresa of Avila said that every difficulty in prayer comes from one fatal flaw: that of praying as if God were absent. I believe that negative theology, while helpful, doesn't take fully into account the fact that when God is silent, He is not absent. "Surely," He has promised, "I am with you always, to the very end of the age" (Matt. 28:20).

At the start of this chapter, I quoted a passage from C. S. Lewis's memoir about his wife's death in which he described God as a "very absent help in times of trouble." However, as he continued to demand explanations for the pain he was enduring, he came to a different conclusion later in the book: "When I lay these questions before God I get no answer. But a rather special sort of 'no answer'. It is not the locked door. It is more like a silent, certainly not uncompassionate gaze. As though He shook his head not in refusal but waving the question. Like, 'Peace, child; you don't understand.'"[19]

Life is often confusing. We may experience the chaos of premature funerals, inner turmoil like that endured privately by Mother Teresa, or even the public dereliction of faith like that suffered by Elie Wiesel in Auschwitz, but God does not leave us alone.

*But Zion said, "The Lord has forsaken me, the Lord*
*has forgotten me."*
*Can a mother forget the baby at her breast*
*and have no compassion on the child she has borne?*

*Though she may forget, I will not forget you!*
*See, I have engraved you on the palms of my hands;*
*your walls are ever before me.*

ISAIAH 49:14-16

· · · ·

In this chapter, we have explored the reality and significance of God's silence as the worst kind of unanswered prayer. We've seen that God sometimes falls silent and appears absent not just in the pages of history but also in the experience of every believer who longs to grow in his or her faith. We have also seen that it is important to embrace these painful seasons and not to deny them or rush through them. But this begs the question of how to do this. How do we move beyond mere endurance to active engagement with the unanswered prayers of our lives so that we can grow through them in eager anticipation of Easter Sunday?

## Love That Will Not Let Me Go

*O Love that will not let me go,*
*I rest my weary soul in thee;*
*I give thee back the life I owe,*
*That in thine ocean depths its flow*
*May richer, fuller be.*

*O Joy that seekest me through pain,*
*I cannot close my heart to thee;*
*I trace the rainbow through the rain,*
*And feel the promise is not vain,*
*That morn shall tearless be.*

*O Cross that liftest up my head,*
*I dare not ask to fly from thee;*
*I lay in dust life's glory dead,*
*And from the ground there blossoms red*
*Life that shall endless be.*

This famous hymn was written by George Matheson on
the eve of his sister's wedding, his own marriage having
been called off when George began to go blind.

## Chapter Eleven

# ENGAGING THE SILENCE

*Because God lives . . . present in absence, praying and responding in silence, the Easter Saturday story which leaves us mute, is also our empowerment for utterance and prayer.*

ALAN E. LEWIS

In April 1960, Martin Luther King, Jr. was emerging as one of the most prominent black leaders in America. The civil rights movement was gathering speed all around him, but opposition was mounting as well (just 18 months earlier, King had been stabbed by a mentally deranged woman in New York City). In this tumultuous atmosphere, the 31-year-old pastor gave a magazine interview outlining his stance with regard to suffering:

> As my sufferings mounted I soon realized that there were two ways that I could respond to my situation: either to react with bitterness or seek to transform the suffering into a creative force. I decided to follow the latter course . . . I have lived these last few years with the conviction that unearned suffering is redemptive.[1]

At the age of 31, with less than 8 years left to live, Martin Luther King, Jr. understood that life's great trials invariably either make us *bitter* or make us *better*. They never leave us unchanged. Mother Teresa succeeded in doing this too by transforming her private struggles with faith into a creative force. But for every person who responds creatively to seasons of despair, there are others who allow their disappointments with God to make them cynical and who abandon Him because He appears to have abandoned them.

The title of this chapter pertains to *engaging* the silence of God. To "engage" means to involve oneself actively with a person, situation or thing in order to release some latent potential. When our prayers go unanswered—and especially when God is silent—we have an important choice to make that can shape the destiny of our lives: "Either to react with bitterness or seek to transform the suffering into a creative force."

In this chapter, I want to offer some practical tools to help you do more than just survive Holy Saturday. I want to help you actively *engage* the silence of God and redeem the disappointments of your unanswered prayers into something creative for God.

### *Looking Back:* Remembering God's Word in the Silence

Even when Jesus was pinned to the beams, gasping for breath and devastated by the apparent abandonment of His Father, His terror found its vocabulary in Scripture. *"Eloi, Eloi, lama sabachthani?"* He cried out in His mother tongue. "My God, my God, why have you forsaken me?" (Mark 15:34). Jesus realized that His agony had been articulated with chilling accuracy in the words of the psalm:

> *My God, my God, why have you forsaken me?*
> *Why are you so far from saving me,*
> *so far from the words of my groaning?*
> *A band of evil men has encircled me,*

*they have pierced my hands and my feet.*
*I can count all my bones; people stare and*
*gloat over me.*
*They divide my garments among them and*
*cast lots for my clothing*
PSALM 22:1,16-18

Far from abandoning the Word of God when He felt abandoned by God, Jesus found the Scriptures more poignant and pertinent than ever. If, as Cantalamessa suggests, Jesus became an atheist at that moment, His atheism somehow still found its context in the truth of the Bible.

When God is silent, the galvanizing revelations that formerly came to our life through the Bible and through the still, small voice may seem little more than a distant memory, but this does not make them any less true. In fact, when God is silent, it becomes especially important to feed vicariously on the words He spoke back in the day when life was an easy conversation of two-way prayer, when the sermon seemed to be aimed directly at our heart and the Bible really was the book we wanted by our bed.

My friend Justin has lost his sense of taste. There are vague hopes of a surgical procedure that might one day restore it to him but, for the last few years, eating has been little more than a flavorless solution to the nutritional needs of his body. Ironically, Elle, his wife, is an accomplished and enthusiastic cook, and whenever we go to their house for dinner, the food is invariably delicious. When God seems absent, His Word (given with such love) seems devoid of the exquisite flavors it once had. Others at the table may be feasting on the same food with delight—"Taste and see!" they say enthusiastically—but for us there is no flavor. God's Word has become bland. And yet, significantly, it remains as nourishing as it ever was and as vital to the well being of our soul.

If we are to engage the silence of God, turning it into a creative force in our lives, we can learn from the way Jesus used Scripture in His moment of abandonment. Although God's Word had become bitter and no longer "sweeter than honey" (Ps. 119:103) on His lips, it remained relevant because it had proved itself painfully true. When God is silent and seems to have left us to suffer alone, the Bible still voices our desperation and contextualizes our doubt. With Job, Jeremiah and those dark psalms of dislocation, we too may fill the silence of God with cries of outrage and lament. And at such times, there can be reassurance in this realization that our circumstances, though painful, have also been articulated (and thus validated) repeatedly in Scripture. Maybe this silence means something after all. Maybe it's leading us somewhere. With a certain tenacity of faith, we identify that somewhere within the silence is the presence of God.

How can He be present yet absent? Perhaps it is like a distant star flickering faintly in the darkness, the light of which we see without knowing for sure whether the source itself is still there. Has the star died, or is it still burning brighter than the sun? We remember times when God seemed to speak to us, or to use us, or to answer our prayer, and we determine to stay true to those moments of certainty even though the actuality is so alien to our current experience. And thus, by the distant light of past encounters, we navigate the darkness, like a mariner steering by the light of long-extinguished stars when every other point of reference has disappeared.

## Sabbath of Doubt

In the darkness of the day before the resurrection, the disciples must surely have recalled the poignant words of Jesus. Maybe they remembered His words merely as irony and pathos, or maybe—for John, Mary Magdalene or Lazarus?—as a star still burning. Lunch on that Sabbath, straight after synagogue, would have begun as it always did, with a blessing spoken out—are you ready for this?—over the bread and wine that were to be served with the meal. If any of the 11 remaining disciples were capable of eating that day, the grace spoken before lunch on Holy Saturday would have stabbed their hearts with remembrance of that Last Supper shared with Jesus. "This is my body," He had said as He broke the bread. "Do this in remembrance of me" (Luke 22:19). Do this in remembrance? It was hard to forget!

Perhaps it would be better to forget. Words from the past could not make Jesus come back to life, nor could they anesthetize the pain of the present. But then again, maybe these echoes still had the power to spark little flickers of "maybe" and "what if" in the hearts of the disciples. If Jesus had known what was coming, might God possibly be concealing a bigger plan? This can be our experience too. When God is silent and our prayers are unanswered—when the Word of God is flavorless in our mouths—there can sometimes still be faint flickers of hope and meaning expressed to us and for us in Scripture.

> *God, God . . . my God!*
> *Why did you dump me miles from nowhere?*
> *Doubled up with pain,*
> *I call to God all the day long.*
> *No answer. Nothing.*
> *I keep at it all night, tossing and turning.*
> *And you! Are you indifferent, above it all,*
> *leaning back on the cushions of Israel's praise?*
> PSALM 22:1-3, *THE MESSAGE*

## *Looking Around:* Encountering God in Other People and Places

I wonder if the disciples attended the synagogue on Holy Saturday. They had probably never missed public worship on the Sabbath before, and we know that such routines tend to become even more important when a person is in a state of shock. So if the followers of Jesus did attend, it's fascinating to consider what passages of Scripture they may have heard and what prayers they may have prayed.

Although no one knows for sure, because it was the High Sabbath in the middle of the Passover celebrations, it's quite likely that on the day that Christ lay dead, the synagogues of Israel studied the story of the Exodus. If so, the pathos would have been unbearable for those who had believed in Jesus. Imagine them sitting there, less than 24 hours after Christ had bled and died, hearing about the blood of the lamb on the doorposts and about the cries of those in Egypt for the death of their firstborn sons. We know that a criminal had already believed in Jesus while dying on the cross and had thus become the first Christian in paradise, even before the resurrection (see Luke 23:42-43)! If a condemned thief had responded to Jesus' death with faith, is it too much to imagine that the day after the crucifixion, some of the synagogue preachers also began to grasp the significance of the previous day's events as they considered the story of the Lamb of God?

Perhaps some preachers did begin to wonder. But elsewhere, in other synagogues, indignant Scribes and Pharisees probably seized the opportunity presented by a Sabbath sermon to quell dissent with snide insinuations about a certain "Son of Pharaoh" who had deservedly died the day before. And if they did make such remarks, were they not correct? Hadn't Jesus become the incarnation of sin—the cursed son of Pharaoh—so that the sons of God might go free? That Sabbath, the friends of Jesus must have been haunted in their grief by so many strange signs.

### The Sign of the Torn Veil

Meanwhile, Nicodemus and Joseph of Arimathea, being men of status, would probably not have worshiped at a provincial synagogue but rather at the Temple itself. They had already put their necks on the line for Jesus, and I suspect they wouldn't have dared to set tongues wagging by the eloquence of their absence the day after Jesus' crucifixion.

Perhaps a few fishermen and tax collectors from out of town could lie low among the crowds on the High Sabbath (especially if their lives were in danger), but not men like Nicodemus and Joseph, entwined as they were in the grave machinations of civic responsibility. If these two men did attend the Temple that day, what did they see? Mark's Gospel tells us that as Jesus breathed His last, "The curtain of the temple was torn in two from top to bottom" (15:38). Is it possible, therefore, that worship in the Temple that day took place against the dramatic backdrop of that torn veil? If so, I wonder what message this spoke into the silence of that day,

Scholars are divided as to which one of the veils in the Temple was torn. Some people argue that it was the curtain between the Holy Place and the Holy of Holies—in which case the spiritual significance would be profound but only the priests could have seen the damage, as ordinary people were not allowed into that area of the Temple. The other thrilling possibility is that the torn curtain might actually have been the outer veil between the Outside Court and the Holy Place—in which case every person who attended the Temple the day after Christ's crucifixion would have witnessed firsthand the torn veil and glimpsed the Holy Place behind it, where only priests were permitted to go.

I want you to visualize this. The outer veil was not, as I used to imagine, merely a big net-curtain wafting in the breeze. The outer veil was made of linen, and it was 90 feet high. That's higher than a four-story building![2] Such huge dimensions would explain why Mark makes a point of saying that it was torn "from top to bottom." Josephus, the first-century Jewish historian, describes four bright colors on this veil that symbolized the four elements of the universe (fire, earth, air and water). Above this, he says, there was a panorama of the heavens.[3]

If it was the outer veil that had been torn, the sight of this towering depiction of the heavens and the elements ripped asunder would have been an unsettling backdrop to the day's rituals. No doubt most of the worshipers would have blamed the damage done to this priceless artifact on the previous day's minor earthquake (see Matt. 27:51). But we know that others, like Nicodemus and Joseph, already had darker theories.

## The Comfort of Bethany
If I had been one of the disciples, I know exactly where I would have spent that Sabbath. I would have gotten myself out of Jerusalem as fast as my little legs could carry me and headed back to Bethany to hide out with Mary, Martha and their brother, Lazarus. With Jesus dead and buried, there would have been no one that I'd have wanted to see more than Lazarus. Lazarus had loved Jesus. Lazarus had been one of the Lord's best friends. And, best of all, Lazarus knew a thing or two about being dead and buried. His very life defied the logic of despair, and the fact that his house was a couple of miles out of town made his home the perfect bolt hole.

It was in Bethany at the dinner party thrown by Simon the Leper the previous week that Mary had wept and anointed Jesus' feet with perfume. That perfume had been expensive, so I imagine its fragrance could still be smelled in the air around Simon's house. And speaking of Simon the Leper, he was another harbinger of hope for the simple reason that thanks to Jesus, he wasn't a leper anymore. In Bethany, the crowds had cheered, "Hosanna." The place had been one of joyful worship. In Bethany, there were many seeds of comfort for a scared and grieving disciple, and perhaps there were also faint whispers hanging in the air like that perfume, suggesting that all was not lost.

I hope you have a place like Bethany that you can go to when you're wrestling with unanswered prayer. It could be a place or a book or a piece of music that reminds you of all the good things God has done in the past. It could be a person like Lazarus whose very being makes the presence and power of God real to you even when life is at its worst. Bethany is a connection point that reminds you of something you once knew for sure: that God can do immeasurably more than all you ask or imagine, that the Kingdom remains a matter of power (see 1 Cor. 4:20) even when there's little evidence of it in your present situation, and that all things are possible for him who believes. Bethany's the kind of community or the kind of family where you can sometimes still smell the perfume of God's presence.

### Learning God's Language

"Christ in you, the hope of glory." That's what Paul told the believers in Colossians 1:27. Sometimes the only place we can find the hope of glory is in one another. Not in prayer, not in the Bible, not in worship, but in community. The nineteenth-century rabbi Menachem Mendel of Rymanov once said that "human beings are God's language." In other words, God speaks to us through people. He speaks to us through doctors and nurses who work so hard to heal and help us, through children who ask for a bedtime story, through friends who know how to make us laugh and when to sit in silence, and through the preacher at church, the documentary on television, and the song on the radio. We expect God's voice to be unmistakable, a rumbling revelation or an insistent inner whisper. Yet for those with the ears to hear, He often speaks most eloquently through the commonplace actions of ordinary, unwitting people.

One morning after a traumatic night in which Samie had been rushed to the hospital, I stumbled downstairs to get break-fast for the kids. As I poured the cereal, I reflected miserably on the fact that Samie had been enjoying a better spell with fewer seizures of late, which is why waking up in the hospital that morning had, I guessed, hit particularly hard. The paramedics had tromped and clomped into the house just after midnight, carrying Samie noisily out to the ambulance, and somehow Hudson and Danny had stayed asleep through it all. So here they were now, slurping their Weetabix in the kitchen, oblivious to the fact that their mummy was not upstairs in bed but was in fact in hospital on the other side of town.

"Okay, let's go!" I said, eyeing the clock. "Time for school," I told Hudson. "Nursery for you, Danny," I said, lifting him out of his chair. *And hospital for me,* I thought. *But what can I say to Samie that could possibly help her feel less depressed and scared?* Turning myself into the "tickle monster," I chased the kids laughing down the hallway and out to the car, almost colliding with the mail carrier as we stepped out the door. "Erm, thanks," I said, taking the let-ters before strapping the boys into their seats. As I did so, I noticed that Danny's hair was standing on end like an electrostatically charged orangutan. For a moment I toyed with the idea of taking him back upstairs for the hairbrush, but I soon decided that I couldn't be bothered. After all, if you can't look like an orangutan when you're two years old, when can you?

After dropping the kids off, I arrived at the hospital, where I found Samie in a ward with six old ladies. The peculiar smell of hospital breakfast still hung in the air. "Morning," I said breezily as I stooped over to kiss her forehead. I don't normally kiss people's foreheads, but somehow it seemed the appropriate target in front of the six old ladies looking on.

I'm lousy at the whole empathetic listening thing. When people share their troubles with me, I invariably leap to find solutions.

The only words of empathy I can ever think of are ridiculous clichés from television programs that no one actually says any more—phrases such as, "I'm sure you'll feel an awful lot better after a good night's sleep." Sometimes I hear myself saying "Mmm, I know how you feel," when I actually haven't a clue how the person feels and, quite frankly, I would prefer not to find out. Occasionally, I respond to a tale of great woe by nodding my head sympathetically and saying "I'm so sorry" when it blatantly isn't my fault that they just failed their driving test for the thirteenth time or that their grandfather has been struck down with dysentery whilst camping in the Canadian Rockies. I don't know much about counseling, but I can tell that this isn't really what it's all about. And when my clichés don't work and there's absolutely nothing practical I can suggest to fix the problem, I get flustered and, like a lot of guys, often resort to talking about the weather or football.

In the hospital that morning I could tell that Samie's situation that morning was going to need world-class empathy and that discussing football was probably not such a great idea. Stalling for time, I handed Samie the mail, and that was when God intervened and spoke to her. The first envelope she opened turned out to be a real, bona fide, bolt-from-the-blue, thank-you-Jesus Word from God. It was a greeting card signed by at least 30 members of a church in Sheffield, assuring us in multiple ways of their ongoing love and prayers. The arrival of that card at that precise moment spoke to us eloquently about God's concern and even His presence with us on that bleak morning in that ward with the six old ladies. Baz Gascoine, the big-hearted church leader behind the unexpected card, later told me that he had just felt led to send it the previous Sunday, several days before Samie's hospitalization. It wasn't hard to see God's hand in the timing of its arrival or to find His love expressed in the doodles, Bible verses and spidery ink. Those scribbles were, to us, God's language spoken eloquently just when we needed to know that we were not alone.

The University of Wisconsin's Center for the Study of Pain conducted an experiment several years ago in which researchers timed how long volunteers could keep their feet in buckets of freezing water. They discovered something very remarkable: Whenever a companion was allowed in the room with the person whose feet were being frozen, he or she could endure the cold for twice as long as those who suffered alone. "The presence of another caring person doubles the amount of pain a person can endure," the researchers said.[4] The same is undoubtedly true of emotional pain, and here again, we see that "human beings are the language of God."

### *Speaking Out:* Expressing God's Word in the Silence

As I've been writing this book, I've been receiving regular prayer bulletins tracking the deteriorating condition of Rob Lacey, a guy I know who has been fighting a losing battle with cancer. Steadily, in spite of our prayers, the ugly, agonizing actuality of "unmiracles" has worked itself out in Rob's body and in his young family. The process has been complicated and darkened by the fact that Rob was "healed" of cancer four years ago in answer to desperate and determined prayer. Because Rob is pretty well known as an actor and author, his miraculous recovery received plenty of exposure at the time.

For many reasons, I've wanted to tell you about Rob—to share his story that is Good Friday, Holy Saturday and Easter

Sunday all rolled into one—but it has all seemed too bewildering and too immediate, and I just haven't known where to begin. Then I came across an article by a guy named Ben Irwin who had flown 4,000 miles to see Rob just days before he had died. Ben's article managed to say everything that I've wanted to say, only better. Ben has kindly agreed to let me include it in this chapter.

## Five Minutes with Rob

Recently my wife and I traveled to Wales to visit a friend who was dying of cancer. When we left a week later, I wondered how to begin putting the pieces of my faith back together.

As my wife and I navigated the maze of hospital corridors, I braced myself to face the worst. But nothing could have prepared me for the sight that greeted us as we walked into Rob's room. The person lying in front of me barely resembled the one I had last seen less than a year before. The weight loss was dramatic; he looked like a skeleton with flesh hung loosely over his bones. It took all his might to prop himself on his elbows as I sat down beside him . . .

It was the third time in 10 years Rob had battled cancer. The first diagnosis came six months after he was married. The cancer returned a few years later, about the time Rob and his wife were expecting their first child.

A couple of years into Rob's second bout with cancer—one that was supposed to end his life—it began to look like a miracle was happening. Gradually the cancer disappeared; the doctors could only scratch their heads. There was, the doctors admitted, no medical explanation for the cancer's disappearance. So Rob and his family did the only thing anyone can do in a situation like this: they basked in God's incomprehensible favor.

Fast-forward four years. The cancer came back—initially in his bladder, then his lymph nodes, too. To add a touch of cruel irony, less than a month before he died, Rob's wife gave birth to their second child, a beautiful baby girl.[5]

Confronted by the tragedy of this incredibly talented young husband and father fading away in the prime of life, Ben Irwin had many questions for God.

It seems almost trivial, reflecting on what happened to me that day we visited my friend lying in a hospital bed, clinging to his life. But the fact is, I left Rob's side a different person: my theology—all my neatly arranged ideas about God and His role in our lives—had come crashing down.

If God is in complete control, doesn't that make Him responsible for Rob's slow, torturous death? Isn't He to blame for robbing a wife of her husband, depriving a son of his dad and denying a baby girl even the memory of her father? What grand purpose, what divine scheme could ever justify this cruelty?

On the other hand, even if God doesn't actually cause these things to happen—if He simply *allows* them to take place—is He any less responsible? If I had the cure for AIDS but did not share it with those suffering from the virus, society would hold me accountable for their deaths. Is God any less responsible if He has the power to cure cancer but does nothing?

That night when I crawled into bed, I was raging on the inside—furious with God for allowing my friend to die. Stunned that He was making Rob's wife and children endure all this.

The next day we went to see Rob one last time. He was asleep. Rest being such a precious commodity in his weakened condition, we chose not to disturb him. But as I sat at the nurse's station, writing our goodbye on a scrap of paper, I sensed something that had been absent the day before: God's presence.

It wasn't overpowering. The air was not thick with it. It was small, subtle—barely perceptible. I didn't leave the hospital with answers to any of the questions that plagued my mind the day before. My theology and my ideas about God were still in a state of upheaval. But in their place emerged a new idea: Whatever else God may or may not be, He is present in our pain. He suffers with us.

Why He doesn't step in and simply put an end to the suffering now, I don't know. Believing that someday He'll make everything right doesn't make life easier now. But still, the fact that God was with Rob in the midst of his suffering was, at least, something. It was almost as if, on some level, God had cancer, too.

"He took up our infirmities and bore our diseases . . ." (Matt. 8:17, *TNIV*). He didn't just "sympathize" with us. And He didn't just bear our "spiritual" sickness. The text says He actually carried our diseases . . .

In the end, we traveled 4,000 miles to spend five minutes with Rob. But I wouldn't trade those five minutes for anything in the world . . . Sometimes it's not enough to tell a suffering friend you're praying for them. Sometimes you have to become the answer to your own prayer . . .

Our last night in Wales, as we gathered with mutual friends to pray for Rob, I realized that God is present in the midst of suffering because we are present in it.

We are God's presence.[6]

## Being the Presence in the Absence

South African archbishop Desmond Tutu once recounted the story of a Jewish man in a concentration camp who had been forced to clean the toilets. The man knelt with his hands immersed, swabbing and scrubbing away at the filth, and as he did this, his Nazi guard sought to humiliate him further. "Where is your God now?" he sneered. Quietly, without removing his hands from the toilet, the prisoner replied, "He is right here with me in the muck."[7]

Holy Saturday is the day on which we wonder, *Where is God?* Yet the answer may be that He is right there with us in the muck. When we are present in a situation—no matter how terrible it may be—He cannot be absent. Whenever life gets tough and we cry out to God for help, our desire is always to be airlifted out of the theater of war. But more often than not, instead of *airlifting* us to safety, God *parachutes* down to join us in the muck and chaos of our situation. I doubt that the Jewish man cleaning the toilets had nice spiritual feelings to confirm the truth of his conviction that day, but he was right to assert that the presence of God was there with him and in him.

So, too, was Ben Irwin right to assert that in the face of cancer, "God is present in the midst of suffering because we are present." At Rob's bedside, Ben and his wife realized that the presence of God is neither a feeling nor a theory but a physical reality fleshed out in our lives whenever we share in Christ's sufferings with love. Ben and his wife had become God's language of love to a man about to die. And Rob Lacey had been—and *is*—God's language, too.

. . . .

With hindsight, we know that Holy Saturday was not the end of the world. It was the space between two worlds—a day on the very cusp of beginning. Living as we do with the hindsight of Easter Sunday, we can endure our Holy Saturdays with a certain optimism not afforded the disciples that day. God may be silent, but we know that He will speak soon. Many of our prayers will go unanswered, but not for long! We may even be dying, but on our Holy Saturday, we have reason—good reason—to believe in the resurrection awaiting us on Sunday.

Like Lazarus and Mary Magdalene, we can look back at all that Jesus has done for us in the past with grateful hearts, even if we don't know where He is right now. But unlike them, we can also look to the future with realistic hope that Sunday is coming and the best is yet to come. As we walk around from day to day waiting for a breakthrough in our career, our family, our health, our bank balance, our sexuality, our ministry, our best friend's illness, our marriage, or our daughter who's turned her back on Jesus, we do so with our hope in Jesus, risen from the dead. "And hope does not disappoint us" (Rom. 5:5).

At several points in the preceding pages, I cited a theologian called Alan E. Lewis, whose life's work culminated in an extraordinary book entitled *Between Cross and Resurrection*. Lewis was one of the very few theologians ever to explore, in any depth, the profound meanings of Holy Saturday that we have barely scratched in these two chapters. While writing his brilliant book, Lewis was diagnosed with terminal cancer, and so theology became autobiography as he found himself enduring his own Holy Saturday. The book finishes with a powerful prayer, written by Lewis as he prepared to die, which was read aloud at his funeral. On the following page are the last few lines of that prayer from a dying man whose life had been dedicated to exploring and engaging the silence of God.

## Prayer

*Hear our prayer for a world still living an Easter Saturday existence, oppressed and lonely, guilty of godlessness and convinced of godforsakenness. Be still tomorrow the God you are today, and yesterday already were: God with us in the grave, but pulling thus the sting of death and promising in your final kingdom an even greater victory of abundant grace and life over the magnitude of sin and death. And for your blessed burial, into which we were baptized, may you be glorified for evermore. Amen.*

ALAN E. LEWIS (1944-1994)

# WHEN

## Every Prayer Is Answered

*I have seen the Lord!*
John 20:18

It's been the weekend from hell and now, at dawn on the first day of the week, Mary Magdalene is weeping at the tomb of Jesus. The questions we have asked in this book were Mary's long before they became ours: *How* is she going to endure the overwhelming of her soul with such sorrow? *Why* have her hopes and even her prayers come to nothing? And *where* on earth is God when Jesus lies dead in the grave? In deep trauma Mary Magdalene comes to pay her last respects. And so she sees the answer to all her prayers through tears.

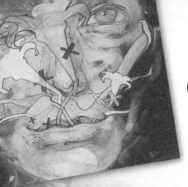

## Chapter Twelve

# LIVING HOPE

*Praise be to the God and Father of our Lord Jesus Christ! In his great mercy he has given us new birth into a living hope through the resurrection of Jesus Christ from the dead.*
THE APOSTLE PETER, 1 PETER 1:3

The Indian poet Tagore tells the story of a beggar who sees a golden carriage approaching from afar "like a gorgeous dream." Realizing that it is the carriage of the king, the beggar prays for riches. This, he believes, is the greatest opportunity of his life.

Sure enough, the carriage stops where the beggar stands and the king climbs out with a smile. But then, the strangest thing happens: The king stretches out his empty hand and asks the beggar, "What have you to give me?" Confused and uncertain, the beggar reaches into his bag and takes out a grain of corn—only one, and the smallest. Is this a joke? Slowly, he places it in the king's palm.

At the end of the day when the beggar empties his bag on the floor, he is surprised to discover a single grain of pure gold—but only one, and the smallest. "I bitterly wept," the beggar said, "and wished that I had the heart to give my all."[1]

· · · ·

Sometimes the King of kings confuses and disappoints us. He appears to ridicule our misery: He who has so much asks even more of us who have so little!

Perhaps this happens when we're sick in the hospital and, instead of stretching out His hand to heal us (which is what we really need), He asks us to love our neighbor—the woman snoring like a freight train, night after night, in the next bed. Perhaps we're enveloped in the thick gloom of depression and the King expects us to worship as if the world were not gray. To *rejoice* for Christ's sake! Perhaps this happens when we're close to breaking, stressed out of our little minds, and He sincerely expects us to attend the church potluck supper.

Time passes. The King, who could have answered our prayers easily, seems in fact to have left us poorer. But then at the end of the day comes the pouring out of our lives. That is when at last we may find that there is gold in our hands, molded to the shape of our sacrifices. We look back and see how He used our time in the hospital to comfort others. We recall that when we were stressed to the point of breaking, it was at the church potluck supper, of all places, where we laughed until the tears rolled down our cheeks.

There is a divine alchemy at work in all faithful suffering. We look back and realize that it was actually our disappointments and not our plaudits that the Lord has transformed to gold. Now we know what once we doubted, "That in all things"—even in our unanswered prayers—"God works for the good of those who love him, who have been called according to his purpose" (Rom. 8:28).

## The Apostle to the Apostles

Mary Magdalene was, almost certainly, the same person as Mary of Bethany, the sinful yet extravagant worshiper who poured out perfume and wept her tears upon the feet of Jesus at a dinner party less than a week before He died.[2] We know for sure that she had been set free from multiple demonic strangleholds and that in her gratitude she became one of the wealthy women who supported Jesus financially.

Mary Magdalene was also one of only five people whom the Bible records as being at the foot of Jesus' cross when He died. Mary stayed there right to the end, and when Jesus' body was taken down from the cross, she followed Joseph of Arimathea to see where they laid His corpse. We assume that she went out at dusk on Holy Saturday (when the Sabbath had officially finished) to purchase the spices for Jesus' body. Dawn the next day found Mary Magdalene returning to the burial garden, only to discover that Jesus' body was missing. "They have taken my Lord away," she said aghast, "and I don't know where they have put him" (John 20:13). After all she had endured, she still described Jesus as her Lord.

When my prayers are not answered, I often become resentful or apathetic. But Mary Magdalene poured out her worship consistently, just as she had poured out her perfume and her tears on Jesus' feet and just as she had poured her resources into His ministry. Unlike the beggar in Tagore's parable, she had reached into her sack and emptied it for the King. And so it was Mary Magdalene who encountered Jesus Christ before anyone else on Easter morning.

> "Woman," he said, "why are you crying? Who is it you are looking for?"
>
> Thinking he was the gardener, she said, "Sir, if you have carried him away, tell me where you have put him, and I will get him."
>
> Jesus said to her, "Mary."
>
> She turned toward him and cried out in Aramaic, "Rabboni!" (which means Teacher).
>
> Jesus said, "Do not hold on to me, for I have not yet returned to the Father. Go instead to my brothers and

tell them, 'I am returning to my Father and your Father, to my God and your God.'"

Mary Magdalene went to the disciples with the news: "I have seen the Lord!" (John 20:15-18).

How very beautiful it is that the first person on Earth to see Jesus after His resurrection does so through tears. And perhaps it's the tears—or perhaps it's the twilight or simply the impossibility of the reality and the fact that she's been seeing His face everywhere anyway all weekend—but when Mary first sees the Lord, she mistakes Him for a gardener! This moment alone makes me want to follow Christ for the rest of my life (I'm weeping as I type). How can we fail to love such a Lord? Here is the Alpha and Omega, Creator of the rolling spheres, the One whose resurrection from the dead heralds the bright dawning of a new dispensation. The earth has quaked and angels worship, but He Himself is mistaken for a humble, bumbling horticulturalist with dirt beneath his fingernails at the start of a working day.

This, then, is the great revelation. And, of course, it doesn't come to a man—not to Pilate or Caiaphas or even to Peter or John. It comes first to a woman, and a bad woman at that—one from whom Jesus had cast seven demonic powers and who (according to Catholic traditions) may even have been a prostitute. Mary was a bad woman who had become a gracious woman, generous and faithful to the end.

The first words of the New Covenant are a question. Not an announcement, not an answer, but a quietly considerate question addressed to a weeping woman: "Why," Jesus wants to know, "are you weeping?" And for anyone like Mary, anyone like you and me, who has journeyed through the darkness of Maundy Thursday and the despair of Good Friday to reach this garden tomb, it's a stupid question. But it's also a profound question and, with hindsight, even a funny one, too. Jesus, the

God you may confuse with a gardener, simply speaks Mary's name. Easter dawns with a question and a name.

Instinctively, Mary moves to touch, but Jesus warns her, "Do not hold on to me, for I have not yet returned to the Father. Go instead to my brothers and tell them, 'I am returning to my Father and your Father, to my God and your God.'" Mary runs to tell the disciples the incredible news: Jesus has risen from the grave! What's more, He's not returning to heaven in a huff with His so-called "friends." He calls them His brothers and wants them to know that His God is, explicitly, their God. His Abba, Father is theirs. They are closer to His heart than ever before.

For this commission, Mary Magdalene is sometimes recognized as the apostle to the apostles, the first witness to the resurrection! Mary's life had been transformed utterly by Jesus. This former victim, who had been faithful through many trials, becomes the apostle to the apostles, the primary recipient of the good news that Jesus Christ is alive!

## The Refiner's Fire

The transformation that came to Mary has happened to millions of people, but it is not automatic. The simple fact of the matter is that Mary Magdalene saw the Lord first because she was the most extravagant and diligent in her loyalty through suffering.

Jesus still reveals Himself first of all to (and through) those who endure suffering faithfully without ceasing to worship. "Blessed are the meek," He says. "Blessed are those who mourn . . . those who thirst" (Matt. 5:4-6). Eventually, and usually gradually, Jesus blesses our grief. Perhaps our past, like Mary's, is cratered with guilty secrets and littered with low self-esteem. Maybe our present reality remains painful and disappointing. But Good Friday (when we don't know why the darkness is prevailing) and Holy Saturday (when we don't know where God has gone) give way like the winter to the summer. Easter Sunday comes and we, of all people, become messengers of ultimate hope.

Samie and I are friends with an elderly lady named Sheila Giffard-Smith, whose occasional words, seasoned as they are with a lifetime of loyalty to Jesus, have often been a great source of comfort to us. Sheila's sensitivity to our struggles may be attributed to the fact that she has suffered chronic migraine headaches for most of her adult life. For Sheila, the condition (which affects one in 10 Americans) began quite dramatically when she was just eight years old. She learned that her mother, who had left home two years earlier, was never coming back because she was having an affair with the family doctor. Sheila suffered her first migraine the first time she went to stay with her mother and the doctor. The stress on her eight-year-old mind triggered the condition that would affect the rest of her life. Sheila never stayed with her mother again.

Whenever her eyes "went funny" at boarding school, Sheila would simply be left in a darkened room with a sick-bowl until it had passed. In adulthood, the enforced unreliability of frequent migraines barred Sheila from promotion as a teacher and undermined her socially. "It was this 'letting others down' more than anything else, that drove me to start praying earnestly for healing," she recalls. "I truly desired to be free to serve the Lord."

However, Sheila's prayers were not answered, and gradually she adopted Amy Carmichael's maxim: "In acceptance lies peace." Remarkably, she began to look for reasons to praise God in the midst of her migraines. "And there was always something!" she says. No one knows why Sheila's prayers were not answered. What we do know is that Sheila has a depth of character and a ministry that could only have been forged through years of pain. A condition that could easily have made her bitter has, in fact, refined her character into something beautiful for God.

## Who's to Blame?

*You are living and searching in error,*
*because God means movement and not explanation.*

ELIE WIESEL[3]

One day when Samie and I were particularly discouraged by our own situation, we received a card from Sheila that was, as usual, full of scriptural encouragement. That day we also received an e-mail from a crusade evangelist in South America with the amazing news that several hundred Brazilians had been praying for Samie's healing! However, the e-mail went on to inform us that they had discerned certain "root problems" in Samie's past. None of these people had ever met her, but they urged Samie to repent of the sins they had identified so that the healing they had claimed for her could come into effect.

I confess that my blood boiled. A man who had never met Samie seemed to be diagnosing that the agony of her illness was somehow her fault. Even if his discernment had been right (which it patently wasn't), his delivery would still have been unkind. The e-mail revealed far more about the nature of his faith than it did about Samie's. It seemed to me that he, like many others I have met, couldn't cope with the possibility of unanswered prayer. He was not prepared to take no for an answer, and therefore he had learned to scrabble around for something, or someone, to blame whenever the facts threatened to destabilize his watertight theories of what God should do in a given situation. We see this same tendency in Job's comforters who hated the way his suffering called into question their God-in-a-box theology, fearing that what had happened to Job might happen to them.[4]

Sitting there that day, comparing the Brazilian's message with Sheila's, I was reminded that people who suffer unanswered prayers can often have a far greater sensitivity and resemblance to Jesus than those who continually seek to sidestep pain in the name of faith. Sheila has a depth of character forged in the fires of faithful endurance. As W. H. Auden says:

> Under the look of fatigue, the attack of migraine
>   and the sigh
> There is always another story, there is more than
>   meets the eye.[5]

One day, Jesus cured 10 men of leprosy and then sent them away to get checked over by the priests. Only one of these men—and a Samaritan at that—returned to say thank-you. "Were not all ten cleansed?" exclaimed Jesus. "Where are the other nine? Was no one found to return and give praise to God except this foreigner?" (Luke 17:17-18). This story does not merely teach us a lesson about manners but also makes an important point about priorities: All 10 men were equally healed, yet only one truly worshiped. The other nine considered their answered prayer more thrilling than the presence of the Answerer. They took their healing gladly, but they missed the greatest miracle of all: the presence of God!

On another occasion, Jesus predicted that many would experience miracles yet never become His friends (see Matt. 7:22-23). As a result, they would be cast into hell, rejected by Jesus, even though they had witnessed so many dramatic and dynamic answers to prayer. In sharp contrast, we may be sure that people like Sheila who have trusted Jesus through many disappointments will be welcomed into His presence. Who, then, is the most blessed? Jesus leaves us in doubt:

> *Blessed are the poor in spirit,*
> *for theirs is the kingdom of heaven.*

*Blessed are those who mourn,*
*for they will be comforted.*
*Blessed are the meek,*
*for they will inherit the earth*
MATTHEW 5:3-5

Sheila Giffard-Smith recently wrote me a letter looking back on her 72 years of debilitating illness with remarkable serenity. She said, "My dependence on the Lord in my need has drawn me ever closer to Him, discovering *His* strength in my weakness, *His* presence in my pain. So looking back, I can say that I almost feel sorry for those who go through life with such freedom from trouble that they never discover the greatest gift of God's strength! Now, at the age of 80, I feel so blessed."

Like Mary Magdalene (and perhaps unlike that Brazilian), Sheila understands that encountering Jesus is even more desirable than miracles and explanations. It was an encounter with God that silenced Job's questions (see Job 40–41). It is an encounter with God that we all need most.

An unknown soldier of the American Civil War captured these priorities in a famous verse about the blessings of unanswered prayer:

I asked for strength that I might achieve;
He made me weak that I might obey.
I asked for health that I might do greater things;
I was given grace that I might do better things.
I asked for riches that I might be happy;
I was given poverty that I might be wise.
I asked for power that I might have the praise of men;
I was given weakness that I might feel the need of God.
I asked for all things that I might enjoy life;
I was given life that I might enjoy all things.

I received nothing that I asked for, all that I hoped for.
My prayer was answered, I was most blessed.

## Questions That Heal

It's interesting to note how many times after His resurrection Jesus introduced Himself to people by asking them questions. Good Friday had left a mess, and Jesus was systematically dealing with the consequences of chaos in the lives of His friends by provoking them to respond to His presence.

Jesus' question for Mary Magdalene, "Why are you crying?" (John 20:13) targeted her *pain*. His question for the two men on the road to Emmaus, "What are you discussing . . . Don't you understand?" (Luke 24:17-25) targeted their *confusion*. His question to the disciples, "Why are you troubled, and why do doubts rise in your minds?" (Luke 24:38) targeted their *crisis of faith*. And then He cooked breakfast for Peter and asked him a question that targeted his *guilt*: "Do you truly love me?" (John 21:15).

The journey through Maundy Thursday, Good Friday and Holy Saturday will create a mess in your life as well. But Jesus loves you too much to leave you for long in pain, confusion, doubt or a state of unbelief. He wants to help you deal with your disappointments.

Perhaps your experiences of unanswered prayer have left you hurting and disorientated like Mary Magdalene. If so, He asks you the question He asked her: "Why are you crying?" So tell Him! Lament. Rant, if you need to. And when you are done, stop and hear the way He speaks your name.

Maybe your disappointments in prayer have left you confused like those earnest men on the road to Emmaus. If this is the case, don't run away from the questions. Allow Jesus to explain the Scriptures to you by His Spirit. He wants to help you make sense of what you're going through. Study and think.

Discuss these matters with friends. Perhaps, as you talk, there will be moments when you realize that Jesus has joined the conversation, just as He did on the road to Emmaus. Perhaps you could gather a group of friends and go through the Discussion Guide at the end of this book together.

Maybe unanswered prayer has created a quiet crisis of faith in your life. Like the disciples, who could hardly believe it when Jesus appeared in their midst, your old confidence in God has been eroded. You are older and wiser, which is good, but you are also suspicious and weary. Imagine Jesus stepping through the locked doors of your heart and asking, "Why are you troubled, and why do you doubt?" Tell Him! If God seems absent, you may find it helpful to explore some of the negative theology introduced in chapter 10. Honestly sharing your disappointments with others will also be important (see chapter 4), as will an appropriation of the keys to growing in faith (see chapter 9). You would not be the first, of course, to tell Jesus, "I do believe, help me in my unbelief!"

Or maybe in your journey through disappointment you have occasionally given in to the temptation to sin. Like Peter, you have been scared and said things you should not have said and held your tongue when you should have spoken up. Perhaps you too have sometimes felt like giving up and sinned anonymously with servant girls and strangers. Jesus may seek you out in the things you love to do. After all, that is how He sought Peter—on the beach after a long night fishing—helping him to confess his love again, once for each denial.

When we suffer, Jesus comes with questions to refine and enhance our humanity. He of all people understands that this process of dealing with the mess created by our disappointments in prayer can hurt terribly. He knows that without His help, we will become bitter not better, and that we will lick our wounds like a dog or curl up in a ball of self-protection like a hedgehog. But if, like Mary, we will continue to worship, even at the grave of everything we ever believed in, our grief will turn to gold. The greatest miracle in the world—greater than any healing or any revelation—is the grace unleashed by a life refined through suffering. It is a grace that was first released when Jesus endured abandonment and death so that Mary Magdalene, and millions since, might receive a living hope that can no longer die.

> *Praise be to the God and Father of our Lord Jesus Christ! In his great mercy he has given us new birth into a living hope through the resurrection of Jesus Christ from the dead . . . In this you greatly rejoice, though now for a little while you may have had to suffer grief in all kinds of trials. These have come so that your faith—of greater worth than gold, which perishes even though refined by fire—may be proved genuine and may result in praise, glory and honor when Jesus Christ is revealed.*
>
> 1 PETER 1:3,6-7

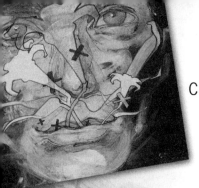

Chapter Thirteen

# BEYOND MIRACLES

*If only for this life we have hope in Christ, we are to be pitied more than all men. But Christ has indeed been raised from the dead, the firstfruits of those who have fallen asleep.*

THE APOSTLE PAUL, 1 CORINTHIANS 15:19-20

My favorite building in all the world is La Templa Sagrada Família (The Church of the Holy Family), Antoni Gaudí's breathtaking, yet unfinished, basilica in Barcelona, Spain. Erupting magnificently from the sidewalk like a towering mountain of melting, dribbling wax, it is astonishing and unique. The first time I stepped out of the subway and saw this monumental entity, the experience was, for me, literally breathtaking. And once inside, I discovered that every curve, every stone slab and swooping beam of the vast edifice, down to the most meticulous detail, seeks somehow to articulate the gospel of Christ's life, death and resurrection.

For the architect Gaudí, La Sagrada Família was the unfinished summation of his life's work. For several years he actually lived on the building site, breathing the dust, and drawing his ultimate inspiration from the organic symmetry of creation as well as the teachings of the Church. As the building rose skyward from its foundations in great, grinding hallelujahs, Gaudí's fame also soared. Kings and queens came to see the building site, imagining what it would one day become. But then, in old age,

Gaudí was killed, run over by a tram. Because of his ragged attire and empty pockets, cab drivers refused to pick him up, thinking he was a tramp, and he was eventually taken to a pauper's hospital. Nobody recognized the great man until his friends eventually tracked him down the next day. They tried to move him into a nicer hospital, but Gaudí refused, reportedly saying, "I belong here among the poor." He died two days later and was buried in the midst of his unfinished masterpiece.

Gaudí had begun planning La Sagrada Familia in the 1880s and was still working on it the day he died, some 40 years later. Other architects have since continued to apply and interpret his designs, but the basilica will not be finished until 2026, at the earliest. Gaudi's vast project reminds me that we are all called to pour our lives into something bigger than ourselves. "My client," joked Gaudí on one occasion, "is not in a hurry."

Life is not a short story. I am not the star. And so, like Gaudí giving his life to the construction of an edifice that outshone and outlasted him, we too contribute what we can to the epic story of God, a tale with many characters, vast battle scenes, a million interweaving subplots and many perplexing twists and turns.

In the book of Revelation, the prayers of the ages are described as incense rising to the throne of God. It's an insight that can help us make sense of the part our unanswered prayers will ultimately play in the fulfillment of God's epic. In Revelation 5, John sees the Lamb that was slain standing before the throne of God with sole authority to unlock the scroll of God's purposes in salvation and judgment. In the midst of this extraordinary scene, John sees our prayers, gathered together and soon to be poured out in one vast Amen: "The four living creatures and the twenty-four elders fell down before the Lamb. Each one had a harp and they were holding golden bowls full of incense, which are the prayers of the saints" (Rev. 5:8).

It's awesome to imagine that our unanswered prayers—all the frustrations, the tears, the dashed hopes—are being stored up by God in those golden bowls and may, eventually, become our most powerful contribution to the world. Let me say it again: Our unanswered prayers may be the real ministry of our lives. As Tim Chester writes in *The Message of Prayer*:

> Prayers we think of as directed to the present are in fact being stored up to be answered on the final day. When we pray for those suffering ill health we are expressing our longing for the day when there will be no more sickness (Rev. 21:4). When we pray for God to end wars and oppression we are expressing our longing for the day when the kingdoms of this world will become the Kingdom of our God and of his Christ (Rev. 11:15). When we pray for mercy on those suffering natural disasters we are expressing our longing for the day when creation itself will be remade (Rev. 21:1). . . . The prayers we think have gone unanswered may in fact be stored up in the bowls of incense held by the twenty-four elders, waiting for a greater fulfillment than ever we anticipated. . . . Many of your prayers are lodged there and one day they will determine the ultimate course of history.[1]

Gaudí's basilica will eventually incorporate three façades, each articulating a different aspect of Christ's life. Gaudí, in his generation, created the Façade of the Nativity, ornately exploring and celebrating the birth and life of Jesus. In our generation, the second façade has almost been completed: that of the Passion of the Christ. While this wing remains true to the original design made by Gaudí, it also reflects the nuances of our time. It is refreshingly different yet aesthetically and structurally the same.

Two generations have already combined their insights, technological abilities and craftsmanship in this one act of worship, and yet it will be many years before the cranes are dismantled and anyone can say a final Amen to the prayer of Gaudí's life. Who knows whether we will see La Templa Sagrada Familia completed in our lifetime? My pretensions are dwarfed, my self-importance hushed, by a story so much bigger than myself. La Sagrada Familia, like many of Europe's great cathedrals, contextualizes my problems helpfully. But what of the third, unfinished dimension of Gaudí's imagination? Work is just beginning on the final structure, The Glory Façade. At last, we have the money, the time and the technical ability to start expressing Gaudí's ideas about the wonder of the resurrected Christ who reigns on high and will return in glory.

I regard this laborious process of construction as a powerful depiction of Christian experience. We are grateful beyond words for the objective reality of His nativity and crucifixion by which we have been redeemed. The messages of Christmas and Easter tower over us like the first two façades of Gaudí's basilica. But we await the completion of the story when Christ's glory will fully be revealed and His temple will be complete. As the apostle Paul says, "In him the whole building is joined together and rises to become a holy temple in the Lord. And in him you too are being built together to become a dwelling in which God lives by his Spirit" (Eph. 2:21-22).

## Imagining Heaven

*Where, O death, is your victory?*
*Where, O death, is your sting?*
1 Corinthians 15:55

When we seek to describe the glory of God, whether in stone, metal, music or words, we inevitably enter the realm of metaphor. When Samie and I were facing the stark possibility that she would die at the age of 30, I was dismayed to discover that I had no meaningful metaphors for the afterlife, no vision at all for the Kingdom to come. I was not excited by the prospect of sitting on a cloud plucking a harp. Neither was I thrilled at the idea of an unending worship service. (Forgive me, but it's true.) Continually throwing crowns down on the ground before God sounded painful. The idea that Samie would become a serene spirit and no longer my wife was nothing short of spooky. My imagination, I discovered, was bereft of any imagery or vocabulary that could grant genuine comfort and joy at the prospect of resurrection from the grave.

Heaven is, according to the apostle Paul, a mystery (see 1 Cor. 15:41-51), and I have no problem with that. It's my love of mystery that makes me want to explore life (and now death, too) through the tantalizing possibilities of music, literature and film and through Catalonian basilicas and complex relationships. According to Albert Einstein, "The most beautiful thing we can experience is the mysterious . . . He to whom this emotion is a stranger is as good as dead." Mystery is pregnant with meaning. But there is nothing less mysterious than an empty room without shadows or clutter, which was precisely the state of my imagination with regard to eternity. The life and death of Jesus were real to me. But the third façade—the glory of the resurrection—had not yet been constructed in my inner reality.

I approached a pastor and admitted to him that I had no particular desire to go to heaven (not that I was volunteering for the alternative). I asked him to help me, explaining that I needed someone to cast for me a vision of heaven that would, literally, be worth dying for. The pastor listened to me caringly and responded with many words. But the more he talked, the more it became clear that although he had a spectacular vision for the next 30 or so years of life on Earth, he had no vision whatsoever for eternity. I suspect that although he was older than me, he had simply not yet been forced to stare for himself into the abyss, wondering, *What's next?*

The contemporary Western Church at large seems to me to have little belief in the afterlife. We are so temporal and comfortable. We can perpetuate the delusions of our own immortality for longer than any previous generation, but ultimately, unless our death comes instantaneously in early life, we must think about such things. We will be the poorer if we do not. And so I began a solemn, lifelong pilgrimage that some might deem a little morose. My aim? To find a thrilling vision for the eternity we will spend with Jesus.

Like a child in a sweet shop, I quickly discovered that there are glories all around. The writings of the theologian N. T. Wright have helped me begin my pilgrimage by explaining that life after death will not be a disembodied spirit world but a physical one and that, controversially, it will not be in a distant heaven but here on a renewed Earth. "The great majority of Christian expressions of hope through the middle ages, the reformation, and the counter-reformation periods have been misleading," Wright says, arguing that they were rooted in pagan-Greek thinking instead of biblical ideas. "Heaven is not the Christian's ultimate destination. For renewed bodies we need a renewed cosmos, including a renewed earth. That is what the New Testament promises." He continues:

> What then do the New Testament writers mean when they speak of an inheritance waiting for us in heaven? This has been much misunderstood, with awesome results in traditions of thought, prayer, life and art.

The point of such passages, as in 1 Peter 1.4, 2 Corinthians 5.1, Philippians 3.20, and so forth, is not that one must "go to heaven," as in much-popular imagination, in order to enjoy the inheritance there. It is rather that "heaven" is the place where God stores up his plans and purposes for the future. If I tell a friend that there is beer in the fridge, that doesn't mean he has to get into the fridge in order to enjoy the beer![2]

We know that Jesus was different yet the same after His resurrection. He was recognizable, yet not easily so. He could walk through walls, yet He also enjoyed real relationships, expressed deep emotion, cooked breakfast on a beach and bore the physical marks of His crucifixion. Several times, He sat down to eat hot meals, full of flavors and aromas, wrapped in conversation. Remarkably, His appearance was not striking. He had risen from the dead, and yet no one gave Him a second look in the street! Perhaps our resurrection bodies, though different, will therefore be surprisingly normal.

As I began to cultivate a more tangible vision for eternity, I also found it helpful to identify the kind of places where I would love to spend a few thousand years. For instance, there is a piece of countryside five miles from my house where a white windmill stands under a very big sky above rolling fields of grass and barley. Whenever I go there these days, I imagine that this might be a glimpse of heaven—not yours, necessarily, but mine. In the misty distance I can make out little English villages tucked in the creases of the hills, promising me ancient pubs where wet dogs lie on the flagstones by inglenook fireplaces and conversation is punctuated by laughter and the clinking of glasses. On clear days, I can see the place where Samie and I got married, and far away on the horizon, I can just make out the city of Portsmouth, where we became parents and where my football team plays to gasps, groans and cheers through the winter months. Embracing this amazing vista is the arc of an ever-changing ocean, sometimes belligerent and sometimes sparkling blue.

Inquisitive souls may find a glimpse of eternity in various places—from a windmill in England to a church in Barcelona and from the Sistine Chapel to a dusty, old study haunted with books. Great literature, music and cinema can do the same (arguably, all good art combines the three facades of life, death and unfinished glory). For instance, the film *Finding Neverland*, about the life of J. M. Barrie, left my friends and me stunned and weeping in the foyer of a California cinema. We sat there praying, traumatized yet resensitized, as the crowds filed past eating popcorn. And then, of course, there is Tolkien's epic *The Lord of the Ring* trilogy, not least this scene from *The Return of the King*:

> But Sam lay back, and stared with open mouth, and for a moment, between bewilderment and great joy, he could not answer. At last he gasped: "Gandalf! I thought you were dead! But then I thought that I was dead myself. Is everything sad going to come untrue? What's happened to the world?"
>
> "A great Shadow has departed," said Gandalf, and then he laughed, and the sound was like music, or like water in a parched land; and as he listened the thought came to Sam that he had not heard laughter, the pure sound of merriment, for days upon days without count. It fell upon his ears like the echo of all the joys he had ever known. But he himself burst into tears. Then, as a sweet rain will pass down a wind of spring and the sun will shine out the clearer, his tears ceased, and his laughter welled up, and laughing he sprang from his bed.

"How do I feel?" he cried. "Well, I don't know how to say it. I feel, I feel"—he waved his arms in the air—"I feel like spring after winter, and sun on the leaves; and like trumpets and harps and all the songs I have ever heard!"[3]

One day when "everything sad will come untrue," we will rise, feeling "like trumpets and harps and all the songs [we] have ever heard." The Glory Façade will soar to the sky, completing the story of Christ's birth, death and resurrection in the temple of our lives. Perhaps in the age to come, I will sometimes sit quietly by my windmill. You will sit in your sacred place. Such metaphors are limited, but they are helping me cultivate a joyous vision for the eternal prospect of resurrection.

## A Vision of Jesus

As a young woman, my Aunty Cleeve had lived a flamboyant life full of music and fashion. She was always fascinated by people, especially artistic people, and when she eventually became a Christian, her faith was vibrant and contagious. But in old age, knowing that her death was imminent, she became increasingly anxious as her past misdemeanors returned to haunt her.

However, the last time Samie and I saw Aunty Cleeve, her countenance was bright. As soon as we stepped into her little room at the care home, we could sense the peace of God's presence. Initially she noticed Samie's fashionable, knee-length boots and began reminiscing about a similar pair she had worn in the 1930s, but before long, the conversation turned to weightier matters. A few days before our visit, something extraordinary had happened that had, she said with an expression of surprised delight, taken away her fear of dying entirely. She spoke quietly and carefully about a visitation she had received from Jesus. One night, she said, He had actually appeared to her, right by the bed. My Aunty Cleeve, so wracked with fear at the prospect of death, had seen the Lord. That was all. No words were exchanged. No words were necessary. From that moment, death had lost its sting.

Whether or not we receive the reassurance of such a vision of Jesus (and few people do), Christians share a wonderful hope. We do not "grieve like the rest of men, who have no hope," writes the apostle Paul (1 Thess. 4:14). Why not? Because, unlike them, "We believe that Jesus died and rose again."

The bitter futility of bereavement without faith in Jesus was brought home to me by a tragic event that took place just 100 yards from my front door. An 18-year-old named Karl was recently killed in a car crash at the end of our road. His friends had evidently gathered by the lamppost where he died, because the next morning there were flowers and empty beer cans (one left unopened with a note explaining that it was a gift for Karl). Although I didn't know Karl, it seemed to matter to me that he had died just yards from our front door, so I went to pay my respects, too. When I did, I noticed that one of his friends had written the following sad poem and had propped it against some flowers:

*A thousand words can't bring you back*
*We know because we've tried,*
*Neither will a thousand tears*
*We know because we've cried.*
*You left behind broken hearts*
*And happy memories too,*
*But we never wanted memories*
*We only wanted you.*

*RIP, mate.*

The ink on this desperate poem had blurred in the rain. Over following weeks, the colored paper around the flowers went moldy and the flowers themselves died. Today, as I drive past this slowly rotting shrine, it reminds me of the futility of life without Christ. It seems particularly tragic when compared to the hopeful experiences of people like my Aunty Cleeve, or to the glorious visions expressed by Tolkien and Gaudi, or to the actual encounter of Mary Magdalene with the risen Jesus Christ.

Of course, many Christians remain terrified by death. They haven't seen Jesus as Mary Magdalene or my Aunty Cleeve did and they approach eternity with many doubts and deep regrets. The eighteenth-century Englishman John Bunyan, who was imprisoned for preaching without a license, addressed precisely this issue in perhaps the most famous Christian allegory of all time. As the hero, simply called Christian, traverses the trials of life, he eventually reaches the river of death that he knows he must cross. However, unlike his companion, Hopeful, Christian is terrified:

> Then they addressed themselves to the water; and entering, Christian began to sink, and crying out to his good friend Hopeful, he said, "I sink in deep waters, the billows go over my head, all his waves go over me . . ."
>
> Then said the other, "Be of good cheer, my brother, I feel the bottom, and it is good." Then said Christian, "Ah my friend, the sorrows of death have compassed me about, I shall not see the land that flows with milk and honey." And with that, a great darkness and horror fell upon Christian, so that he could not see before him; also here he in a great measure lost his senses, so that he could neither remember nor orderly talk of any of those sweet refreshments that he had met with in the

way of his pilgrimage ... Then said Hopeful ... "These troubles and distresses that you go through in these waters are no sign that God hath forsaken you, but are sent to try you whether you will call to mind that which heretofore you have received of his goodness, and live upon him in your distresses."

Then I saw in my dream that Christian was as in a muse awhile; to whom also Hopeful added this words, "Be of good cheer, Jesus Christ maketh thee whole." And with that, Christian brake out with a loud voice, "Oh I see him again! And he tells me, *When thou passest through the waters, I will be with thee; and when through the rivers, they shall not overflow thee. . . .*" Christian therefore presently found ground to stand upon; and so it followed that the rest of the river was but shallow. Thus they got over.[4]

We approach the silence of God, and especially death, in different ways. Some people, like Hopeful, are full of faith to the end. But others, like Christian, face death with horror. They are plagued with guilt and may even doubt their salvation. But Bunyan's message for both types of people is the same. Both Hopeful and Christian crossed that river, one with faith and one with fear. Both received the reward for their faithful pilgrimage through many trials, for, as Jesus says, "he who stands firm to the end will be saved" (Matt. 24:13).

· · · ·

When I wake at night and look at Samie sleeping quietly next to me, I must face the possibility that, though we pray with all our hearts for the completion of her healing, it may never happen. She may suffer from epilepsy for the rest of her life. Worse still, the tumor might grow back again. It's been a long time since that first seizure when I thought I was watching Samie die. Danny was just seven weeks old back then, and now he's six and Hudson's eight. The other day, they came out of school to find Samie lying on the playground, shaking and twitching in front of all the other moms. Meanwhile I was kneeling beside her, praying for an end to the seizure as usual, without any apparent success.

But whether the future brings miraculous answers to prayer or ongoing suffering and silence, nothing can take away the things God has taught us and done in us through Samie's illness. As the prophet Isaiah says, "The grass withers and the flowers fall, but the word of our God stands forever" (40:8). Reluctantly, I acknowledge that "though outwardly we are wasting away, yet inwardly we are being renewed day by day. For our light and momentary troubles are achieving for us an eternal glory that far outweighs them all" (2 Cor. 4:16-17).

We see this glorious redemption of suffering displayed in the lives of so many of the people mentioned in this book. It's evident in Floyd McClung, who was willing to choose God's glory even if it was time for his daughter to die. We see it in Barbara Fisher, who found faith for dying and in so doing spoke God's word into my life. We see it in Rob Morris, who has dedicated his life to the rescue of children from sexual slavery. We see it in Margaret Lee, who was strangled by cancer yet able to list its limitations and the eternal qualities of God's love.

And if our story has helped in any way to ease the pain of your unanswered prayers, then to God be the glory. Somehow, He has conspired to bring a little comfort through a chronic illness and a chronic coward like me.

*Praise be to the God and Father of our Lord Jesus Christ,*
*the Father of compassion and the God of all comfort,*
*who comforts us in all our troubles,*
*so that we can comfort those in any trouble*
*with the comfort we ourselves have received from God.*

2 CORINTHIANS 1:3-4

# AFTERWORD

*For no matter how many promises God has made,
they are "Yes" in Christ.
And so through him the "Amen" is spoken
by us to the glory of God*
2 CORINTHIANS 1:20

I am thrilled that Pete has written *God on Mute*. These last few years have been a difficult and painful journey for both of us, but they have also enabled us to learn more of God's heart and to draw a little closer to Him on our journey.

Recalling events and memories of the last five years (in order to capture as honestly as possible how our lives have played out since the tumor was first discovered) has surprised us both. At times it has brought us to tears—sometimes in the middle of the night, crying out to God in old and in new ways. At other times, we've been left thanking Him in amazement at the great things He has done.

This really is the book I was looking for when I first found myself crying out for some hope, help and answers following my diagnosis. So my prayer is that our honesty in the hard times (although in this I do think Pete has described me more favorably than I deserve) can help someone, somewhere, who is struggling with his or her own unanswered prayers. I don't always understand God's ways in my life, but I'm absolutely certain that He can be trusted.

Samie Greig
Guildford, England

# Appendix A

# PERSONAL CHECKLIST

*CAUTION:* Making sense of unanswered prayer is seldom simple, so I offer this Personal Checklist with a measure of caution. Each of us, of course, is unique, and the factors at work in our situation are complex and probably painful. What's more, God Himself interacts with these factors in mysterious ways that invariably confound our nice neat charts and tables! I offer this checklist, therefore, merely as a simplistic summary of the biblical explanations and responses outlined previously in this book.

| | WHY ISN'T MY PRAYER WORKING? | WHAT CAN I DO ABOUT IT? |
|---|---|---|
| **GOD'S WORLD—(CHAPTER 7)** | **1. COMMON SENSE (pp. 112-113)** Am I asking God to do something stupid, meaningless or illogical? | Consider praying in a different way or just dong something practical yourself! |
| | **2. CONTRADICTION (pp. 114-117)** Are my prayers likely to be conflicting with those of someone else? | Remember that you share the planet with over 6 billion other people, and thank God that in saying no to you He's probably blessing someone else. |
| | **3. LAWS OF NATURE (pp. 117-120)** Are my prayers potentially detrimental to the natural order or to the lives of others? | Matt. 8:23-27 Don't stop praying—God can and does do miracles over the natural order! But remember, although your prayer seems so reasonable, in saying no to you, God may be protecting many others. |
| | **4. LIFE IS TOUGH (pp. 120-126)** Am I expecting God to spare me from stuff that's just common human experience because of the Fall? | John 16:33; Rom. 12:12; 2 Cor. 4:16-18 Discuss your situation with God and with your friends. Are you experiencing a direct satanic attack or a by-product of the Fall? Is God asking you to pray against this or for grace to endure it *with* Him? |

| WHY ISN'T MY PRAYER WORKING? | WHAT CAN I DO ABOUT IT? |
|---|---|
| **5. DOCTRINE (pp. 126-129)** | **1 Tim. 4:16** |
| Does my prayer reflect God's character and His promises in the Bible? Might it be out of line with His will for my life? | Talk to someone sensible about the thing you're asking God to do. Does that person think it's in line with what God wants? If so, go to item 13 in this list. If not, don't moderate your expectations; elevate them to what God has for you! |
| **6. SECOND BEST (pp. 137-139)** | **Jer. 29:11-12; 1 Cor. 2:9-11** |
| Although my desire in prayer is for something good, is it possible that God has something even better in store for me? | With this one, only time will tell whether God is saying no because it's not the best for you or simply if He is saying "not yet." Keep asking but hold your prayers lightly, remembering all the ways that God has given you the best in the past. |
| **7. MOTIVE (pp. 139-141)** | **Jas. 4:2-3** |
| Are my prayers essentially just selfish? | Assuming that you want something that is not intrinsically sinful, feel free to chat with God about how much you'd like whatever it is—the way a kid might with his dad—but don't expect or insist on it in prayer. Also, make sure that you're not coveting something that belongs to someone else! |
| **8. RELATIONSHIP (pp. 142-144)** | **2 Cor. 12:7-10; Phil. 3:10** |
| Is there an opportunity here for going deeper in my relationship with God? | Remember that the ultimate answer is the Answerer. Take time to worship and thank God. Turn your prayers into a conversation and get rid of the shopping list. Are you willing to trust Him even if the answer is no? |
| **9. FREE WILL (pp. 146-153)** | **Gen. 2:16; John 7:17** |
| Am I expecting God to override someone's free will? | Pray a small step at a time and pray creatively into the situation, remembering that while God won't control a person, He will allow you to influence that |
| **10. INFLUENCE (pp. 153-155)** | |
| Am I trying to exercise ungodly power over a person's life in prayer? | person's situation in prayer. For example, "Please make John become a Christian" might become, "Please send a Christian to talk to John." |
| **11. SATANIC OPPOSITION (pp. 162-172)** | **Dan. 10; Eph. 6:10-18** |
| Is my prayer in line with God's will but experiencing specific demonic resistance? | Learn about spiritual warfare. Study what the Bible says about your authority in Christ. Wield the Sword of the Spirit, which is the Word of God. Find |

GOD'S WILL—(CHAPTER 8)

| WHY ISN'T MY PRAYER WORKING? | WHAT CAN I DO ABOUT IT? |
|---|---|
| | Scriptures that you can use in prayer. Get others to share the prayer burden with you. Ask God to reveal any particular keys that could unlock the situation. Make sure you spend more time worshiping Jesus than thinking about Satan. Also, try fasting. |
| **12. FAITH (pp. 172-180)** Do I really believe that God can do this? Am I out of my league? | **Dan. 3:16; Mark 9:24; 11:23-24** Could you perhaps start smaller and work up to this? Keys to growing in faith include worshiping, fasting, and memorizing God's promises. (See the full list in chapter 9.) |
| **13. PERSEVERANCE (pp. 180-184)** Do I want it enough to keep praying? | **Luke 18:1** Don't give up! Find a way of praying regularly into this situation, and make a habit of it. |
| **14. SIN (pp. 184-187)** Honesty time: Is there secret sin you need to confess? | **Mark 11:25; Jas. 5:16** Find someone you trust who is a Christian and confess your sin. If there are strongholds in your life, ask a mature person to help you walk free. Also, consider whether there is anyone whom you need to apologize to or forgive. |
| **15. JUSTICE (pp. 187-188)** Am I actively seeking to express God's love for the poor? | **Isa. 58** Make friends with just one person in your community who is marginalized in some way. Make sure you budget time and money each month for hospitality. Get educated about the challenges facing the poor at home and in the developing world. Get political! |
| **16. NONE OF THE ABOVE** Am I trying to find answers where I need instead just to trust? | **1 Cor. 13:12-13; 2 Cor. 12:7-10** Ouch! You're doing all the right stuff, but your situation doesn't make sense. Be real with God. Hold on to Him like a hurting kid who doesn't understand. You really need your friends right now. |

GOD'S WAR—(CHAPTER 9)

EXPLORING THE SILENCE—(CHAPTER 10)

# HEROES OF THE FAITH AND UNANSWERED PRAYER

It's okay to struggle with unanswered prayer. So have all the great heroes of the faith. Here are just a few examples:

**Job (afflicted son of Israel, c. before 2000 B.C.)**
I cry out to you, O God, but you do not answer; I stand up, but you merely look at me (Job 30:20).

**Enoch, Noah, Abraham (patriarchs of Israel, c. 1900 B.C.)**
All these people were still living by faith when they died. They did not receive the things promised (Heb. 11:13).

**David, son of Jesse (second king of Israel, 1005-965 B.C.)**
David pleaded with God for the child. He fasted and went into his house and spent the nights lying on the ground . . . On the seventh day the child died (2 Sam. 12:16,18).

**Elijah (Hebrew prophet, c. 900 B.C.)**
He came to a broom tree, sat down under it and prayed that he might die (1 Kings 19:4).

**Jonah (Hebrew prophet, c. eighth century B.C.)**
"Now, O LORD, take away my life, for it is better for me to die than to live." But the LORD replied, "Have you any right to be angry?" (Jon. 4:3-4).

**Jeremiah (Hebrew prophet, c. seventh century B.C.)**
You have covered yourself with a cloud so that no prayer can get through to you (Lam. 3: 44).

**Jesus**
I pray also for those who will believe in me . . . that all of them may be one, Father, just as you are in me and I am in you . . . May they be brought to complete unity (John 17:20-22).

My God, my God, why have you forsaken me? (Mark 15:34).

**The Disciples**
The disciples came to Jesus privately and said, "Why couldn't we drive [the demon] out?" (Matt. 17:19).

**Saint Paul**
There was given me a thorn in my flesh, a messenger of Satan, to torment me. Three times I pleaded with the Lord to take it away from me. But he said to me "My grace is sufficient for you for my power is made perfect in weakness" (2 Cor. 12:7-8).

**Saint John of the Cross (Carmelite mystic, 1542-1591)**
"The dark night of the soul . . . in this time of dryness, spiritual people undergo great trials . . . they believe that spiritual blessings are a thing of the past, and that God has abandoned them."

**Martin Luther (German monk, theologian and Church reformer, 1483-1546)**
On the death of his daughter, aged 13, in 1542: "My little daughter [Magdalena] is dead. It is marvelous that how sick at heart it has left me, so much do I grieve for her . . . Even the death of Christ is unable to take all this away as it should . . . I am angry with myself that I am unable to rejoice from my heart."

### J. Hudson Taylor (missionary to China, 1832-1905)

Suffering mental and physical breakdown on hearing news of the massacre of 58 of his missionaries and 21 children in China: "I cannot read; I cannot think; I cannot even pray; but I can trust."

### J.O. Fraser (pioneer missionary to China, 1909-1938)

"'Does God answer prayer?' loomed larger and larger as a tormenting question. 'Does he know and care?'"

### C. S. Lewis (author and scholar, 1898-1963)

"What chokes every prayer and every hope is the memory of all the prayers [Joy] and I offered and all the false hopes we had . . . Step by step we were 'led up the garden path.' Time after time, when He seemed most gracious He was really preparing the next torture."

### Mother Teresa (founder of the Sisters of Charity, 1910-1999)

"I feel that God does not want me, that God is not God, and that God does not exist."

### Henri Nouwen (Catholic priest and writer, 1932-1996)

"So what about my life of prayer? Do I like to pray? Do I want to pray? Do I spend time praying? Frankly, the answer is no to all three questions. After sixty-three years of life and thirty-eight years of priesthood, my prayer seems as dead as a rock . . . The truth is that I do not feel much, if anything when I pray."

### Ruth Bell Graham
### (wife of evangelist Billy Graham, 1920-present)

"God has not always answered my prayers. If He had, I would have married the wrong man several times!"

# DISCUSSION GUIDE FOR SMALL GROUPS

## By Pete Greig and Stephanie Heald

We designed this Discussion Guide for use by friends, small groups and book clubs, although individuals may find it a useful tool in their personal devotional times as well. It uses each chapter of *God on Mute* as a springboard for honest dialogue and prayer. Its aim is to bring healing and build faith by equipping people to process and apply the important issues raised in this book thoughtfully and prayerfully in a safe context.

### Why Take Groups Through the *God on Mute* Discussion Guide?

There is strong evidence that God's people are being mobilized globally to intercede on a scale quite unprecedented in our time. A revival of prayer is touching churches, university campuses, entire denominations, cities and even nations. It's a thrilling moment to be alive for, as any student of Church history knows, such movements of prayer have invariably preceded great outpourings of God's power.

However, at such a time, it is particularly important to think about prayer biblically and to reject hype or we risk sowing long-term disappointment in our desire for an immediate harvest. Many people have sincere questions and even disappointments regarding prayer and we must address these concerns diligently, intelligently, and above all, *faithfully*. Without such interaction, I believe that the foundations of the burgeoning prayer movement (not to mention the foundations of our own personal prayer lives) will prove to be shaky when the storms of testing come. As I think about it now, I realize that my desire is not so much for an explosion of prayer—a phenomenon that lasts a short time and leaves a mess—but for millions of small fires to be ignited and tended in such a way that they will burn for many years in every heart, every family and every community that loves the name of Jesus and longs for His return.

· · · ·

## Unanswered Prayer and Individual Christians

Many people have given up on God because their experiences of unanswered prayer were never dealt with appropriately. An even larger number of people have lost their faith imperceptibly. Remaining in church, they may continue to call themselves Christians but gradually downgrade their expectations of what God can do in their lives, and thus, they lose the passion that once burned so brightly. However, it doesn't have to be this way if we will just help individuals to process their disappointments courageously and biblically. Why?

- So that no "root of bitterness" can grow up in our lives (Heb. 12:15)
- So that wounds and disappointments may be healed (see Jas 5:16)
- So that others may stand with us, sharing our burdens and stirring us up to persevere (see Gal. 6:2)
- So that we do not lose heart (see 2 Cor. 4:16)
- So that others may listen to the Lord on our behalf and help us know how to pray (see 1 Cor. 2:12-14)

- So that others may bring wisdom to our situation and share insights into possible reasons for our struggle (see Jas. 1:2-5)
- So that others may encourage us with stories of *answered* prayer and remind us of the promises of the Bible that will increase our faith (see Heb. 10:24-25)
- So that we can grow in faith and authority through our struggles
- So that we can be helped to recognize and trust the hand of God in our present situation

## Unanswered Prayer and Churches

Unanswered prayer doesn't just affect individuals. I can think of many wonderful communities that have been damaged and depleted because, while they mobilized themselves to prayer and celebrated encouragements publicly, they never addressed the accompanying experiences of disappointment.

For instance, a large church in England received a remarkable prophetic word assuring them that the Lord was going to give them a particularly prominent facility as an auditorium in their locale. They responded with great faith, prayed, fasted and gave money sacrificially. They continued to pray like this for several years, but the owners always refused to sell the building to them. Eventually, the large church became dispirited—as the proverb says, "Hope deferred makes the heart sick" (Prov. 13:12)—and they entered a long-term decline, significantly influenced by disappointments that can be traced back to this large-scale, corporate experience of unanswered prayer.

Many years ago, another church—this one in America—cried out to God for the healing of their pastor's wife who was dying of cancer. There were prayer vigils, days of fasting, remissions and encouragements, but ultimately she died. It's a tragedy that has been brushed under the carpet ever since. The widowed pastor, who had not prepared himself for the possibility of losing his wife, never showed any trace of his grief to his congregation. No one mentions it publicly but privately many questions are still being asked because the community has never had the opportunity to acknowledge and learn from this painful disappointment.

At university, I was one of the leaders of the little group of 30 Christians on campus, and we became convinced that God was going to bless us with growth so that we would be 100 strong by the end of the academic year. We responded with half-nights of prayer, stocked up on discipleship materials for new Christians "in faith," launched a student newspaper full of testimonies and delivered it round every door on campus, and engaged enthusiastically in relational evangelism. However, in spite of so much faith, a year later the group had grown to just 35. I remember feeling disappointed and embarrassed.

It's not easy to admit our disappointments in prayer, but discussing them honestly, in an appropriate group setting, can be releasing, enlightening, encouraging, healing and even faith building.

• • • •

## Using This Guide

You can use this Discussion Guide at various levels:

- *Alone.* Although this is a guide for group discussion, you can still use the questions to help with your own times of reflection.

- *With a spouse, prayer partner or other friend.* We often pray with others, so it can be appropriate to admit and process our disappointments together, too.

• *In a small group / reading circle.* A skillful facilitator will draw out the honest thoughts of all the group members, ensuring a healthy balance between mutual edification, honesty and spiritual encouragement. Remember that this is a guide and not a rule, and always work hard to engender a climate that is prayerfully compassionate and sensitive to the realities of people's deep pain.

> *All praise to the God and Father of our Master,*
> *Jesus the Messiah! Father of all mercy! God of all*
> *healing counsel! He comes alongside us when we go*
> *through hard times, and before you know it,*
> *he brings us alongside someone else who is going*
> *through hard times so that we can be there for that*
> *person just as God was there for us.*
>
> 2 CORINTHIANS 1:3-4, *THE MESSAGE*

## Chapter One
## Confetti

**Exploration: Praying Like a Man Falling Downstairs**
Think back to a time of crisis, perhaps after an accident, a failed relationship or sudden bereavement. Spend a few moments, alone or in pairs, thinking or talking through the details of that time—how you felt and how you responded.

• Can you remember if or how you prayed at that time?

*It's okay to pray like a six-year-old or a man falling down stairs. In fact, it's more than okay; it's possibly the most important kind of prayer there can be* (page 41).

· Were you aware of God's presence at that time? What words would you use to describe it?

*Strangely, I was also becoming aware of a kind of inner warmth. It was the comfort of huddling into a thick coat with deep pockets on a bitterly cold night. Doctors would probably call it shock, but to me it felt a lot like the presence of God* (page 36).

· Can you remember how (or if) you prayed in the following weeks? Can you relate to Pete's fear of not praying enough, not fasting enough, not having enough faith or of simply running out of words?

*When our souls, like Christ's, are overwhelmed with sorrow to the point of death, we do not necessarily pray like Jesus. In fact, we may barely pray at all* (page 39).

## Meditation
Was there a particular verse of Scripture that you held on to at that time? Read it now, or look up Philippians 4:6. Then read Psalm 23 and rewrite it in your own words, relating it to your experience.

### Chapter Two
### Seeking Magic Fruit and
### Finding Tears

*When God is silent in response to our deepest and most desperate prayers—saying neither yes with a miracle nor no with a clear sign that would at least let us know He had heard us—it is natural to conclude that God doesn't care* (page 46).

## Exploration: Doxology in the Darkness

Read and reflect on the following Scripture passages. Take your time.

- Zechariah 2:8: For whoever touches you, touches the apple of his eye.
- Zephaniah 3:17: The LORD your God . . . will take great delight in you, he will quiet you with his love, he will rejoice over you with singing.
- Isaiah 49:16: See, I have engraved you on the palms of my hands.
- Psalm 139:5,7: You hem me in—behind and before . . . where can I flee from your presence?

How closely do these passages fit your picture of God as your Father, specifically how He cares for you personally? Why do you think this is so?

*But I do know that the very best thing about our lives—the most incredible thing we've got going for us—is that the Creator of a million stars is entirely and eternally good, that He is utterly caught up in the details of our situation, and that He cares for us more than we care for ourselves* (page 54).

## Meditation: Abba, Father

Read the prayer on page 56. Keeping in mind that "the power of prayer depends almost entirely upon our apprehension of who it is with whom we speak,"[1] spend some time praying in pairs or alone.

## Pray

Ask the Lord to deepen your understanding of Him as your heavenly Father in whatever situation you may be facing.

## Chapter Three
## Into the Mystery

Exploration: Downsizing God

Pete talks about psychoanalyzing God and downsizing God. What are some of the ways we do this?

> *More often, they say things that sound very spiritual and faith-filled such as, "Prayer isn't about changing reality. It's about changing the way we* look *at reality"* (page 63).

Arbitrary Miracles

How can a God of love allow suffering? This is perhaps the fundamental question with which we must all wrestle. Read one answer in Job 38:1–42:6 and Matthew 10:29-31.

Meditation: Possibilities

> *Living with unanswered prayer, I need a big God; an awesome, unspeakably amazing God; a death-defying, eternal God; a God who dies in Siberian concentration camps and senseless car crashes in order to destroy death and release an indestructible life. I need a God whose promises are certain; a God who's been there before and can walk with me and counsel me and pray for me and prepare a place for me and make all things work together for good* (page 71).

When have you had a revelation of the awesomeness of God's power? Are there particular people, places or circumstances that open your mind to the greatness of God? What has been your response? Pray for a fresh vision of God's power in your life or situation. Take time to worship God.

*"He will wipe every tear from their eyes. There will be*
*no more death or mourning or crying or pain, for the*
*old order of things has passed away." He who was seat-*
*ed on the throne said, "I am making everything new!"*
*Then he said . . . "He who overcomes will inherit all*
*this, and I will be his God and he will be my son."*

REVELATION 21:4-5,7

## Chapter Four
## Naked Prayer

Exploration: Honest to God

*The thing that keeps God out of our lives is not our sin. It is our*
*compulsion to pretend, to cover up our nakedness with fig*
*leaves, to climb sycamore trees in order to see without being*
*seen* (page 78).

What are the tricks that you use to avoid God or to hide
from Him? Why?

### Meditation: Learning to Lament
Read Psalm 89:46-52, Luke 18:11-14 and Matthew 5:4. What do
these Scriptures tell you about honesty in prayer?

*Together*
Take a straw poll of your favorite (or least favorite) contemporary worship songs and discuss the lyrics. Use a songbook if
you have one on hand. Are there any songs that you find particularly helpful or unhelpful? Why? You may want to play the
U2 track "I Still Haven't Found What I'm Looking For" and
discuss why this song caused an outcry from disappointed
Christians when it was first released. Or, have each person take

a Bible, flick through the book of Psalms and choose a stanza that seems particularly honest. Have the person read the passage to the group.

*Alone*
Write a song, prayer or poem to God in the simplest, most honest terms you can find. Tell Him how you feel, about your situation, about yourself, about Him. Religious-sounding words that you would not naturally use (such as "faithfulness" or "righteousness") are banned!

## Chapter Five
## A Darker Trust

*The power to choose God's will instead of one's own personal preferences is, according to Scripture, the defining human opportunity. In the Garden of Eden, our ancestors first prayed the tragic prayer that we have been praying ever since: "Not Your will . . ." they said to God, greedily eyeing the fruit of knowledge and power, "Not Your will but our will be done"* (page 93-94).

### Exploration: Memories of Easter
Read Genesis 22:1-19 and one or more of the following accounts of Gethsemane:

- Luke 22:39-46
- Matthew 26:36-45
- Mark 14:32-42

When—either recently or in the distant past—have you had to relinquish your own will and accept the Lord's will? How do these passages affect your understanding of that time?

*You may already be wondering whether some of your unanswered prayers have, in fact, been answered. Maybe God has simply been replying to your prayers with a loving but firm no. I don't suggest this lightly. It may well be the most painful possibility you have ever had to consider, and it may also seem to fly in the face of everything you know of God's heart and will* (page 96).

Compare the time you've already mentioned (when you had to relinquish your will to God's) with another time when you believed that it was God's will for you to fight circumstances instead. How did you know God's will in these two different situations?

### Meditation: Moving Heaven and Earth

Pete suggests that coming to terms with God's will may sometimes take you through the stages of grief: denial, anger, bargaining, depression and acceptance. Can you identify any of these stages in your own experience? You may even be experiencing one of these currently. Discuss them or write them down.

### Chapter Six
### Wondering Why

### Exploration: Asking Why

Sometimes our prayers are answered, but not in quite the way we expect. Sometimes half a miracle can be harder than none at all. We may spend the rest of our lives waiting for the other half.

In what ways has the Lord used pain or incomplete answers to prayer in your own life or in the lives of others?

*Through our relatively moderate suffering, Samie and I have learned to cherish life with dimensions of gratitude that we could never have known without all the pain. How can we not thank God for doctors, nurses and anticonvulsing drugs, for our gorgeous children, and for the kindness of family and miracles God does in other situations? The journey of life proves itself more wonderful and more terrifying than we could ever have anticipated* (page 111).

## Meditation: Thanksgiving

What are some of the things you have learned to thank God for in the midst of painful times? Spend some time thanking God for the traces of His goodness amidst pain. (Remember that this does not mean thanking God for the suffering itself but rather for His activity within and in spite of it.)

*Happy are they who bear their share of the world's pain; in the long run they will know more happiness than those who avoid it.*

MATTHEW 5:4, *PHILLIPS*

## Chapter Seven
## God's World

### Exploration: Tough Life

Choose two of the following questions for discussion:

- What are your hopes for your life, your work, your family, your friends or your home?

- Pete's friend Mike states, "When things are sort of ticking along nicely in life as they sometimes do . . . you really need to treasure those times, because they're not normal" (page 122). What things have brought you close to the point of realizing that life is "fundamentally tough"?

• Share some of the unanswered prayers you have prayed that may be attributed to the complexity of creation?

• What do you make of Francis Schaeffer's observation that "our prayers for ourselves are almost entirely aimed at getting rid of the negative at any cost rather than praying that the negatives be faced in the proper attitude"?[2]

## Meditation: Faith and the Fall

Read Luke 22:31-32 and 1 Peter 4:12-19 and answer the following:

• These verses were written to Christians who were facing persecution for their faith. What can we learn from this about responding to other kinds of suffering?

• The apostle Paul longs not just "to know Christ and the power of his resurrection" but also "the fellowship of sharing in his sufferings" (Phil. 3:10). What do you think this means? Why are we called to do this?

> The Christian witness, and our ultimate hope, is not merely a miraculous succession of miraculous escapes from all human affliction. Rather it is the joy of a deepening relationship with the "man of sorrows familiar with suffering" (Isa. 53:3) who loves us and lives in us (page 125).

## Pray

Thank God for the immense beauty and complexity of creation. You may find it helpful to thumb through the pages of *National Geographic* or watch a recording from the Discovery Channel.

## Chapter Eight
## God's Will

### Exploration: God's Will Is Best
Which prayers are you now incredibly glad that God hasn't answered?

### Recognizing God's Ways
Read Isaiah 55:8-9, James 4:2-3 and 1 John 5:14-15. What are some of the things that have helped you to recognize God's ways and pray according to His will? How can you put these into practice?

> *It is when we pray "according to his will" that God hears and acts, which means that miracles happen only when our prayers harmonize with God's broad desires for our lives* (page 141).

### God's Will Is Relationship
Can you trace how pain, persevering in prayer and crying out to God day after day have drawn you closer to the Lord?

> *When we decide that we want Him more than we want His stuff— the most amazing thing happens. We are rewired and our requests are either altered as we grow to know and prefer what He wants for us or they are simply answered because, in seeking first the kingdom of God, "all these things" are given to us as well* (page 144).

### Going for a Fistful of Converts
If God chooses to limit His powers and to allow people free will, how exactly can you pray for friends and family who don't yet know Him?

**Pray**
Pray through the Prayer of Surrender by George MacDonald on page 158.

## Chapter Nine
## God's War

### Exploration: The Fight of Your Life

> *As objects of hostility, our call is to stand firm, never doubting the reality of the battle raging against our lives nor the victory that is ours to come* (page 170).

How does the idea of being an "object of hostility" strike you? Do you recognize it in your life? How do you deal with it?

### Standing with Courage
Consider the following questions:

- What is the scariest thing God has asked you to do? What helped you to face it?

- What are your hardest mundane struggles? What victories have you seen?

> *For most of us, [the battle] rarely feels or looks heroic: Instead, it takes the mundane form of a daily struggle, sacrificing ourselves not just once but repeatedly* (see Rom. 12:1), *preferring others, holding our tongues when we want to criticize and trusting God when we feel like quitting. . . . It's just that we never realized that winning could sometimes hurt like hell* (page 172).

## Standing in Faith

What are some of the ways God has used to increase your faith? Reread Pete's list of faith-building exercises on pages 261-263. Choose a couple items from the list and determine to try them out this week.

> *Faith in God comes from getting to know God's faithfulness.* . . .
> *Faith is a pair of open hands* (page 173).

## Standing in Perseverance

Read Luke 18:1-8. What are the reasons that you should pray and not give up?

## Standing with Integrity

James 5:16 states, "The prayer of a righteous [person] is powerful and effective." Do you know a righteous person whose prayers just seem to get answered? What can you learn from him or her?

## Pray

Pray through the "Help Me to Stand" prayer found on page 189.

## Chapter Ten
## Exploring the Silence

### Exploration: Exploring Silence

Sit in complete silence for two minutes, noting the sounds that become audible when you become still. How do you respond to silence? Do you try to fill the gaps in the conversation? Do you relax? Do you have to have music or background noise? When do you find it easiest to hear God?

## When God Goes Missing

Reflect on Eugene Petersen's statement: "The story in which God does his saving work, arises among a people whose primary experience of God is his absence. . . . This seemingly unending stretch of the experience of the absence of God, is reproduced in most of our lives and most of us don't know what to make of it."[3]

## Why Is God Absent?

Answer the following questions:

- If our primary calling in life is to love God with all our hearts and minds and with all our soul and strength, why does He hide from us? Why does God wrap Himself in a cloud?

- Martin Luther argues that God withdraws to draw us into deeper relationship with Him. Pete suggests that God is silent partly to teach us to live without adult supervision, to learn to ride without stabilizers. What do you think?

  *I believe that negative theology, while helpful, doesn't take fully into account the fact that when God is silent, He is not absent* (page 208).

- Go for a walk and think through a time when it felt like God was absent. Ask Him to show you how He saw that time.

  *When I lay these questions before God I get no answer. But a rather special sort of "no answer." It is not the locked door. It is more like a silent, certainly not*

*uncompassionate gaze. As though He shook his head*
*not in refusal but waving the question. Like, "Peace,*
*child; you don't understand."*[4]

## Chapter Eleven
## Engaging the Silence

*Life's great trials invariably either make us bitter or make us*
*better. They never leave us unchanged* (page 211).

*If only to save myself from bitterness, I have attempted to see*
*my personal ordeals as an opportunity to transform myself and*
*heal the people involved in the tragic situation.*[5]

Pete suggests we try to find ways to creatively engage with
the silence by remembering, looking for and speaking out about
the way God has spoken and moved.

### Looking Back: Remembering God's Word in the Silence
What Scriptures have you found most helpful on your journey?
Look them up and meditate on them. Try reading Psalms 18, 22,
23, 88, 89:46-52, or leaf through Job, Jeremiah, Lamentations
and the Gospels. Find a Bible-study series that suits you and
work your way through a single book of the Bible, such as Tom
Wright's *Mark for Everyone* (London: SPCK Publishing, 2001).
Also, think about the last time you remember God being close
to you and speaking clearly. Go over what you can remember in
your mind.

### Looking Around: Encountering God in Other People and Places
What concrete signs of God's goodness do you have to hold on
to? What prayers has He answered in the past that are now evi-

dent in your life? Is there someone who makes it easier for you to believe? Perhaps you could phone him or her or, better still, visit that person this week.

### Speaking Out: Expressing God's Word in the Silence

Try to affirm what you learn or know to be true—what God has done for you in the past, that He loves you, or whatever. Affirm this out loud, in conversation or in prayer. Then write a prayer to God, telling Him why you love Him. Share your testimony, honestly, with someone who doesn't yet know the Lord.

### Pray

Pray through the prayer by Alan E. Lewis found on page 229.

## Chapter Twelve
## Living Hope

### The Refiner's Fire

> *There is a divine alchemy at work in all faithful suffering. We look back and realize that it was actually our disappointments and not our plaudits that the Lord has transformed to gold* (page 233).

Look up Romans 8:28. How do you respond to this promise? Are you able to apply it to your own circumstances?

### Apostles

Read and reflect on one or more of the Gospel accounts of the resurrection: Matthew 28, Mark 16, Luke 24 or John 20–21. Take your time if you are doing this alone, and as you read, try to put yourself in the place of Mary or Peter. What question do you think the Lord might ask you? Can you think how you might show your love for the Lord—in however small a way?

## Chapter 13
## Beyond Miracles

Look up 1 Peter 1:4, 2 Corinthians 5:1 and Philippians 3:20. Answer the following:

- How clear is your picture of heaven? How do you imagine spending eternity?

- What do you imagine you have waiting for you in heaven?

Only the Word of God lasts forever. Whether through miraculous answers to prayer or through ongoing suffering and silence, it is only the things God says to us and does in us that will live on. These things alone endure.

# ENDNOTES

**Introduction**
1. Karl Barth, *Prayer and Preaching* (London, UK: S.C.M. Press, 1964), p. 19.
2. Annie Dillard, *Pilgrim at Tinker Creek* (New York: Harper Perennial 1998), p. 205.

**Chapter One: Confetti**
1. Karl Barth, *Church Dogmatics*, vol. 3, part 3, ed. G. W. Bromiley and T. F. Torrance (Edinburgh, UK: T and T Clarke Publishers, 1960), p. 268.
2. Ibid.

**Chapter Two: Seeking Magic Fruit and Finding Tears**
1. Andrew Murray, *With Christ in the School of Prayer* (Old Tappan, NJ: Spire Publishers, 1965), p. 68.
2. C. S. Lewis, *The Magician's Nephew* (New York: HarperCollins Publishers, 1983), pp. 159-160.
3. Ibid., p. 168.
4. C. S. Lewis, *A Grief Observed* (London: Faber, 1961), pp. 26-27.
5. Bertrand Russell, *The Autobiography of Bertrand Russell* (New York: Routledge, 2000), p. 194.
6. Roger Steer, *J. Hudson Taylor: A Man in Christ* (Littleton, CO: OMF Books, 1990), p. 356.
7. Brennan Manning, *Ruthless Trust* (London: SPCK Publishing, 2002), p. 37.
8. Jenny Robertson, *Windows to Eternity* (Oxford, UK: BRF Publishing, 1999), n.p.

**Chapter Three: Into the Mystery**
1. John Kirvan, *God Hunger* (Notre Dame, IN: Sorin Books, 1999), p. 50.
2. The term "theodicy" was coined in 1710 by the German philosopher Gottfried Leibniz in an essay in which he set out to demonstrate that the evil in the world does not conflict with the goodness of God.
3. Harold S. Kushner, *When Bad Things Happen to Good People* (New York: Shocken Books, 1981), pp. 158-159. Kushner's argument is based on the work of the Christian theologian Dorothee Sölle, who argued that the Holocaust makes the traditional Judeo-Christian doctrine of God's omnipotence untenable.
4. Ibid., p. 45.
5. C. G Jung, *Answer to Job,* trans. R. F. C. Hull (Abingdon, UK: Routledge Classics, 1952), p. 2.
6. Ibid., p. 15.
7. Of the three positions outlined here, perhaps the mystical one is the most "Christian." This position has been explored by mystics such as Saint John of the Cross and by the contemporary "negative" theologians. The strengths and weaknesses of this position will be examined in chapter 10.

8. Elie Wiesel, *The Night Trilogy: Night, Dawn, The Accident* (New York: Hill and Wang, 1987), pp. 73-75.

9. Reeve Robert Brenner, *The Faith and Doubt of Holocaust Survivors* (New York: The Free Press, 1980), pp. 103-105.

10. Kushner, *When Bad Things Happen to Good People*, pp. 99-100.

11. W. H. Auden, *For the Time Being: Advent* (New York: Random House, 1976), p. 274.

12. Bert Ghezzi, *The Sign of the Cross: Recovering the Power of Ancient Prayer* (Chicago: Loyola Press, 2004), pp. 3-5. I have done my best to source this story back to the original, but without success. I seem to recall having read it, but the possibility remains that it is apocryphal.

**Chapter Four: Naked Prayer**

1. Dorothee Solle, *Suffering* (Philadelphia, PA: Fortress Press, 1975), p. 76.

2. Bono, introduction to *Selections from the Book of Psalms* (New York: Grove Press, 1999), p. viii.

3. I am so grateful to Cecily Kellogg for allowing me to quote from her blog, which is called "And I Wasted All That Money On Birth Control" and may be found at http://zia.blogs.com/wastedbirthcontrol.

4. Eugene Peterson, *Christ Plays in Ten Thousand Places: A Conversation in Spiritual Theology* (Grand Rapids, MI: Wm. B. Eerdmans Publishing, 2005), n.p.

5. Walter Brueggemann *The Prophetic Imagination* (Philadelphia, PA: Fortress Press, 2001), p. 57.

6. Richard Foster, *Prayer: Finding the Heart's True Home* (San Francisco: Harper-SanFrancisco, 1992), p. 24.

7. Joseph M. Scriven, "What a Friend We Have in Jesus," 1855.

**Chapter Five: A Darker Trust**

1. Floyd McLung, *Living on the Devil's Doorstep* (Nashville, TN: W Publishing Group, 1988), p. 39.

2. Barry K. Ray, MD, Manuel C. Vallejo, MD, Mitchell D. Creinin, MD, et al., "Amniotic Fluid Embolism with Second Trimester Pregnancy: A Case Report," *Canadian Journal of Anesthesia*, vol. 51, May 29, 2003, pp. 139-144. http://www.cja-jca.org/cgi/content/full/51/2/139.

3. Dylan Thomas, *The Poems* (London: J.M. Dent and Sons, 1971).

4. Joan Chittister, quoted in Jim Wallis and Joyce Hollyday, eds., *Clouds of Witnesses* (Maryknoll, NY: Orbis Books, 2005).

5. The Schomburg Center for Research in Black Culture, *Standing in the Need of Prayer* (New York: Free Press, 2003), p. 145.

**Chapter Seven: God's World**

1. C. S. Lewis, *The Problem of Pain* (New York: HarperCollins Publishers, 2001), p. 18.

2. Jesus invites us—and Paul recommends—that we pray about the details of our lives (see Matt. 7:7; Eph. 6:18; Phil. 4:6).

3. C. S. Lewis, *The Problem of Pain,* p. 25.
4. Ibid., p. 21.
5. Ibid., p. 5.
6. C. S. Lewis, *God in the Dock* (Grand Rapids, MI: Wm. B. Eerdmans Publishing Company, 1994), n.p.
7. G. K. Chesterton, *Orthodoxy* (Thirsk, UK: House of Stratus, 2001), p. 80.
8. Alexander Solzhenitsyn, *One Day in the Life of Ivan Denisovich* (New York: Signet Classics, 1998), p. 139.
9. Ibid.
10. Francis Schaeffer, *True Spirituality* (Wheaton, IL: Tyndale House, 1971), pp. 26-27.
11. D.M. Lloyd-Jones, *The Christian Warfare* (Edinburgh, UK: The Banner of Truth, 1976), p. 115.
12. Alan E. Lewis, *Between Cross and Resurrection* (Grand Rapids, MI: Wm. B. Eerdmans Publishing Company, 2003), p. 425.

**Chapter Eight: God's Will**

1. P.T. Forsythe, *The Soul of Prayer* (Vancouver, Canada: Regent College, 2002), p. 12.
2. Annie Dillard, *Pilgrim at Tinker's Creek* (New York: Bantam Books, 1974), p. 16.
3. Eileen Crossman, *Mountain Rain* (Littleton, CO: OMF Books, 1982), p. 89.
4. Arthur Green and Barry W. Holtz, *Your Word Is Fire* (New York: Paulist Press, 1977), p. 24.
5. John Newton, *Letters of John Newton* (Edinburgh, UK: Banner of Truth, 1960), n.p.
6. Forsythe, *The Soul of Prayer,* p. 18.
7. C. S. Lewis, *The Problem of Pain* (New York: HarperCollins, 2002), p. 25.
8. Alan E. Lewis, *Between Cross and Resurrection* (Grand Rapids, MI: Wm. B. Eerdmans Publishing Company, 2003), p. 414. Lewis says that "God is dependence rendered infinite."
9. Barbara Brown Taylor, *When God Is Silent* (Cambridge, MA: Cowley Publications, 1998), n.p.
10. Francis Thompson, "The Hound of Heaven," 1910.
11. George MacDonald, *Diary of an Old Soul* (London: SPCK Publishing, 2001), p. 46.

**Chapter Nine: God's War**

1. Walter Lippmann, quoted in Phillip Yancey, *Rumors of Another World* (Grand Rapids, MI: Zondervan Publishing House, 2003), p. 119.
2. Ibid.
3. Chris Cook, "Demon Possession and Mental Illness," Kent Institute of Medicine and Health Science, University of Kent at Canterbury, May 11, 1997.

4. C. S. Lewis, *The Screwtape Letters* (London: Fount, 1986), p. 9.

5. Tom Wright, *The Epistles of Paul to the Colossians and to Philemon: An Introductory Commentary* (Downers Grove, IL: InterVarsity Press, 1986), p. 114.

6. John Paul Jackson, *Needless Casualties of War* (North Sutton, NH: Streams Publishing House, 1999), p. 32.

7. George Eldon Ladd, *The Gospel of the Kingdom* (Grand Rapids, MI: Wm. B. Eerdmans Publishing Company, 1959), p. 39.

8. "Omaha Beach," Wikipedia.com. http://en.wikipedia.org/wiki/Omaha_Beach (accessed November 2006).

9. Chuck Lowe, *Territorial Spirits and World Evangelization* (Littleton, CO: OMF Books, 1998), p. 70.

10. Arthur Wallis, *God's Chosen Fast* (Oldbury, UK: Christian Literature Crusade, 1986), n.p.

11. Martin Luther, *Faith and Freedom* (New York: Vintage Classics, 2002), p. 95.

12. Brennan Manning, *Ruthless Trust* (London: SPCK Publishing, 2002), p. 13.

13. Dallas Willard, *Hearing God* (Downers Grove, IL: InterVarsity Press, 1999), p. 199.

14 Journal entry of J. O. Fraser dated February 6, 1916, quoted in Geraldine Taylor, *Behind the Ranges* (Littleton, CO: OMF Books, 1944), p. 89.

15. Ibid., p. 156

16. Ibid.

17. Augustine, *The City of God* (New York: The Modern Library, 1994), p. 327.

18. Martin Luther, quoted in J. Pelikan and H. Lehmann, eds., *Luther's Works* (St Louis, MO: Concordia Publishers, 1974), p. 105.

19. Lewis, *The Screwtape Letters,* pp. 44-46

**Chapter Ten: Exploring the Silence**

1. Rabindranath Tagore, *Gitanjali* (Boston, MA: Digireads.com, 2005), p. 25.

2. C. S. Lewis, *A Grief Observed* (London: Faber, 1961), pp. 5-7.

3. Eugene Peterson, *Christ Plays in Ten Thousand Places* (Grand Rapids, MI: Wm. B. Eerdmans Publishing Company), p. 153.

4. Ibid.

5. Martin Luther, cited in Alan E. Lewis, *Between Cross and Resurrection A Theology of Holy Saturday* (Grand Rapids, MI: Wm. B. Eerdmans Publishing Company, 2001), p. 2.

6. See Craig L. Blomberg, *The Historical Reliability of John's Gospel* (Downer's Grove, IL: InterVarsity Press, 1998), p. 265.

7. *Il Segreto di Madre Teresa* (Mother Teresa's Secret), cited in Bruce Johnston, "Mother Teresa's Diary Reveals Her Crisis of Faith," Telegraph.co.uk, November 29, 2002.

8. Mother Teresa, cited in Bruce Johnston and Brigid Delany, "Does God Exist? The Agony of Teresa," November 30, 2002. http:/www.smh.com.au/articles/2002/11/ 29/1038386314539.html (accessed November 2006).

9. Johnston, "Mother Teresa's Diary Reveals Her Crisis of Faith."

10. Fr. Cyril Halley, cited in Bruce Johnston and Brigid Delany, "Does God Exist? The Agony of Teresa."

11. Tim Chester, *The Message of Prayer* (Downer's Grove, IL: InterVarsity Press, 2003), p. 240.

12. Elie Wiesel, *Night* (New York: Bantam Books, 1982), p. 62.

13. Jürgen Moltmann, *The Crucified God* (London: SCM Press, 1999), pp. 273-274.

14. Rudolf Bultmann, cited in Moltmann, *The Crucified God,* p. 148.

15. Albert Camus, cited in Moltmann, *The Crucified God,* p. 226. Some would counter with Hebrews 12:2, which says that Jesus "for the joy set before him endured the cross, scorning its shame." However, it is clear from Christ's cry of dereliction that in the actual moments prior to His death, Jesus was neither scorning the shame of the cross nor anticipating the joy set before Him in a way that alleviated the extreme physical, mental and spiritual crisis.

16. Raniero Cantalamessa, "The Rocks Were Split," Third Lent Meditation to the Papal Household, April 7, 2006. http://www.cantalamessa .org/en/2006quaresi ma3.htm (accessed November 2006). Cantalamessa distinguishes between what he calls active atheism and the passive atheism of those who experience the abandonment of God: "There is, in fact, an active atheism, culpable, which consists in rejecting God, and there is a passive atheism, of punishment and expiation, which consists in being rejected or feeling rejected, by God."

17. P.T. Forsythe, *The Soul of Prayer* (Vancouver, B.C.: Regent College Publishing, 1997), p. 12

18. R. S. Thomas, *Later Poems: 1972-1982* (London: MacMillan London Ltd., 1983), p. 23.

19. Lewis, *A Grief Observed,* pp. 58-59.

**Chapter Eleven: Engaging the Silence**

1. Martin Luther King, Jr., "Suffering and Faith," *Christian Century Magazine*, April 27, 1960.

2. Pelletier, cited in Raymond E. Brown, *The Death of the Messiah,* vol. 2 (New York: Doubleday Books, 1994), p. 1112

3. Flavius Josephus, *The Jewish War,* 5.5.4, no. 213-14, cited in Brown, *The Death of the Messiah,* p. 1112.

4. Kushner, cited in Brown, *The Death of the Messiah,* p. xiv.

5. Ben Irwin, "Five Minutes with Rob," first published in *Relevant* magazine, May 23, 2006. Rob Lacey, father, husband and author of *The*

*Word on the Street*, a modern retelling of the Bible, passed away on May 1, 2006. You can learn more about his books at his website: www.thewordonthestreet.co.uk.

6. Ibid.

7. Archbishop Desmond Tutu, speech delivered before the South African Truth and Reconciliation Commission, September 11, 2002. http://www.cathedral.org/cathedral/worship/911images/dt020911.shtml (accessed November 2006).

**Chapter Twelve: Living Hope**

1. Ranindranath Tagore, *Gitanjali* (New York: Penguin Classics, 2005), p. 272.

2. While the Synoptic Gospels are less clear on this point, John's Gospel almost certainly views Mary Magdalene and Mary of Bethany as the same person. The alleged "evidence" for Dan Brown's novel *The Da Vinci Code* (which suggests that Mary Magdalene was, in fact, Jesus' wife and the leader of the Early Church) is historically errant, as it is based on certain Gnostic texts written after the biblical Gospels.

3. Elie Wiesel, *Legends of Our Time* (New York: Holt, Rinehart, Winston, Inc., 1968), p. 93.

4. Gregory A. Boyd, *Is God to Blame?* (Downers Grove, IL: Intervarsity Press, 2003), p. 161.

5. W. H. Auden, *Twelve Songs* (song VIII) from *Collected Poems* (New York: Vintage International, 1991), p. 135.

**Chapter Thirteen: Beyond Miracles**

1. Tim Chester, *The Message of Prayer* (Downers Grove, IL: InterVarsity Press, 2003), p. 243.

2. N. T. Wright, "Jesus' Resurrection and Christian Origins," originally published in *Gregorianum*, vol, 83, no. 4, 2002, pp. 615–635.

3. J.R.R. Tolkien, *The Return of the King* (New York: Ballantine Books, 1978), p. 283.

4. John Bunyan, *The Pilgrim's Progress* (New York: Penguin Classics, 1987), pp. 136-138.

**Appendix C: Discussion Guide for Small Groups**

1. Andrew Murray, *With Christ in the School of Prayer* (Old Tappan, NJ: Spire Publishers, 1965), p. 68.

2. Francis Schaeffer, *True Spirituality* (Wheaton, IL: Tyndale House, 1971), pp. 26-27.

3. Eugene Peterson, *Christ Plays in Ten Thousand Places* (Grand Rapids, MI: Wm. B. Eerdmans Publishing Company), p. 153.

4. C. S. Lewis, *A Grief Observed* (London: Faber, 1961), pp. 58-59.

5. Martin Luther King, Jr., "Suffering and Faith," *Christian Century Magazine*, April 27, 1960.

# ACKNOWLEDGMENTS

I'm extremely grateful to those who trawled through the manuscript of this book in its various stages of evolution. The mistakes are all mine but these people have made *God on Mute* much better than it would otherwise have been: James Greig, Gill and Peter Greig-Allen, Carla and Steve Harding, Phil Togwell, and especially the legendary Stephanie Heald.

Thanks are also due to Linnea Spransy, Brian McLaren, Friar Jon Peterson, Rev. Mike Fox, Roger Forster, Mike Ash and the Tall Skinny Kiwi for their input. I'm also indebted, once again, to Richard Herkes, Les Moir and Carolyn Owen at Kingsway (Survivor) and to Alex Field, Bill Greig III, and Roger Thompson at Regal Books.

Thank you to those brave souls who allowed me to tell their stories: Sheila Giffard-Smith, Mike and Jo King, Rob Morris, Greg Russinger, Misha and Lionel Thompson, Floyd and Sally McClung, Cecily Kellogg and Ben Irwin.

I also wish to express my deep gratitude to those whose practical and prayerful commitment makes this crazy life possible: Andy and Andrea for giving me a place to write, Helen Monkton for keeping my back in shape, Susan and Peter in Canada, Will and Dani in Switzerland, Tony and Jo in Zambia, Roger and Donna in Tulsa, Andrew and Linda, Baz and Linda, Ken and Fiona, Richard and Steph and, of course, to Daniel B., wherever you may be right now.

**And Finally . . .**
Samie, words fail me. There are almost 80,000 of them between the covers of this book and yet I can't find the ones that will convey how much I love you and how grateful I am that you are still here with me each day. Thank you for letting me tell your story.

Hudson and Danny, you're not allowed to read this book until you're at least 16! However, you did help to write it in ways you will never know. You boys have loved, supported and spoken God's words to me continually throughout the difficult experiences described in this book and you, in turn, have been loved and prayed for by people all over the world in a way that makes you very special. Whatever happens, never stop trusting God.

# ABOUT THE AUTHOR AND THE ARTIST

**Pete Greig** is an author, church-planter and one of the founding leaders of 24-7prayer, a ministry that has grown unexpectedly from a single night-and-day "prayer room" into an international, interdenominational Christian community of people committed to prayer, mission and justice. Thanks to an innovative approach to spirituality and culture, 24-7 prayer has captured the attention of newspapers and magazines from *Rolling Stone* to *Readers Digest* and has been the subject of an acclaimed British television documentary. Proposed by *Relevant* magazine as one of the top 50 "revolutionary leaders" of his generation, Pete is a popular speaker and writer, whose books, including *Red Moon Rising* and *The Vision and the Vow*, have been translated into a number of languages. Pete is married to Samie and they have two children. They live in Guildford, England, where they are active members of a missional community.

· · · ·

**Linnea Spransy** is an artist in residence at the 24-7 Boiler Room in Kansas City, Missouri. A graduate of the Yale MFA program, she has already had a number of exhibitions, including one at the Cristine Wang Gallery in New York and another in Kunming, China.

# ADDITIONAL RESOURCES

**24-7**

*Red Moon Rising: The Adventure of Faith and the Power of
Prayer*
by Pete Greig and Dave Roberts
The amazing story of the birth of the 24-7 Prayer
movement
(Relevant/USA, 2003; Survivor/UK, 2004 ;
Brockhaus/Germany, 2005;
Päivä/Finland, 2005; Torch Trust for the Blind
[audio]/UK, 2006)

*The Vision and the Vow: Rules of Life and Rhythms of Grace*
by Pete Greig
A contemporary call to discipleship exploring
the words of Pete Greig's poem "The Vision,"
which has touched more than one million people
(Survivor/UK, 2004; Relevant/USA, 2004)

*The 24-7 Prayer Manual: A Guide to Creating and
Sustaining Holy Space in the Real World*
Everything you need to know to set up and run
a night-and-day prayer room
(Survivor/UK, 2003; Cook Communications/
USA, 2005)

*Lord of the Ring: A Journey in Search of Count Zinzendorf*
by Phil Anderson
A fascinating biography of the little-known man who
inspired the modern prayer and missions movements.
(Survivor/UK, 2006; Regal/USA, 2007)

*PunkMonk*
by Andy Freeman and Pete Greig
(Regal/USA, 2007; Survivor/UK, 2007)

# [ 24-7 TITLES ]
## WWW.24-7PRAYER.COM

# The Secret Origins of Praying 24-7 Revealed

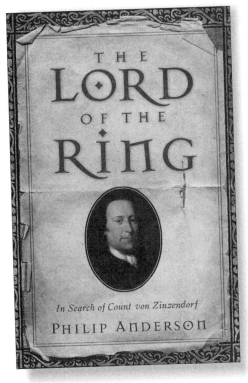

**Lord of the Ring**
978.08307.43278

Part history, part narrative, *The Lord of the Ring* takes readers on a fascinating journey back to the 18th century Moravian renewal movement. Experience the passion of young Count Nikolaus Ludwig von Zinzendorf and his friends as they took a vow to serve Christ their King faithfully in whatever situation of life they found themselves. Signed by the five school friends and illustrated in a medallion made by Zinzendorf's grandmother, the vow of the "Confessors of Christ" is as relevant today as when it first was conceived in 1716. Join Philip Anderson on an aerial road trip via his three-seater plane as he undertakes a 21st century pilgrimage from England to Germany. Anderson retraces the steps of Zinzendorf, reconnects with his legacy and seeks to apply it to life and faith in a new millennium. Learning from the past, readers will discover crucial signposts for grappling with the Church of today's identity and calling as an authentic, relational, missional community.

# More Relevant Resources from Regal